THE TROUBLE WITH HIM

THE FORBIDDEN LOVE SERIES BOOK 3

KAT T. MASEN

The Trouble with Him
The Forbidden Love Series Book 3

Kat T. Masen

Disclaimer: The material in this book contains graphic language and sexual content and is intended for mature audiences, ages 18 and older.

ISBN: 978-1-68564-901-2
Editing by More Than Words Copyediting and Proofreading
Proofing by Nicki at Swish Design & Editing
Cover design by Outlined with Love Designs Cover Image Copyright 2021
First Edition 2021
All Rights Reserved

"That's why it's called falling in love.
You don't force yourself, you just fall." - Unknown

PROLOGUE

AVA

Three Years Ago

Shopping for jewelry is one of life's greatest pleasures. The small pieces, designed to be a girl's best friend, can evoke many emotions. The overwhelming feelings of joy, pride, love, and commitment, even if the so-called ring is for my sister.

Inside the store are glass enclosures showcasing the finest of diamonds. All shine bright, glimmers of hope that maybe one day I'll find my knight in shining armor who will lavish me with a ring to symbolize eternity.

Okay, what the hell is going on here?

I shake my head to rid myself of these thoughts. I'm twenty-two, and I can't think of anything worse than committing to one man for life. It's not that I don't believe in it, but if I settled down with any of my exes, I'd have considered it a jail sentence rather than a precious gift of love and devotion.

My eyes gravitate toward a particular ring, but even then, I am unsure. I certainly like it, but I'm not sure if

Millie will. She's never one to be into jewelry, and most of the items she wears were gifts from Mom and Dad.

I point my finger to the Asscher-cut diamond. "This is beautiful."

"You think Millie will like it?"

"She's not one for extravagant diamonds," I mention, then shrug my shoulders. "She's always been a sentimental old soul."

"Okay, so are you thinking something more vintage?" Austin asks, scratching his head.

"Hmm, maybe." I continue to browse until the shop assistant finally stops gossiping and pays us the attention we deserve. Sales assistants often work on commission, and this chick isn't doing anything to earn this sale.

"Let me guess, engagement ring?" She forces a smile while watching us furtively.

"Yes," we both say in unison.

"I see you were eyeing the Asscher-cut. It would look amazing on you."

My eyes lift, meeting with hers. On closer inspection, the woman should really tone down the false eyelashes. It's one thing to enhance your eyes, but go overboard, and you'll be mistaken for a drag queen. *God, I sound more like Eric every day.*

"It's not for me, it's for my sister," I tell her, then point to Austin. "I'm just helping him choose."

"Oh, well, my apologies. I just thought you two looked like a couple."

Austin laughs beside me. "We get that a lot, don't we, Ava?"

I roll my eyes, letting out a huff. "He's my soon-to-be brother-in-law who is a pain in the ass because he can't decide what ring to choose."

"So, tell me about your girlfriend?"

"She's beautiful, kind, loving, and my best friend," Austin says all in one breath.

I nudge his side, holding in my laughter. "I think she means her taste, you goof."

"Oh," Austin mouths then grins. "She's simple."

"So, more classic, would you say?" the assistant presses, making Austin uncomfortable. Austin turns to me, his eyes pleading for a much-needed life jacket.

"Amelia is simple with her taste," I inform Miss-fake-lashes. "So yes, perhaps something classic."

The assistant bows her head, moving it from left to right as she scans the glass enclosure. She stops suddenly on a small cluster of rings. Then, carefully, she pulls a ring out of the cushion bed it sits in and lifts it closer to us. "How about this?"

"I don't know," Austin mumbles, leaning back while slipping his hands into his pockets. "It is beautiful."

"What are you unsure of?" she questions.

"All of it."

An obnoxious groan leaves my mouth. I pull Austin aside, away from the assistant, ready to give him one of my overbearing pep talks. "Are we back here again? Doubting whether to do it? Dad said yes, so what's the problem?"

"What if Millie says no?"

"She won't say no."

"How do you know?"

"Well, I can't bet my life on it," I admit, but quickly straighten my shoulders to appear confident. "Is there something else you're not telling me?"

Austin lowers his head to raise it again moments later. "No... you're right, Ava. I want to marry Millie, and this is the right thing to do. Give me your hand?"

"What for?"

"I want to slide it on, to practice and see if it feels right."

I bite my lip while shuffling my feet. "Wait, isn't that bad luck?"

Austin cocks his head, his hazel-colored eyes probing me with an annoying smirk.

"Stop being dramatic, Ava. You've got beautiful hands, just like Millie. Now shut up so I can practice."

I stand still as Austin reaches out for my hand. When his fingers touch mine, I hold my breath, terrified the small jolt which electrified throughout my body is a warning of a bad omen.

Slowly, he guides the ring down my finger until it nestles into place. It fits perfectly. He holds onto my hand as we both fall silent.

There is no doubt Millie will feel the same. Austin coming back into her life is a sign they are meant to be together. After all, they were high school sweethearts and lost their virginity to each other.

Then there's the matter of my father's approval. Dad loves Austin and admires his tenacity, not to mention his choice to study medicine. He's always treated him with respect as if Austin were his son. I'm certain it's the reason why he agreed to Austin's proposal, even though Millie is still young.

It did, however, come with a stern string attached. They were not to get married if it interfered with their studying and graduating from college. That is—and will be for the next few years—the number one priority in Austin and Millie's lives.

There are so many reasons as to why this is the right decision. Austin was always meant to be a part of our family, and this is the beginning of what will be a beautiful journey for them both.

Sure, the whole 'Will' saga dragged out longer than it should have, but they were never meant to be together. If they were, they wouldn't have spent the last four years apart. I may not know anything about love, but I know if Will loved her, he would never have left or stayed away for so long.

"Austin," I whisper, then raise my eyes until I'm locked in his unwavering stare. "It's beautiful, and she'll love it."

"You think so?" he almost croaks. "It does look perfect on you."

"I know so."

Austin releases the breath he's been holding to lean forward and place his lips on my cheek. Then, with a gracious smile, he pulls away to turn his attention back to the assistant.

"We'll take it."

ONE

AVA

Present

"**W**hat do you mean my appearance is canceled?"

My manager, Kris, stands beside me with a clipboard in hand and AirPods nestled into her ears. Her fingers type rapidly on the phone while her lips press together into a white slash. I cross my arms, impatiently waiting for an answer as the anger brews on the cusp of unleashing on everyone inside this very room.

Slowly, she lifts her gaze to the mirror to meet mine. "Courtney Rae is the new face for the event tonight."

Upon my reflection in the mirror, my eyes widen with a cold stare. The vein on my forehead comes out of nowhere, prompting my makeup artist, Jonathan, to step away with fear.

My hands fall onto the dresser in front of me as I close my eyes, willing to control the anger bubbling to the surface. This event was planned a year ago, and it was no backyard job. Hosting the biggest party in Miami on New Year's Eve will launch my business to the next level. Over fifty thousand people are attending the concert, big-name musicians performing, and endorsements were thrown at me to help promote. Everything I wear tonight, down to the blush on my cheeks, was strategically planned to advertise on my social media accounts.

This is how I've become a self-made millionaire, and now what? I'm replaced with only five hours' notice? As the seconds pass, the animosity buries deeper within, and any rational thoughts are buried under the blinding rage consuming me.

I stand up in a rush, accidentally knocking a bottle of foundation onto the ground. With my hands on my hips, I glare at the team in front of me.

"I was booked a year ago. There's a contract in place for me to host tonight's event. Give me one reason why Courtney Rae is suddenly replacing me?"

Kris bows her head, shuffling her feet nervously. "She is... how should I say it, younger, but—"

"I'm aware she is nineteen," I cut Kris off, momentarily beyond words. "What does that have to do with anything?"

"They want a young face for their social content," Kris adds.

"I'm twenty-fucking-five!" My voice bounces against the walls, causing it to sound louder in the small room. "I'm not past my goddamn prime."

Kris raises her hands to try and calm me down. "I understand, but, Ava, they want to draw in the younger demographic. Courtney has close to a hundred million followers and is not afraid to remove her clothing. You know how it is."

Of course, I know how it works. The more skin you expose, the more money is thrown your way, and therefore, the more followers you gain. I refuse to become that woman.

My brand was built on me as a person, and it didn't involve scandalous shots compromising my integrity. Sure, I may post a few bikini shots in summer, but it's always done tastefully. If it weren't, I'd have my father to answer to, and he is ruthless when it comes to business, especially when his daughter is involved.

Slamming my fist against the dresser, I raise my hands to my hair to remove the curlers. In a mad rush, my hair becomes tangled, infuriating me more. When all my hair falls loosely against my back, I yank my robe off, revealing the satin gold designer dress I wear underneath.

"Organize my flight back home now," I demand while gathering my belongings. "Get my lawyers on this. This will not be the last they've heard of me."

I refuse to stay in Miami a minute longer, ignoring Kris, who fails hopelessly at trying to calm me down. This isn't the first time I've been bumped for someone younger, but it has been happening more often lately. Each time it does, my confidence shatters, and finding the strength to hold my head up high becomes harder and harder.

The pressure of this industry is too much at times. Unlike Millie, who studied law, my chosen profession is short-lived. What's hot one minute may not be so hot the next, and tonight proved just that.

The flight from Miami gives me too much time to fester in my own thoughts. Thank God it's a private plane, so I can avoid dealing with people. With the new year upon us, it's the perfect time for resolutions or an opportunity to reinvent yourself. In fact, I even posted something on my social media account about how to build a new you in the new year.

The problem is, I can't even practice what I preach.

My life is a *mess*.

When the plane lands at JFK, I welcome being back in New York. On the drive back to my apartment, I decide to surprise my boyfriend, Olivier. We'd gotten into a fight over tonight after he left Miami in a huff only this morning. We had recently moved in together—a decision which didn't go down well with my father. According to Millie, Dad has trust issues and thinks Olivier is after my money. The thought alone is ludicrous. Olivier is a sought-after model who has his own money. Maybe not as much as me, but he isn't broke and living on the streets. Together, we're the perfect couple, and both our followers grew to double the amount when our relationship went viral. Designer brands are desperate to book us, anything from photoshoots to promoting their properties or products. It has been our busiest year, and frankly, Dad has no idea what he is talking about.

I retrieve my phone from my purse, dialing my sister's number. The call connects as Millie and Ashton's faces appear on the screen.

"How is my little man doing?" I ask, unable to hide my smile. "My gosh, Millie, he is so big now."

"I know, right?" Millie grins while brushing Ashton's bronze hair to the side with her fingers. "Time to give him a sibling."

"Wait, you guys are actually trying?"

Millie nods with an enthused smile. "It's even more fun when you're purposely trying to fall pregnant."

I laugh, then release a long-winded breath. "It reminds me of movies when you see the women all like, I'm ovulating, get home quick."

"Yeah." Millie chuckles softly. "Something like that."

"Are you guys all there?"

Millie turns around, adjusting the screen until Will

appears, waving hello. I can tell by his glassy eyes that the festivities started early. No surprises there, New Year's Eve at my parents' house is always a big deal.

"How's my favorite sister-in-law doing?"

"You are so wasted," I tell him while laughing. "You've never called me that. I think it's Addy because she's quiet and barely speaks to you."

"You may have a point there."

"Starting early, are we?"

"Dad brought out beer pong," he drags with an eye roll. "I don't even remember the last time I played it. College, probably."

"Beer pong... classy."

"There's no beer in it," Millie informs me. "It's Sambuca, and it's lethal."

The call is hijacked by Rocky, Eric, and my cousins. They're all as loud and boisterous as each other, fighting for attention until Eric calls for order.

"Ava, darling, what time are you live?" Eric asks.

I purse my lips, then release an annoyed huff. "It's not going to happen. Long story and one I'd rather not get into right now."

Millie opens her mouth to speak, only to pause her movements to collect her thoughts. Her brows draw together, and I know she's concerned.

The others are too drunk to even care. It's times like this I miss my family. I love living in Manhattan, and it's not like I'm completely alone. Andy lives here but is currently traveling for the week in Europe. Rocky and Nikki live in the Upper East Side, though they spend a lot of time on the West Coast because of Will, Millie, and Ashton.

"I miss you guys," I say wistfully.

"Come home tonight?" Millie suggests, lowering her voice. "You'll still make it before midnight."

I offer a half-smile at the suggestion. "It's already nine. Besides, I'm going to surprise Olivier. I felt terrible for leaving him in the first place."

Millie moves the phone away to a quieter room, the door closing behind her.

"Are you guys better now? After the fight this morning?"

It slipped my mind that I had texted Millie after my fight with Olivier. I was angry, and hurt, and Millie is always the person I vent to when it comes to my personal life.

"I think we're both under a lot of pressure. We had three photoshoots back to back this week with very demanding photographers."

Millie smirks. "Honey, it's Vogue."

"God, you sound just like Eric."

She throws her hand to her forehead dramatically. "Oh no... what will become of me? But seriously, maybe tonight will be the night for the two of you to reconnect."

"Hmm..." My mind drifts off to mine and Olivier's relationship. I begin to fidget with the hem of my dress, unsure if I should bring up my concerns. "I have a question for you. You've been married to Will for almost two years now, right? What's the longest time you've gone without sex?"

"Longest? Maybe, like a day."

I sigh heavily. "You're no help."

"Ava, what's going on?"

"We haven't had sex in like three months," I blurt out, relieved to get it off my chest. "I'm probably making a big deal out of it because we've both been busy."

"I mean, sure. But you do sleep in the same bed, right?"

"Yeah, when we're both home at the same time."

"And do you try?"

"Not anymore," I mumble, closing my eyes momentarily. "I gave up after several rejections in a row. I figured, if he wants it, he'll take it."

"Ava," Millie says faintly. "Come home, please? It sounds like you need family right now."

The thought of coming home did sound appealing, but I have a life here and a boyfriend who deserves my attention. I straighten my shoulders, willing to find any confidence left within me.

"I will, soon."

We chat for a few more minutes before wishing each other a happy new year then ending the call.

The streets are chaotic, nothing unusual for New Year's Eve. When the driver finally pulls up at the building, I thank him before exiting.

Harry, our doorman, greets me hello while holding the door open for me. I nod to thank him, then quickly make my way to the elevator.

The doors close, each level lighting up until I reach the penthouse. I purchased this place only a few months ago from a couple embroiled in a nasty divorce. Thanks to Nikki, who represented the wife, she notified me of it coming onto the market. After a great financial year, I made the purchase and moved out of my apartment in Brooklyn.

My fingers punch in the pin code, then I push the door open to a dark apartment. Olivier mentioned nothing about other plans, and just as I'm about to call him, my eyes gravitate down the hall and toward a faint glow coming from beneath the bedroom door.

I remove my heels, allowing my bare feet to walk against the porcelain tiles. With each step I take, my mouth begins to dry, and my breathing falters. I force myself to take a deep breath until the sound of moaning catches my attention.

My stomach hardens, footsteps dragging as my mind conjures up all these scenarios. This is it—he's fucking some other woman who is probably younger than me too.

Without another thought, I open the door to see Olivier in bed, on all fours, with an unknown man behind him.

Letting out a loud gasp, I ignore my weakened muscles and heavy feeling in the pit of my stomach. Quickly, I turn around in a panicked rush, scurrying out of the room and pretending I didn't just see my boyfriend being fucked by another man.

The quick steps become too much, my feet stumbling as I trip over and fall onto my arm. As I lay on the ground, the pain soars through me, making it unbearable to move my wrist.

"Ava, it's not what you think!" Olivier rushes out of the room, now dressed in a pair of boxers.

I crawl along the ground until he tries to help me up. With my wrist and ego bruised, I still manage to swat his hand out of the way.

"Not what I think?" I almost cry while glaring at him. "I don't know how else to interpret it besides the fact that another guy's dick was inside your ass!"

The other guy, a model from the fashion industry, quickly places his clothes on and joins us. I wasn't wrong about the age. The guy is much younger.

Olivier runs his hands through his hair. "I'm sorry, you weren't meant to come home tonight."

I gather the strength to stand up without applying pressure to my wrist. Desperate to alleviate the pain, I head toward the kitchen and retrieve a cold pack from the freezer. Slowly, I apply it onto my wrist, willing the swelling to subside, then search for a bandage.

Olivier follows me to the kitchen, pacing the area between us while he runs his hands through his messy blond hair.

"So, if I didn't come home, how long were you going to keep up this charade?" I beg of him to answer. "It explains why you haven't wanted to touch me."

"Ava, I still love you."

"You love my money, my family's name. But don't you dare say you love me," I fume, releasing my anger toward him. "Love is a powerful feeling, Olivier. I suggest you look deep inside and admit to yourself who you really are and stop pretending. As for me, I'm going to leave. I want you out by tomorrow."

Unable to think straight, I wrap my wrist up with the bandage. I take my purse, only for Olivier to call out, "Ava, please wait!"

My hand rests on the doorknob, but I don't turn around. Olivier doesn't deserve another second of my time. He gave up that privilege the moment he chose to betray me and with another man, of all people.

I open the door, taking a step out, then close it behind me. It's best I don't hover, quickly making my way to the elevator. Inside the confined space, I bow my head with a hitched chest until a loud sob escapes me. My hands clutch onto my stomach as the uncontrolled tears onset a wave of nausea. When the door pings open, my hand instantly covers my mouth as I begin to dry heave.

My breaths come hard and fast, but somewhere amid this breakdown, I realize I am all alone with nowhere to go. Miles away, across the other side of the country, my family celebrates ringing in the new year. All my friends are busy with events I declined because Miami was more important. My appearance was a bust, bumped for a hotter and younger influencer.

And my live-in boyfriend—is gay.

The loneliness is palpable.

The tabloids will have a field day with how miserable my life turned out to be. I can see the headline already— Daughter of Mogul Lex Edwards Falls from Fame.

There is no way to spin anything into a positive tonight.

So, I do the only thing to make it all go away and forget I even exist—I hit up the closest bar with the intent to make my life one giant blur.

TWO

AVA

O ut of every decent bar within walking distance of my building, I end up at some Irish pub called *Alistair's.*

I've never heard nor seen the place in the entire time I've lived in the city, though I was never one to frequent such establishments. I prefer high-end bars with a designer dress code and men who wear suits.

Alistair's is anything but high-class. The crowd is less than desirable, and my Gucci gold dress stands out amongst the denim worn by the lively patrons.

Everything inside the quaint space is made from heavy wood with splashes of green to tie in the Irish theme. There's a wall-mounted flat-screen television over the bar, next to black-and-white photographs of random people.

An odd smell permeates the place, causing me to scrunch my nose upon stepping further inside. Almost everyone is already drunk, dancing to questionable music from some era I'm unfamiliar with. Jugs of beer are served all around me with tall glasses, and the word 'pint' is yelled way too often by the bar staff serving.

People are jolly, cheering on newcomers as if everyone inside the bar is their best friend. It will only be a matter of time before I fall prey to their overbearing social behavior. I already dread it, desperate to wallow in self-pity alone at the bar. There's plenty of laughter and a few playful fights followed by more obnoxious roars.

I need alcohol—stat. And beggars can't be choosers.

"What's the strongest thing you've got?" I yell over the noise to the bartender.

The man is older, perhaps in his fifties, with salt and pepper-colored hair. With a sly grin, his dimples appear which catch my attention. I find myself staring, oddly, until he winks while pulling a bottle of whisky from the shelf behind him.

"This is what you need." The brown liquor is poured from the bottle into the glass. "Macallan neat. Best way to ring in the new year."

I'm not one to enjoy whisky, preferring cocktails and other bright and colorful drinks with umbrellas hanging off the side. But I no longer care about anything or anyone, desperate to forget I even exist right now.

My fingers wrap around the glass as I stare at the amber liquid. Without another thought, I throw it back, allowing the burning sensation to slide down my throat. I let out a rasp as the amused bartender watches on.

"Sweetheart, we nurse, not chug."

Unable to hold back my distaste for the intense flavor, I wrinkle my nose and open my mouth with my tongue pushing slightly forward.

"That was..." My words are caught in my throat as I wonder how my father drinks this stuff. It's his go-to drink for everything. "Strong. Hit me up with another."

I have no idea why I order another, but the smoky flavor

continues to linger, and I feel my limbs falling lighter. Upon recommendation, I nurse the second one until the music becomes somewhat tolerable. It's all old-school mixes, well before I was even born. As I turn to see the folk around me, a guy is wearing a t-shirt that says *Rub me, I'm Lucky.* The tall college-aged man wearing some '80s punk rock orange wig would be lucky as fuck to have anyone rub him. He's what one would call the life of the party, but not someone you'd take back home and into bed.

It could be worse—you could be single in a bar on New Year's Eve after finding your boyfriend in bed with another man.

As the memory rears its ugly head, I call for more drinks. By my fourth, the bar is much more pleasant. I make friends with Alistair, the bartender. It turns out he is married with three kids to some Australian chick. He owns the bar, and his wife is an artist. It's a shame. The more we speak, the more I realize older men can be quite attractive. Maybe, I shouldn't be so picky and extend my age range to accommodate older men. Imagine that—my father would *kill* me.

I remove the black coat I wear as the temperature inside becomes warmer. A few people notice, eyeing me with a sleazy lick of the lips. I ignore them, aware my cocktail dress is somewhat scandalous in a casual joint like this.

There's a brush against my arm as a man squeezes in, a little too close for comfort.

"Hey, gorgeous," he greets, standing at my side while leaning his arm on the bar. "Looks like you could use someone tonight?"

Turning to look at him, I see a typical metrosexual guy with everything so perfect—probably another gay guy. The eyebrows are way too shaped for my liking. Andy and

Jessa's voices ring in my head from the last conversation we had about my choice of men. I'm not that picky. Sure, I like a handsome man, and on occasion, I have nit-picked, but that's out of boredom and usually a sign I need to move on.

Perhaps, I'll try something new. Give this guy the benefit of the doubt.

"Ava Edwards," I introduce myself with a smile. "And you are?"

"Richard." He lowers his head, then lifts his gaze with a simper. "Everhard."

I almost spit out my drink. "Your name is Dick Everhard?"

"If you want it to be."

An exaggerated sigh leaves my mouth. Great, this is what I have to look forward to being single again. And here I was trying to give him the benefit of the doubt, only for him to assume I'm after his dick.

"I think we're done," I drag.

"C'mon, you're hot. A little fun won't hurt you."

I'm about to unleash my inner goddess, though she's long drunk and barely able to stand straight until a familiar scent lingers in the air.

"How about you leave her alone?" The recognizable voice warns Dick.

I turn my body, my gaze lifting to meet the hazel-colored eyes from my past. Unable to hide my joy at seeing a familiar face, I instantly throw my arms around Austin's neck.

"Austin, what are you doing here?" I ask, still in his embrace.

He pulls away, only managing a smile. "Day from hell, to put it bluntly."

I stare at his face, admiring how much he's matured

since the last time I saw him, which would've been two years ago at the Hamptons for Rocky's birthday. The night it all fell apart for him. We touched base after that out of concern since he was part of our family, but we just drifted apart without the common person holding us together anymore.

"It sounds like you need Alistair's strongest stuff." I motion for Alistair to serve us, requesting two Macallan's neat. "Alistair can solve all the world's problems tonight, I'm sure of it."

Alistair grins while serving us. "You're going to break some hearts, Miss Ava."

"First-name basis." Austin chuckles beside me. "How drunk are you?"

"Drunk enough that I've forgotten all about what happened before I walked in here. But sober enough to remember how much fun we used to have together." I clutch onto my stomach as laughter escapes me. "Do you remember when we went camping, and you woke up with a frog on your head?"

Austin shakes his head, unable to hide his amusement. "That was the first and last time I attempted camping. Some memory, huh?"

Our laughs subside, and the giant elephant takes a seat between us. I wasn't sure if I should mention it, opting to order more drinks. Austin drinks two in a row, and while he was never one to shy away from a drink, he doesn't appear to be himself, and something is troubling him.

"Are you okay?" I ask, watching him stealthily.

"Not really." His gaze falls onto the glass in front of him as his finger traces the rim. The moment passes as I wait patiently for him to elaborate, but he continues to remain quiet. Suddenly, his eyes are drawn to the bandage wrapped around my wrist. "What happened to you?"

I bow my head. "Long story."

"Did you bandage this yourself?" He questions while touching my wrist softly.

"Can you tell?"

Austin draws his eyebrows together, turning himself inward to better examine my wrist. I purse my lips, annoyed he pointed it out—a reminder of tonight's misfortunes.

"Please let me look at it?" He pauses, narrowing his eyes while glancing at my frustrated stare. "Don't give me that look, Ava. I'm a first-year resident, and I work in the ER. I've seen way worse than this."

"Fine," I mumble, holding my arm out.

Austin presses softly, asking me if I can move my fingers and where it hurts. I answer him accordingly, ignoring the pain where he presses.

"It looks like it may just be a sprain. That's the good news. But of course, you should get it looked at as soon as possible. An x-ray for starters."

"Okay, Dr. Carter," I joke, my gaze focusing on the beard against his sharp jaw. "It's good to see you again. It's been a while."

Austin wraps my wrist back up, much better than I did. "Aside from this, how have you been?"

"Good, bad, I don't know. Ask me when I'm sober of expensive whisky."

He chuckles softly. "And Millie, how is she?"

"Um, good," is all I say.

"It's okay," Austin assures me. "I have moved on. The joy of studying medicine means no time to sit around and dwell on the past."

"I'm glad to hear. I know it wasn't ideal to end that way."

"That's life, Ava. The good, the bad, and the ugly. There is way worse out there. I'll count myself fortunate to have known your family."

Tilting my head, I wonder who the hell this guy is. This is unlike the Austin I remember. Granted, the last time I saw him, he punched Will in the mouth. Aside from his looks maturing, maybe he has too.

"You've changed," I tell him, honestly.

"It's been two years, Ava. A lot has happened."

"Oh," I mouth. "Like what? Aside from school and work?"

He lowers his head with a knowing smirk. "You're still as nosy as ever."

I dig my elbow into his side while grinning. "Alone on New Year's Eve, there can't be anyone that special in your life."

"The same could be said for you."

"This is depressing."

Austin motions for Alistair to serve us again. "It doesn't have to be. We need to be grateful we are here, in this beautiful city."

"Okay, now you're really scaring me with all your positive vibes, but you know what? I will drink to that. I've got nothing else to lose."

We drink to being alive, to living in Manhattan. We drink when Alistair stops serving and does a rendition of Bon Jovi's "Livin' on a Prayer". It's followed by Richard, aka Dick, serenading Sharon, a fellow patron who just broke up with her husband of twenty years, with an '80s number called "Lady In Red."

We all become the best of friends, and as the night

wears on, the pints come our way, and I don't hesitate in drinking myself into a stupor. I sing along to the songs, surprising myself as I know the lyrics to some thanks to Eric and his love for The Spice Girls.

Alistair yells for everyone to pipe down, announcing the countdown to midnight. I grab Austin's hand, taking him to the dance floor as we gather in a large group. At the top of our drunken lungs, we shout the countdown and yell 'Happy New Year' to each other.

Austin wraps his arms around my waist, pulling me into him. "Happy New Year, Ava."

Resting my hands on his shoulders, I stare into his eyes as we both laugh uncontrollably for no reason at all. "And to you. Who would've thought we'd end up here, sad and pathetic, drunk on pints while Dick tries to score with Sharon?"

"He has game." Austin chuckles, letting out a slight cough. "As do many of the men in here. You're quite the hit tonight."

My shoulders shrug, then I grin. "I'm going to stay single this year, you know, be a selfish bitch and make it all about me. I'm so done with the dating scene. It's exhausting."

"To quote you, you do you, boo."

I burst out laughing at how awkward Austin sounded when saying that. We've both had more than enough to drink, so I toy with bringing up calling Millie. If Austin is fine with saying hello, as I know Millie will be too, it seems like the perfect way to ring in the new year—close the past to bigger and better things moving forward.

"Hey, listen, would it be awkward if I call Millie? She would love to see you?"

Austin dances in front of me, lost in his own groove. He

has always been a good dancer, and they always say that men who can move on the dance floor can move in the bedroom. *Don't even think it.*

"Yeah, it's fine," he yells over the noise.

I pull him away from the dance floor to a quieter section of the bar while dialing her number, and wait for the call to connect. As soon as her face appears, I wave and yell Happy New Year. With a smile on her face, she returns the sentiments.

"So, guess who I ran into?"

"Who?"

Austin bumps into my side, causing me to smack his arm. He waves hello, grinning as Millie raises her brows, surprised to see him.

"Austin?" Her eyes widen as her lips curve upward into a welcoming smile. "What a small world. How have you been?"

"Busy with work...and you?"

"Same, I'm in LA now."

Austin smiles. "Of course, it's home."

"Okay, we just wanted to say hello," I interrupt, pushing him out of the way. "I love you, Millie. Give everyone my love!"

I press the button to end the call accidentally. "Oh shit!"

"What happened?"

"I hung up." I laugh, followed by a hiccup. "Oh well, the night has only begun!"

My hips sway on their own accord to the music, but my phone vibrates in my hand non-stop. I can barely make out the screen, squinting to read the text messages.

Millie: *Did you just hang up on me?*

Millie: *So, you just ran into Austin? Is he okay? I hope he doesn't hate me?*

Millie: *You know what? Don't answer that. Why are you at a pub? I saw an Irish flag behind you.*

Millie: *And what the hell was that music?*

Millie: *Okay, don't answer any of that. Why aren't you with Olivier? Did something happen?*

Millie: *ANSWER THAT*

Geez, my sister is relentless in her pursuit of answers. I decide to ignore her. Besides, she's busy with Will plus a drunk Rocky and Eric. I'm the least of her problems.

Austin and I continue dancing with our new friends until my feet grow tired. If I knew I'd be jumping around all night, I wouldn't have worn these strappy heels which pinch my feet.

Placing my arms around him, I rest my head on his shoulder and losing myself in his comforting hug. He feels like home, and at a time when it feels like my whole world is falling apart, Austin walking into this bar is everything.

A remixed version of Rihanna's songs blares over the speaker, an unusual choice for an Irish bar, but apparently, Alistair is diverse with his music.

"Remember the time we went on a road trip to Lake Tahoe, and it was just you and me? I think Millie had to come later because of some exam."

"Yeah, the trip when your mom and dad were heard, um, in the cellar?"

I shake my head. "Urgh, I purposely forgot that. Thanks for the reminder."

"Anytime, so you were saying?"

"We sang this song in the car during our sing-off. It surprised me you knew the lyrics." I laugh.

"I have sisters."

"That's the excuse you said back then."

"Wait." He slows down, so we're both still. "Are you telling me we have a song?"

"Yeah, but I don't know how I feel about it being a song about monsters. Isn't that a bad omen?"

Austin cocks his head to the side with a sneer. "You and your bad omens. Has anything terrible happened to you yet?"

"Um, where shall I begin?"

"But you're alive, right? And aside from this wrist of yours, you are perfectly healthy."

"I am, but..." I trail off, staring at him oddly.

"So, in my professional opinion, you're not broken, just a little bruised."

I place my hands on his chest. "You know what, you're right? I came here feeling very sorry for myself tonight. And as always, Dr. Carter, you're impeccable with your timing in life."

Austin rubs his chin, a mischievous grin spreading across his face. I can't help but mirror his expression, relaxing my shoulders while enjoying our time together.

"What do you think... another round before Alistair kicks us out?"

I grab his hand, dragging him to the bar. "Alistair, one more for the road. You know what, make it on the house for everyone."

Austin chuckles beside me while Alistair looks concerned. "Ava, sweetheart, that's a fair bit of coin."

"Hey, what's the point of all this coin if I'm fucking miserable," I shout back at him before I grab the microphone, standing on top of the bar. "Drinks are on the house!"

A loud roar erupts from the crowd. People push forward to the bar as Alistair and his wait staff busily begin pouring drinks. I lower my body, though careful to keep my legs in place to avoid a show. My body begins to wobble until I lose my balance, and Austin catches me while I fall into his arms.

"You're crazy, Ava."

I touch his nose with my finger, making him squirm. His eyes spark, the hazel staring back at me as he simpers. For a fleeting moment, my heart stills, but I'm quickly distracted by Alistair sliding two glasses of whisky toward Austin and me.

We both take a glass, raising it to each other to clink them together.

"To new beginnings, a new year," he praises.

"I'll drink to that."

THREE

AUSTIN

"Time of death, eighteen hundred hours and thirteen minutes."

The head physician, Dr. Trainor, quietly advises another doctor to accompany him in delivering the news to the family just outside in the corridor. A necessary task but, nonetheless, emotionally draining.

He's gone.

A kid—just shy of six years old.

All because of an allergic reaction to a peanut butter and jelly sandwich another kid ate beside him.

Inside the ER, the team begins the task of preparing a post-mortem. Despite every trained staff member being called in to assist, we did everything possible to save him from the moment his mother carried him through the doors, hysterical as her son lay in her arms unresponsive.

A colleague, Grayson, places his hand on my shoulder, squeezing it tight. He's a second-year resident, and I'm just shy of completing my first year. Over the past twelve months, I've witnessed deaths and can count every single one of them—drug overdoses, car accidents, heart attacks to name a few.

But never a child.

We work busily now, following protocol as Dr. Trainor leaves the area and heads down the hall. My body tenses, waiting for the shrilling scream, and then—we all stop the moment it echoes down the hallway. A sound so animalistic, it tears your conscience apart, and the questions beg to be answered, could we have done more? The answer, medically speaking, is no. An entire team of professionals did everything and anything to save him.

And that's what I repeat in my head. I've spent years studying, but the first times are always the hardest. All I can do now is put on a brave face and perform my job to help other patients who need my attention. Life must go on, despite a family outside wishing they were dead as well.

Time becomes a blur—the emergency room's relentless energy doesn't allow me a moment to stop. Tonight will be the busiest, with alcohol poisoning being the number one reason for admissions. I'm not rostered on all night, though my shift extends two hours overdue to a couple being admitted for hyperthermia while falling into the Hudson River.

When I officially clock off for the day, I stand inside the staff room with my head against the locker. My eyes are fixated on the ceiling, a blank canvas aside from the blinding fluorescent light. There's a tightness inside my chest that won't dissipate, no matter how hard I try to control my hitched breathing.

The sound of the door opening breaks my trance. A fellow resident, Lane, walks in and notices me standing quietly. She opens her locker and retrieves her items in silence, then pulls her long ginger hair out of the bun it was styled in.

"It was tough today," she says, her voice low while dropping her gaze to the floor. "You did the best you could, Austin. You did everything you could, as did the team."

"Then why does it feel like it wasn't enough?"

"Because he's gone. It was his time, as devastating as that may be," Lane professes softly. "You're going to have times when the world is shining, and you've saved a life. But there are also the darker moments when all efforts were not enough. This is the nature of the beast, and we're bound to face these challenges if not daily."

I think about what she says, but the anger is a force desperate for destruction. What if I tried harder? What if the team tried harder? What if we fought for a bit longer and a miracle occurred? All these questions spin like a vicious cycle inside my exhausted state of mind.

"Listen, shifts over," Lane reminds me, releasing a sigh. "What are your plans tonight? I'm heading to a friend's place for a rooftop party. You're welcome to join me if you have no plans. It's best you get out with people and don't be alone tonight."

My head remains low. "I don't feel like celebrating."

"Fair enough. Just promise me you won't be alone, okay?"

I'm unable to nod nor promise her anything, keeping my words at bay. Lane places her hand on my arm, then leans over and kisses my cheek. "Austin, you're worthy of being here. You've helped so many people who needed you. Please never forget that."

It's almost as if she knows my heinous thoughts, how I feel unworthy of even being on this earth. Why me? Why am I spared my life when somewhere in this city, a family is mourning the loss of their son?

Grabbing my clothes, I change out of my scrubs, slamming the locker door. With my bag slung over my shoulder, I walk the corridors quietly, but all I hear is the shrilling scream repeating in my head.

Lane is right, I can't be alone tonight. With no plans, I decide to go home first to dump my stuff and have a much-needed shower, willing to gain some normality and attempt to wash off today's event.

Under the steaming hot water, my movements are still, allowing the water to cascade down my back. I run my hands through my hair, flashing back to the moment I told my parents I wanted to study medicine, and how proud they were because my grandfather was a heart surgeon prior to his passing.

As I grew older, it's all I could think about. It became my drive when I had to produce high grades to get accepted into Johns Hopkins. Then, as the years passed and fate played somewhat of a part with Millie, the decision to transfer to Columbia University felt like a step in the right direction. I was surrounded by the best, and as far as ERs go, we were the busiest in the city.

I knew it would be challenging, but I find myself questioning my strength when these times present themselves, unsure if I have it in me to go all the way. One day, I'll be in Dr. Trainor's position, delivering news to families just like tonight, and that thought alone brings on another level of fear. Am I born to be this person, or will I fail miserably? Again, the questions plague me endlessly.

The water is so relaxing as I lose track of time. When I finally turn the faucets off, I dry myself then wrap a towel around my waist while walking toward my closet. Not in the mood for anything dressy, I opt for a pair of jeans and my favorite navy hoody. With my white sneakers on, I also grab a jacket, given it's predicted to hit below twenty tonight.

There's a stream of messages on my phone from friends inviting me out tonight and a few women I've hooked up with over the last year, but the more I think about it, the less appealing it is to have to make an effort and pretend everything is great. What I need is a drink, something stiff, then call it a night—alone.

I walk to a bar called Alistair's two blocks over from my apartment. It's an Irish pub, and given this part of the city isn't as busy as some areas like Times Square, I'm hoping to get a seat and drink before midnight.

As I enter Alistair's, the sound is deafening, precisely what I need to drown out the noise in my head. Pubs often cater to a different crowd, much more lively and friendly than some of the upper-class bars Manhattan is known for.

My gaze falls upon a few rowdy patrons, obnoxious on the dance floor with a glass in hand. One, in particular, is relentless in his pursuit of what appears to be a much older woman than him. The sight of it is amusing, and I welcome the distraction.

But then, my eyes unknowingly gravitate to a woman at the bar. The long, lean, tanned legs are crossed with a pair of black opened-toe heels. Jesus, she must have been cold outside. It amazes me how women will do anything for fashion, wearing the skimpiest dresses just to look sexy.

Her body sits on the wooden stool, facing the bar. A jacket had been removed, hanging off the backrest and catching my attention is a bandage wrapped around her wrist. Fuck, my mind thinks the worst—a whole lot of problems and a possible suicide attempt gone wrong. No, don't overthink it, she looks too well put together and confident in her attire.

She releases a laugh, the corner of her mouth lifting. *Okay, relax, it's probably just a minor injury.*

My shoulders loosen, alleviating the momentary tension as I admire her curves in the very revealing gold dress she wears, noticing it barely covers her body. If I'm not mistaken, she's not even wearing a bra.

Fuck, like I need to be thinking with my dick right now.

But something about her draws me in, a moth to a very burning flame. I tilt my head, bewildered by the curiosity until she angles her face giving me a better look at her side profile. Instantly, I recognize the beautiful woman like a friendly ghost from my past. A past I'd long forgotten.

Ava Edwards.

As I take steps closer to her, the man beside Ava appears to be coming on a little too strong, physically. Unwillingly, my fists clench as her face is less than pleased, and my hostility toward this stranger causes my teeth to grind, enough for me to warn him to back the fuck off.

Ava spins on her chair, the emerald eyes meeting mine. For a split moment, I see my past come back. My life with Millie, a lot of 'what-ifs' and a trip down memory lane which hasn't happened in a long while. So many mixed emotions from just one goddamn stare.

The shimmer in her eyes reflects back at me, but there's something about it that causes concern, almost as if she puts up a façade and wants everyone to see a different Ava.

Without a second thought, she throws her arms around me. I allow myself to feel her embrace, the familiar scent which brings a sense of comfort. Ava and I had a friendship for years, thanks to my relationship with Millie, but we drifted apart, and I assumed her ties lay with her new brother-in-law.

We both linger a little too long, and judging by the glass in front of her, she's had a fair bit to drink already.

There's no holding back, heading straight to the liquor to ease the tension as we catch up on life. Neither one of us appears to be in the best of moods, denying the truth of the cross we bear because tonight is supposed to be a time to celebrate life.

I enjoy the whisky served, though bourbon is a personal preference. In the end, nothing matters. Whatever can erase my memories, and the quicker, the better.

The close proximity gives me a chance to raise the topic of her injury, which is bandaged poorly in my professional opinion. Thankfully, she allows me to examine her wrist, which appears to be a minor sprain. Still, I suggest she have it x-rayed in case there's further damage.

With Ava beside me, I forget about earlier tonight as we drink our worries away and dance to the music that plays. Ava is always one to be the life of the party, and right now, I welcome her outgoing personality and overbearing need to drink ourselves into a stupor.

Then, it becomes the moment we've all been waiting for. The clock strikes midnight, prompting us to ring in the new year the only way we can—more drinking and dancing.

The crowd becomes even rowdier after midnight. A few grab the microphone, singing their renditions of pop classics. Some men get lucky, disappearing with women they'd only just met. I lose count of how many drinks I've chugged, my limbs falling numb while I enjoy dancing as if the world outside this pub doesn't exist.

Then, Ava asks if it's okay to call Millie, to which I agree. Like I give a fuck anymore. That boat has long sailed, and I fucked a hell of a lot of women to get over her. It worked, obviously, since seeing her on the screen doesn't evoke any romantic feelings. It is, however, surreal to see her again, and even though she didn't confirm the words, I'd heard through the grapevine she'd gotten married and adopted a son. I don't ask questions. It's not my place to get involved in her life anymore.

The damage is done, and Millie has her billionaire prince charming.

After ending the call abruptly, thanks to Ava's accidental finger slip, she offers drinks on the house, to which everyone cheers. I laugh, keeping my opinion to myself. If anyone has the money, it's the daughter of Lex Edwards.

Alistair yells for the final round, which is met with a lot of boos. I bring my phone closer to me, the blurry screen appearing to be after two in the morning.

Ava slides another glass to me, despite my focus being questionable and words slurred.

"So, where to now?" she whines with a frown. "I'm not ready for bed."

"I don't want to be alone tonight," I tell her honestly, downing the whisky in one go. I'd become immune, there no longer being a burn.

"Let's go to your place?"

I turn to face her, tilting my head. "My place?"

"Look, I would offer my place, but that's only if you don't mind watching two men fucking each other?"

"I beg your pardon?"

"Yes, Austin. I said it. A penis in another man's asshole. So, your place?"

I don't even know where to begin with that conversation, assuming she lives with gay roommates, but who gives a fuck—my place isn't far, which is a bonus.

We stumble because walking would be a far cry from how we get home. The only thing which keeps us alive and protected from dying of hyperthermia is our duet of "Islands in the Stream." A few homeless people shout, telling us to shut up.

When we finally reach my apartment, it's slightly better but still cold. I turn on the heat and yell out for Jonah, my roommate, but remember he was at some party tonight.

"This is your place?" Ava questions while removing her jacket and throwing it on the sofa. "It's cute."

I laugh, almost stumbling on my own feet, to which I hold onto the wall for balance.

"Cute? I should probably be offended."

"Okay, small. But hey, I get it. You're a doctor and probably barely spend time here." Ava giggles, letting out a hiccup. "I'm guessing your refrigerator has only Chinese takeout boxes."

"Far from the truth," I contest.

She opens the door, her eyes widening because Chinese take-out isn't something I enjoy unless absolutely necessary. Jonah is a gym buff, and he doesn't consume anything unless it comes in a shake.

"Okay, who's the health nut? And is that Kale I see?"

"As you said, Miss Edwards, I am a doctor. I kind of know the importance of taking care of my body."

Ava closes the refrigerator door, then glances my way with a simper.

"I can tell." She nods, biting her bottom lip. "You look good. Though, you've always looked good. Guess I couldn't admit that before without being crucified, huh?"

I lean against the wall, crossing my arms with a grin. "You're not so bad yourself."

"I'm old," she blurts out.

"Old? Come on, Ava. You're gorgeous. Like a fine wine that gets better with age."

"You're just saying that because you're standing with me inside your kitchen. I'm washed up. A potential has-been. Everyone wants younger women. I'm not even good enough that my boyfriend had to go fuck some other guy."

She rests against the refrigerator, closing her eyes. The fabric of the silk dress she wears clings to her curves, and it's confirmed under this lighting—there's no bra. *Don't even think about it.*

"Ava, what's going on?"

"I don't know anymore." She lowers her head, unable to look at me. "I am nothing."

Moving closer to her, I raise her chin with my finger. As I stare into her eyes, I remember all the times we were together, from back in high school to the big moments when Millie was around. Ava is gorgeous and always has been. I'm not one to compare her to her sister, but all four Edwards daughters are absolutely stunning in their own right.

And yes, if the truth were to be told, there were moments which passed between us. But like anything forbidden, you back off to avoid dangerous territory.

"You, Ava, are worth everything. So, you're not a teenager? You're a beautiful twenty-five-year-old woman who any man would be lucky to have."

My gaze falls momentarily toward her lips, pink and supple, but I scold myself for pushing the boundaries, knowing we shouldn't even be doing this.

"Austin," she croaks.

I breathe, swallowing the lump inside my throat to answer with a simple. "Yes?"

Ava's shoulders curl over her chest, her bottom lip now

trembling. "If any man is lucky to have me, why am I alone tonight?"

"You're not alone," I remind her with a low voice, struggling to control my urge to prove her wrong. My fingertip grazes the strap of her dress as I see her suck in a breath.

"No, I'm not...alone," she manages to let out.

"Ava..."

"Austin," she counters breathlessly. "Choose me, please. Just for tonight."

I raise my eyes to meet hers, begging myself to do the right thing but slowly losing the battle as she becomes too irresistible with her plea. *Don't do it. Think of the consequences.*

Fuck the consequences.

My lips crash onto hers as my body grows hot and feverish. She moans in my mouth, running her hands through the back of my hair. My hands wrap beneath her legs as I carry her toward my room, laying her flat on the bed. As I climb on top of her, pressing against her body, we lose ourselves in heated kisses, barely able to come up for air.

Her skin tastes of sin, an addictive taste I can't seem to get enough of. It's forbidden, because she's my ex-fiancée's sister. But the dangerous position we find ourselves in only adds to the adrenaline rush overcoming me. My kisses consume every groove and crevice, desperate to continue the deep moans she expels.

Pressing my cock against her, I'm eager to remove my pants and be inside her as if my life depends on it, but instead, I drag her strap down, exposing her beautiful tits in the pale moonlight that filters through the window.

My thirst to taste them becomes my only focus as I run my tongue down until I circle her nipples, causing her back to arch. They're so fucking sexy, firm, and round, fitting in my hand perfectly. Desperate to remove my jeans, I manage to drag them off with my boxers, allowing my cock to spring free.

Ava breathes heavily, sliding her hand between us to grasp my shaft. The moment her soft fingers wrap around me, my body jerks with a long-winded groan escaping my dry mouth. Slowly, she begins stroking me, but I warn her we need protection, despite our inability to think straight and fuck like maniacs.

Leaning over, I pull my nightstand drawer open to retrieve a condom. In the dark, I fumble with the corner of the packet, ripping it open and sliding it on within a matter of seconds. This isn't my first rodeo, and I've mastered the art to protect myself in record time.

"Ava," I call softly, giving her a chance to pull away. "Are you sure? Once we do this, we can't undo it."

"No one has to know," she whispers, cupping my face in her hands while bringing me in for a deep kiss. "It's just between us."

Her confidence erases my hesitation. It will be *our* little secret.

Dirty, raw, and completely off-limits.

As I enter her, she gasps loudly, beautiful as she lies beneath me. I'm unable to control my movements, desperate to finish but wanting to savor the moment.

I shift my body, wanting to see her on top of me, so she's riding me with her tits in full view. My hands fall behind my back, watching her with a heated stare as I lick my lips, desperate to bite her nipples which stand erect.

"Austin," she moans. *"Don't stop, please."*

Even if I try, I can't, so far beyond thinking rationally. I wrap my hand around her nape, pulling her down to taste her lips. They're soft, sweet, and taste so damn irresistible.

But even in the dark room, with barely any light to cast our shadows, I'm drawn to Ava's movements. The tilt of her head, the veins in her neck while she continues to call my name.

The way she makes me feel like a *man*.

Resistance is futile, and I want her in every way possible. I want to own her, only for this moment, determined to fulfill this newly created fantasy.

I demand she gets on all fours.

It's time to give her what she wants.

My hands firmly grip her hips, thrusting in and out as my eyes shut, barely able to control the urge to come. Within minutes, Ava's body tenses, and she calls out my name while coming, pushing me over the edge. The heated rush spreads all over my body, impairing my vision to become a burst of stars like a sky full of fireworks. My grunts slow down while I try to catch my breath until the only sound in the room is our heavy breathing as we both come down from the high.

Sliding myself out of her, I gently remove the condom and toss it in the trash near the nightstand. Unable to find any energy, I fall onto the bed beside her, the two of us silent until Ava sits up.

"I should go home." She attempts to stand but loses her balance. I pull her back into the bed, knowing we've both had too much to drink to go anywhere or do anything else.

"You're drunk, and it wouldn't be safe. Stay here."

"But..."

"But what?" I demand, thinking how unsafe it is outside on the streets right now. Throw in the fact that she's a beautiful woman. There's no chance in hell I'll allow it. "You're staying here, and that's final."

"Okay," she agrees, keeping it simple. "Hey, Austin? Happy New Year."

I close my eyes with a grin, but my head begins to spin as the night finally catches up with me. My lips move as I mumble the sentiment in return, but then it all becomes too much, and sleep is imminent. I turn to my side, making myself comfortable, and welcome her warm body beside me.

"Good night, Ava," I whisper, then reach out to pull her body close to me.

She doesn't pull away nor say another word. And before I can even speak, she is fast asleep in my arms, her gentle snores like music to my ears.

It's just one night. That's all it'll ever be.

Our secret.

One night between two people who desperately needed only one thing.

Companionship.

FOUR

AVA

My head is pounding like a woodpecker constantly banging one spot.

Unable to open my eyes, they feel like they're sewn together, impossible to open the lead weight—ramifications from last night's events whatever they were.

I can't even think without it all hurting.

With a slight groan, I rub my eyes before opening them again, slowly, to be met with daylight. The sun is shining through the windows, something I'd normally enjoy but not this morning. I sit up, trying to make sense of everything.

I know the pounding head is because of the alcohol I consumed last night, but I don't recall how I got home or who I came home with.

The sheets against my bare skin are unfamiliar, cheap in texture, unlike the Egyptian cotton sheets which adorn my king-size bed. My mother taught me to spare no expense when it came to bed linen. A good night's rest is the best way to start the day, according to her.

So is having someone between your legs, for argument's sake.

Using every muscle in my body to sit up, I let out another groan until my eyes snap open. Slowly, I turn to my right, my gaze landing on the exposed torso cut to definition. The pit of my stomach churns as my eyes gravitate to the face of the man beside me.

"Shit," I mumble, followed by a hard swallow.

Austin's eyes flutter, and as they open wide, they focus on me in a dazed state.

I pull the sheet up, covering my breasts, aware I'm stark naked.

"Ava," he croaks, then clears his throat. "Why are... oh shit."

He covers his face with his hands, rubbing it vigorously while letting out a sigh. The memory of last night is hazed, though pieces fall into place of just how intimate we were. Me, in bed with a man who is my sister's ex-fiancé. What a terrible way to ring in the new year, certain that all the bad luck of yesterday was a warning of things to come.

I clutch the sheet tighter, my back still exposed. Then, in a panicked state, I scour the area around me for my clothes, spotting them across the room. Great, if I take the sheet with me, chances are Austin will be completely naked as well.

"So..." I drag, fiddling with a loose thread on the end of the sheet. "We um..."

"I think so. I mean, yes."

"I... I..." My words stumble, still shocked at the situation I've found myself in. "I was upset."

"Me too," he lowers his voice.

I turn to face his direction, waiting for him to elaborate, only to be met with an awkward silence. "You were? I mean, I vaguely remember when you walked into the bar, your eyes were bloodshot."

"A patient died in the ER yesterday."

"I'm sorry."

"He was a kid."

My stomach becomes even heavier, a wave of nausea causing me to shiver.

"How awful. Understandably, you're upset," I say softly, unsure how to express my emotions right now. I duck my chin, licking my lips to quench my dry mouth and feeling somewhat vulnerable as we continue to be in the same bed. "I'm so sorry you had to go through that, Austin. I feel terrible for pushing you to party last night."

"No, Ava," he mentions with a slightly annoyed tone. "You were exactly what I needed. The thing is, there is nothing anyone could've done in that room to save him. We did everything we were trained to do, but I questioned my ability and if I have what it takes to practice medicine for the rest of my life. And then, you're there, inside an Irish bar, of all places."

"But..." I trail off, unsure how to bring up the predicament we find ourselves in. "We ended up here, in bed."

"We did."

I'm distracted by how amazing his body looks as he lays with his head resting on his arm, staring at the ceiling. Beneath the sheet, my nipples harden, making me conscious. This is all kinds of wrong. I barely remember last night. I was so drunk, and while bits and pieces are clearer than others, I couldn't even answer who made the first move. Not that it matters now, the damage is done.

My shoulders weigh heavy as the guilt sets in. Austin is Millie's ex-fiancé. How is she going to react when she hears I slept with him? *You don't tell her, idiot.*

"I'm going to use your bathroom."

I drag the sheet with me, refusing to turn around in case

I catch a glimpse of him completely exposed. As I assume he's getting dressed, he shuffles behind me, then I lean down to retrieve my clothes from the bedroom floor.

The moment the bathroom door closes, my stomach makes a churning sound, but I manage to suppress the feeling of being sick. Instead, I quickly make my way to the basin, turning on the faucet to run some water to wash my face. After a few splashes, I grab some tissues and wipe my face down. As I stare at my reflection in the mirror, the dark circles around my eyes make me look like a zombie. In my entire life, I don't think I've ever looked so worn out, both physically and emotionally.

My hands clutch onto the basin as I drop my head and close my eyes for just a moment. Yesterday started a chain of reactions from the moment I was told my services were no longer needed. From that moment, the Universe had it in for me—of that, I'm sure. It's obvious in my previous life, I had pissed someone off.

But then, Austin's voice replays in my head. *"A patient died in the ER yesterday, a kid."*

My eyes snap wide open as my stare fixates on the mirror. I take a deep breath before dressing in my clothes, then leave the bathroom.

When I enter the room again, Austin is wearing sweats and a tee. His hair is a wild mess yet beautifully sitting on his head like it's been styled to portray a bad boy in a photo-shoot. The only thing is, Austin is anything but a bad boy. Instead, he's a kind, loving, intelligent man—who would never purposely hurt any woman.

The perfect catch if he wasn't my sister's ex.

"Listen, I should go."

"Ava, what happened last night can stay between us. Nobody has to know. Nobody needs to know."

I nod, torn between my conscience and why a part of me wanted to stay. To feel loved, if only for a minute.

"You're right. No one has to know. It was just one night, and we were both hurting."

"Will you be okay?"

"Me?" I force a smile, then glance at him one more time before he moves closer to me, and we're only inches apart. "You know me. I'm good at smiling for the camera."

He laces his hand around my neck to draw me in, planting a kiss on my forehead. His lips linger, and just for a moment, I wonder what it would be like. But the thoughts are like poison to my already fragile ego. "Thank you for last night."

"Anytime," I whisper, then laugh softly. "I mean, not anytime, but you know what I mean."

Slowly, he pulls away though his stare continues to drill deep inside my soul. While lost in thought, the momentary silence is the closure we both need to say goodbye once and for all.

My feet move slowly toward the door when Austin calls out, "Ava?"

I turn around. "Yeah?"

"For what it's worth, it was good."

"Just good?" I question with a sly grin.

"If I tell the truth, chances are, I'll drag you back in here." His smirk is unrelenting, the perfect mix of naughty and nice. "Take care, okay?"

"I will, Austin. And you too."

As I close the door, I release the breath I didn't realize I'd been holding in. Outside, the air is cold as I button up my coat and extend my arm to hail the cab not too far in the distance. The cab ride of shame back to my apartment feels slow and tedious despite the empty streets after a night of celebrations.

When I'm finally standing outside my door, the reality of what lies on the other side begins to stir unwanted feelings of resentment.

I had it all—fame, money, a sexy boyfriend.

But I'm all alone, now.

And that hits harder than the sight of Olivier's things gone from our bedroom.

My heels click against the marble floors as I exit the elevator and enter the lobby. It's the first day back in the office after the four-day holiday weekend, and my mood has shifted from feeling sorry for myself to just angry at life in general. During the time alone, I made up a lie to everyone saying I'd come down with a head cold—a great excuse to avoid calls and messages because I needed sleep.

Millie got all mother hen on me, worried about my well-being, but I continued to lie because it was easier than telling the truth, for now.

Eliza, my receptionist, is wearing an awfully low-cut top—coral color with some weird pattern I don't care for. Beside her, Lilliana, my Chief of Marketing—is also dressed rather sexy. I bite down to keep my mouth shut but suspect the reason why they're showing so much skin despite the tenacious snow outside—is sitting inside my office.

"Good morning, ladies," I greet, forcing a smile.

"Good morning, Ava." Eliza grins overbearingly. "Your father is waiting inside your office."

"Of course he is," I mumble beneath my breath. "Do me

a favor? Place a jacket on because I can tell you now my father only has eyes for my mom."

Walking to my office, I don't turn back to see her reaction. Behind the glass doors, I see my father is on the phone, standing next to the window. The moment he lays eyes on me, he ends his call.

"Ava." He sighs with a loving smile. "Happy New Year, sweetheart."

I fall into his embrace as he kisses my hair, something Dad has always done for as long as I can remember. The smell of his aftershave lingers in the air, calming my anger as his presence shifts the room's energy.

"Thanks, Dad," I tell him, then slowly pull away. "To what do I owe this visit?"

He motions for me to sit, and even in my own office, he still dominates the room. I admire the suit he wears—Armani, of course. They love to style him. As I recall, Mom mentioned years ago they often send new clothes to him. He is an influencer in his own right, and despite his ignorance, I'm aware there are several online accounts dedicated to him. It's comical until photos come up shirtless from his younger years and there are eggplant emojis in the captions.

"Just checking in on my daughter. Anything wrong with that?"

I cross my legs, resting my hands on my knees. "I love you, Dad, but you've got an agenda, and I'm assuming it's about what happened in Miami."

He keeps his gaze fixed. "Maybe, I am concerned about you."

"It's bullshit, okay?" I mouth, trying to control my temper. "How dare they pull a last-minute thing like that on me. I'm about to walk into a meeting in which people's jobs are on the line. I don't know how this happened, but someone is going to pay. Do you know how many people I have to answer to because everything I was supposed to do was endorsed?"

"Ava, you have every right to be upset. I wish you'd called me that night. I would have gotten my people onto it."

"C'mon, Dad, I wasn't going to ruin your night too." I sigh dejectedly. "I'm a big girl. Therefore, I pay people the big bucks to sort out messes like Miami. This isn't the first bump in the road, and it sure as hell won't be the last."

"The offer is there," he reminds me calmly.

"I know," I respond, releasing a breath. "So, tell me, how was New Year's Eve?"

"Let's see... Rocky ended up naked in the pool. Ashton fell asleep by eight. Your mother drank too many Jell-O shots."

"It's not a party without Rocky naked in the pool." I laugh, shaking my head. "Age has not tamed him."

"Aside from that, it was a good night." His expression shifts, the smile wavering as his eyes fixate on me with concern. "How about you?"

"Oh yeah, it was fine. Just went out."

He continues to gaze at me, stilling his movements to observe my reaction to his question better. It's almost become second nature to be silently interrogated by Dad. Though, we've always had a strong relationship. When it came to Millie, they used to butt heads a lot, probably because Millie is so much like Mom. The two of them often sided with one another, which only riled up Dad. Plus, they were both argumentative, part of being a lawyer.

As for my relationship with him, we've always remained close, more so than with Mom at times. I definitely got away with more growing up, hence why I was dubbed his 'favorite'. Only by my sisters, though, he never actually said it out loud.

It's not like it's a competition, but Mom is busy these days doing the grandparent thing, which ties her bond to Millie. I guess it's natural, given that Will and Millie are in that stage of their lives.

"Look, Dad. I don't want to hear I told you so. Save the lecture for another time," I warn him as best as I can. "I'm trying to work through things right now."

"Ava, it's me," he assures me, softening his tone. "I'm not going to lecture you. You're an adult now, a very successful one at that."

"Here's the short version, Dad." I take a deep breath, then release quickly. "I walked into my apartment and caught Olivier in bed with some guy's dick in his ass."

Dad scowls, shaking his head in silence. "I'm sorry, Ava."

"What's there to be sorry about, Dad? I'm an idiot. I got caught up in how great we looked on the outside while ignoring the signs. They were all there. And guess what I have to do now? Pretend none of this happened."

"We've all had scandal happen in our lives. Trust me, present company included. Keep your head high and always remain professional," he advises, straightening his posture. It's almost like he did it on purpose as I follow suit, bringing back the confidence which has crumbled over the last few days. "Nasty comments will be said. Just have your publicist make one blanket statement. It's important Olivier does the same."

"C'mon, Dad, what are people going to say when they find out he's gay?"

"To be honest, Ava, people will voice their opinion on you, then move on. Olivier's life will change forever. A straight man coming out is never easy. While I disagree with how he handled your relationship, you have to understand he has a bigger issue at hand. There are a lot of people in this world who don't support same-sex relationships. If you can find it in your heart to close that chapter in your life, be the woman I raised you to be and support him as a friend. Now is not the time to air your anger in public."

"You're right, Dad. It won't be easy for him."

"I'm taking it your mother and sisters don't know?"

I shake my head. "I didn't want to talk about it. I'm humiliated, Dad."

"You've got the Edwards blood. This will make you stronger. Now listen, I have a meeting downtown, and then I'm flying back home tonight. When are you coming home?"

"Soon, I promise. I'll schedule a shoot or something, so I can claim it as a business expense."

"Now, that's the girl I raised," he bemuses.

"Smart and an angel, right?"

"I don't know about angel...you've had your moments."

I throw an amused glance at him. "Don't tarnish my reputation as an angel. Just admit it, Millie has been more of a headache than me."

"You got me there, kid. Though Alexa is proving to be a very challenging daughter." He chuckles softly. "Okay, listen. I need to meet Will."

"Will is here?" I ask, unaware of his visit to the city. "I might see if he is free for dinner tonight."

"Just text him," Dad suggests, then rises from the chair. "Now, go to your meeting and make sure you show them who's boss."

"Always do, Dad." I wink with a lopsided grin. "I've learned from the best."

~

Will had a last-minute change of plans. A client he was supposed to meet for dinner came down with some infectious bug. When Will told me he could meet for dinner, I welcomed the chance to catch up with him since it has been a while since we saw each other last.

"My favorite brother-in-law," I greet while leaning over to hug Will.

"What do you want?" He pulls away, scrutinizing me with his blue eyes. Just like Dad, he's wearing a designer suit. Armani, again, of course. Like two peas in a billionaire pod. "You're in trouble, aren't you?"

I take a seat at the table, ignoring his stare while I place the napkin on my lap then motion for the waiter to serve us. I need wine—stat. This restaurant, Luciano's, makes the best pasta in the city and is known for stocking vintage wine.

"What makes you think I'm in trouble?"

"Because you're making my wife's life hell by giving her the runaround and not answering her texts."

The waiter stops at our table, and without even looking at the menu, I know exactly what I want. Will takes a moment, then orders a steak medium done. When the young man leaves, Will focuses his attention back onto me.

Pushing my shoulders back, I inhale deeply. "I'm trying to process things rather than get all dramatic. Let's be honest here... when Millie and I are together, things can get out of control with our emotions."

"Oh, you think?" he responds sarcastically. "The two of you on the phone is like listening to some overbearing soap opera."

"Yes, see? I guess it's why I'm trying to work through this rather than act irrationally."

As I sit across from Will, the truth is still a hard pill to swallow. I'm scared to talk to Millie because the guilt would eat away at me. But, in reverse thinking, I have nothing to be guilty about, technically. Will and Millie are happily married with a son. It's not like she'd be jealous. She has the love of her life, her soulmate.

Yet, it doesn't make what happened with Austin and me less forbidden.

He is still, and forever will be—her ex-fiancé.

"What's going on, Ava? This isn't like you."

"Olivier and I broke up."

He nods, eyeing me. "I'm sorry. Amelia mentioned you guys had some issues."

My eyes widen, suddenly annoyed at my sister. "Does she tell you everything?"

"No, and to be honest, most of the time, I'm not listening if it's about girl drama." Will purses his lips as the waiter arrives with a bottle of wine. When the wine is poured, we both take a long drink. "If that's any consolation."

"And I slept with someone," I blurt out of nowhere despite my annoyance. "You know, rebound fuck. Not that I mentioned that to Dad this morning."

"It's probably best you don't," Will agrees. "So what? We've all done it. Don't beat yourself up over it."

"I'm not that bad of a person, and it was just one night," I admit, trying to convince myself once again.

As I twist the napkin between my fingers, I glance at Will, wondering if he could read my thoughts? Imagine if he found out, it wouldn't go down pleasantly. When it comes to Millie, Will is over-protective in an alpha male way. He prefers to think she has no past, and he's been the only one.

I clear my throat, then continue, "We both needed comfort for different reasons and agreed it was a one-time thing."

"What's the problem then? It sounds to me like you have your sex life under control."

"I do. I mean, there's still the issue with Olivier."

"Don't waste your time, Ava. What are you looking for, anyway? You're twenty-five, just have fun. It's too young to settle."

"Oh really?" I laugh, leaning back into my chair. "Too young? Did you not propose and marry my sister when she was of the same age?"

"That's different."

I cross my arms in amusement. "Please explain, Mr. Romano?"

"Well, for starters, no one else was going to touch her."

"Keep going, Lex Junior."

Will cringes, hating when I use that nickname on him. "Stop giving me that look. Amelia was always meant to be my wife, end of the story."

"You know what? You are right. Maybe I need to stay single for a while, swear off men."

As Will raises the glass to his lips, he chuckles behind it. "How long will that last?"

"What? You don't think I can stay single?"

"Edwards girls are born to break hearts. Somewhere, out there, a man, or maybe several men, just felt the earth move at your admission. I give you one month."

"One month? I'm going to prove you wrong, Romano."

Will sits back in his chair with a cocky grin, then

extends his hand. "Happy to shake on it, sister-in-law dearest."

"You're a billionaire," I remind him with a satisfied smile. "You should be placing money where your mouth is."

Extending my hand, I follow through with a handshake while I snort at his smug expression. Despite Will being irrecoverably in love with Millie, he was bred the same way as all men. Always thinking with their dick and assuming women are the same, that we all need a man.

Well, I'm not just any woman.

I'm *Ava Edwards*.

And I refuse to let any part of me break again all because of a man.

FIVE

AVA

They say bad luck comes in threes.

From the humiliating event in Miami to Olivier in bed with another man, then to add icing to a screwed-up cake, Olivier decided to run his mouth.

One, two, and fucking—three.

To deflect from his sexuality, Olivier chose to leak private information about me—who I previously dated to a list of men I had slept with before our relationship. Although most of it was a lie, the list was rather impressive if I was an outsider looking in. High-profile billionaires, A-list celebrities, and there was also a prince mentioned.

I should be so goddamn lucky.

But then Olivier took it to another level by leaking a topless photo of me taken on a secluded island during a getaway. Of course, it went viral.

I want to *kill* him.

My legal team went in guns blazing, working nonstop to protect my brand and everything I worked so hard for.

The whole ordeal is a nightmare, dragging on for a month passed. It's a mistake I vow never to repeat. How could I be so naïve to trust a man and even have him move in with me when clearly, I didn't know him at all?

Love and intimate relationships aren't worth all the turmoil. Sure, I bet against Will, but I have no qualms about staying single. More than ever, not worrying about a lover sounds perfectly fine.

Then there's the matter of my father.

To say he isn't impressed is an understatement. I've seen him angry when business deals were compromised, and more notably, when Will and Amelia's affair leaked, but this is the next level of rage. He's on the warpath, and the person caught in the crossfire is, unfortunately, my mother.

"I'm sorry, Mom," I say quietly over the speaker, unable to get out of bed. My eyes glance at the clock on the nightstand, noting the time and quickly calculating how early it is for Mom. She has always been an early riser, much like myself, but the stress of life has worn me out of late. "This is a never-ending mess."

"Ava, this isn't your fault," she reminds me, softening her tone. There's always something in her voice that calms me down. Unlike my reactive father, Mom is rational. "People do things when they're hurt."

"But I don't understand? I've done nothing to hurt him. He left me for another man. I've said nothing regarding his sexuality nor tarnished his name at all. Aside from a blank statement saying we parted ways, I'm innocent here."

My eyes close while I pinch the bridge of my nose, tired of this constant state of despair I've been finding myself in. The ripple of bad luck is like poison seeping through my veins, a slow, agonizing pain that makes it impossible to fight against.

"You will get through this, honey. You're strong and so much like your father it's crazy."

"Speaking of Dad..."

Mom clears her throat. "He has already left for the office."

Dad is also an early riser but heading to the office at five in the morning is enough to tell me he is not coping, still on a mission to destroy Olivier.

"He hasn't returned my calls or my texts. I know he is angry, but that holiday was on a private island. I wasn't walking around in public."

A loud sigh escapes Mom. "You know your father, Ava. If someone comes after someone he loves, he won't stop until that person pays the price."

"Wha... what does that mean?" I panic slightly. "What will he do to Olivier?"

"Honestly? I'd say he'll be hit up with a lawsuit as well as a forced public apology."

I throw my head back against the pillow, releasing a groan. "God, Mom, what the hell is going on with me?"

"You're experiencing life. The ups and downs."

"More like downs."

"It won't always be this way, Ava. First, you need to remember who you are. Grieve this relationship, then hold your head up high and show the world you won't take shit from any other man."

I laugh softly. "So you haven't heard of the bet I made with Will? I swore off men for a while."

"Oh, Ava, taking my mom hat off for a moment," she conveys with a faint chuckle, then continues, "a girl needs to get laid sometimes."

"Are you sure you didn't put Eric's hat on?"

"Too many years as his best friend. I'm ruined."

Releasing a sigh, I fidget with the edge of my duvet. "But I'm serious, Mom. I've dated men and just experienced living with someone. Men are hard work. I don't need all the bullshit that comes with falling in love. I get you and Dad did it, Millie and Will. I mean, sure, it looks nice, but heartache is brutal."

"No argument from me. It is hard work. I've gone through my share of heartache," she reminds me wistfully. "But sometimes, life doesn't allow you to avoid the inevitable. Falling in love can be the best or worst time of your life. It's not always a fairy-tale ending."

"So, what you're saying is, I'm screwed even if I try to control everything?"

"What I'm saying is that sometimes you don't get a choice in where life takes you. Take, for example, Adriana. She never expected to lose her husband and at such a young age. Then add to that grief, trying to raise a baby."

Mom gives me a lot to think about. Always the realist, whereas Dad is the opposite. He creates the life he wants and doesn't feed into the whole 'life is where it takes you.'

"I know what you think because you and your father are so alike." Mom breaks my thoughts, bringing the attention back onto her words. "Ava, you've been fortunate so far, and that's not to say it won't continue that way. But right now, you're hitting some unfortunate bumps. You will get through this even if it feels like you can't."

"I know, Mom." I take a deep breath, hop out of bed, straight to my closet, and pick an outfit for today. The spring weather is warm, warranting a sleeveless dress with a mini-jacket for when the cooler air sets in later in the day. "Listen, I should go. My publicist is driving me crazy, and I'm already late to his meeting."

"How is your new publicist going?" Mom teases.

"Eric is a blessing and a curse. Professionally, he's excellent. But, personally, he is driving me insane. If I could show you the photo dump of women with bangs he disapproves of in my phone, you'd be shocked."

"Hmm, not really. You'd be surprised at what he continues to send me, given I am married. You would think I don't need pictures of sweaty men at the gym. Half these men are young enough to be my son."

I burst out laughing. "That's our Eric."

"Eric, no," I argue while sitting in the white leather chair across from him. "I don't need some guy on my arm if you think I must attend this event tonight."

"Honey cakes, your beaver is looking sad and depressed. Everyone knows the best way to attract a man is by having another man on your arm."

"Firstly, my beaver is fine. And who even uses that term anymore? That's something an old person would say."

"Excuse me. I don't look a day over thirty-five."

"Botox has been kind to you," I drag, then fake a smile. "And to my second point, I will attend alone if I must go."

Eric lets out an annoyed huff, pursing his lips while eyeing me dubiously.

"Will you do all of us a favor and call off the I-don't-need-a man act? You're screaming for a good bang-bang up your coochie. Maybe even the back door. That's if you're even adventurous enough to taste a bit of chocolate over vanilla."

Wrinkling my nose, I keep my lips firmly shut, disgusted he used the words back door and chocolate in the same sentence. But as always, Eric has got me thinking.

Okay, so I haven't gotten laid recently and only because it hasn't even crossed my mind. The last time I was intimate with a man was New Year's Eve, a secret I still carry to this day. On occasion, to clear my conscience, I think about telling Eric but know I must take that one to the grave. I can't afford a leak to Amelia.

"Both doors are just fine," I rush, steering the conversation back to what we were initially discussing. "Now, about tonight, dress code?"

Just before Eric speaks, my phone vibrates in my hand as my father's caller ID appears. I excuse myself to take the call, moving toward the window.

"Hey, Dad."

"Ava," he simply greets, his tone void of any emotion. "Returning your numerous calls."

"Look, I know you're angry at me. I'm angry at myself for trusting Olivier. And I just want to say I appreciate you stepping in. I know you threw a lot of money to have those photos removed..." I trail off, aware of the silence coming from his end.

"I have a meeting I need to get to."

"Uh... sure," I mumble, unable to shake the guilt riddling me. "Dad, I love you."

A long, low sigh filters through the speaker. "I love you too, Ava. I'll call you tonight."

We hang up the phone, but even after his sentiment, it doesn't erase the pain and suffering I've put him through. I try my best to suppress the thoughts, yet the more I try, the more my stomach churns from the stress of it all. Dad never asks for much from me, but I know this is something he won't quickly move on from.

"No luck with Lex?"

I turn to face Eric, shrugging my shoulders. "I guess he

needs to cool down."

"Of course he needs time to cool down." Eric throws his hands up in the air, all dramatic as usual. "We are talking about THE great Lex Edwards. Once, when you were like three and in some playground, a boy pushed you over, and Lex got into a fight with the mother. The poor woman left in tears."

"Oh... how horrible."

"Look, in Lex's defense, the woman was too busy trying to flirt with another dad who clearly had a wedding ring on. But listen, don't get hung up on him. We have a fabulous event to attend tonight, and you're hot property."

"Right," I mutter, no longer in a forgiving mood. The last thing I feel like doing is being social. "Do I have to go? I'm not paid for this, just pulling in a favor for you."

Eric tilts his head, appearing rather offended by my comment.

"I'll call in that favor since I've been working hard to get your titties removed off every site possible!" He raises his voice, then straightens his shoulders. "Okay, rant over."

I roll my eyes at him. "Whatever. I'll see you tonight."

Eric waves his hand, dressed head-to-toe in a white suit with a blush pink-colored silk shirt beneath it. Under the lights, he literally stands out like a pink elephant in the room.

"Ava, darling! You made it and gorgeous as usual." Eric kisses both my cheeks before grabbing my hands. "How amazing is this place?"

My eyes scan the area, admiring the leafy atmosphere under the night sky. The outdoor space is designed well, geared at entertaining with tables and chairs positioned to cater to larger groups. The décor itself is quite modest, but the bar is the showcase of the entire rooftop. The long countertop is lit from beneath in neon lights, as are the shelves housing glass bottles of every liquor you can think of. The bartenders are all cute, perhaps young, but still attractive in their uniforms.

And then, there's the masterpiece on the wall, a signature of the bar's name—Luna. I raise my phone, take a photo, and send it to my cousin Luna, only to remember she's in South America with her parents and most likely doesn't have the best phone reception.

"It's a pretty nice place," I say while still admiring the surroundings. "I mean, how can you go wrong with a rooftop bar?"

"Exactly," Eric echoes my thoughts. "It is Manhattan, after all."

Eric's expression soon falters when his gaze falls upon a man across the room laughing. "Great, look who's here."

Turning in the opposite direction, I note the man in a flamboyant lavender suit, laughing way too hard to the point it comes across as so fake. "That guy?"

"Yes, it's only George Maurice. Look at him, acting like a starving whore."

"And he is?"

"My competition, darling. The Ava to the Amelia."

I touch the base of my neck, then tilt my head to the side while pursuing my lips.

"Um, excuse me? I'm not in competition with my sister," I question Eric with annoyance.

"Oh, right," Eric mumbles, uninterested, then coughs. "I must have my wires crossed with someone else."

Slowly, my skin tingles as the temperature rises. I watch him furtively, wondering whether he knows about my night with Austin. Of course, I haven't told a soul, and I highly doubt Austin would broadcast it to anyone either. But then, we are talking about Eric Kennedy. He can read people's minds like a gifted vampire, only dressed in designer clothes with perfectly shaped brows.

"You know what?" I huff, annoyed at his comment. "I'm going to get a drink."

I walk toward the bar and call out for a drink, not in the mood for the champagne being served. An uneasy feeling washes over me, leaving my stomach unsettled. I narrow it down to not having eaten since the morning after trying these new diet pills a company is pushing me to promote. It's been two days, and if anything, I've been feeling less like my usual self.

The bar staff is busy but stop quickly to take my order of a martini. Suddenly, a scent lingers in the air, intoxicating with its masculinity, or maybe I've been single for too long.

"Josh," a man calls beside me, the tone unforgiving and more of a demand. "Get the girls to move faster."

The Australian accent is the focal point of my attention, standing out amongst locals attending this launch party. I try to get a better glimpse with one eye of the man beside me, but all I can catch is the frustrated stare of the tall stature. Slowly, I revert my eyes to the glass served in front of me, then take a sip without seeming too obvious I tried to check him out.

"Is the champagne not good enough for you?"

"Excuse me?" I glance sideways, then lift my head to stare into the deepest blue eyes I've ever seen. His comment comes across as rude and arrogant, not matching the handsome face watching me while waiting for an answer. "I felt like a martini. Is there something wrong with that?"

"Of course not. You are Ava Edwards, are you not?"

Annoyed by his dismissive glance when mouthing my name, I take it he has a problem with me, and after this week, I have no issue starting a fight. So what's the worst that can happen, anyway? Everyone thinks they know me, and I'm sick of people assuming they know it all.

"And you are?"

"Lochie Fletcher, the owner of this fine establishment."

"This is your bar?" My eyes widen as I scan the space again. "Why didn't you say something earlier?"

"Considering we've been conversing for less than a minute, at what point did you want me to throw that in?"

"Well, Lochie... " I bow my head with a smile, shaking off my earlier annoyance, "... you got me there. So, how did you know my name?"

He rubs his beard, though it's neat and well-groomed, accentuating his sharp jawline.

"I was told of the guest list, and you were marked as a VIP."

"That's my publicist, over there. The one with the resting bitch face. Chances are, he marked the both of us as VIPs."

"Let me guess, Eric Kennedy?"

I nod. "Pain in my ass but worth every cent."

A man joins us, insisting Lochie is introduced to some important people. He excuses himself politely, following the man until an older crowd focuses their attention on him. His smile is flawless as he talks, lighting up his entire face, followed by a hearty laugh.

A few times, I catch him in a stolen glance until a woman wraps her hands around his waist. My ribs grow tight, restricting my breathing, torn between admiring how beautiful she is to my disappointment over the whole situation.

"What's with the resting bitch face?" Eric asks, returning with a glass of champagne in his hand.

"Same could be said about you."

"George was flaunting his new client list, and frankly, he can go to hell."

"My my, Eric, jealousy looks ugly on you."

"Whatever." He huffs while adjusting his cuffs to then lift his chin. "There are a few people I want you to meet, including a very handsome heir who happens to own a yacht club in Montauk."

"Eric, I'm not interested in meeting anyone to hook up with," I tell him, discouraged by my previous attempt with Lochie.

"Honey, you know what they say about a big boat?"

I raise my brows. "Enlighten me, Eric?"

"Strong stern."

"What?"

"Back end..."

"I'm waiting for you to connect this to a dick somehow?"

"I was getting there. You just threw me off. But since you asked..."

"No." I hold my hand up. "I've sworn off men. I don't need to talk about dick, think about dick, let alone get involved with a dick. This year will be dedicated to me."

Eric stares at me blankly, uninterested in my response. Then, blatantly ignoring me, he links his arm into mine and showcases me around the rooftop like some King Charles Cavalier at a prestigious dog show.

I meet the boat guy, who's full of himself it pains me to even entertain his advances. At what point he thought his bright white veneers would be a turn-on is beyond me. Even Eric stares rudely until I nudge him to snap out of it.

The night wears on, which includes a speech from Lochie thanking everyone for coming. The guests applaud, followed by a live band. I let out a yawn, noting it's still early for me.

"Listen, Eric," I begin with, trying to suppress another yawn on the brink of escaping. "I'm tired. Do you mind if I go?"

"A beauty must get her beauty sleep."

"Funny that. You didn't say that two weeks ago when you made me stay at that gay club until four in the morning."

Eric lets out a loose laugh. "Sweetie, never underestimate how selfish I can be when naked men are dancing near me."

Kissing both his cheeks, I remind him about my photoshoot at The Plaza tomorrow. As I walk toward the exit, I stop at the elevator, press the button, and check my phone while waiting.

"Leaving already?"

I lift my head, pursing my lips only to half-smile. "Yes, I am. Congratulations again on your opening."

"So, that's it?" Lochie juts his chin, raising his brows with a smug glance. "You're just leaving?"

"It's late, and I'm tired... " I admit, then continue, "... besides, I'm sure your girlfriend wouldn't appreciate you spending time with other women."

"Girlfriend?" he questions, followed by a laugh. "I think you mean my sister if you're wondering who that woman was with her arms around me."

"Oh," I mouth, annoyed I even mentioned it.

Lochie moves in closer and motions for me to hand him my phone. I'm not sure why I pass it over to a complete stranger, watching him text something quickly.

But, instead, he hands it back over with a mischievous grin.

"It was nice meeting you, Ava."

He grazes his finger down my arm, causing me to break out in goosebumps. With a deep gaze, his eyes drink me in, leaving me breathless. Slowly, he pulls away and walks back to the party.

Releasing the breath I'm holding in, I am taken aback by the sheer force of his touch. Maybe I am wrong, being single is a stupid idea. Why should I deprive myself of a sexy man?

And then, the elevator doors ping open. I enter, still flustered from his touch, then remember he wrote something in my phone. Quickly, I scroll to my messages, where he sent a text message to a number that I assume is his.

You're gorgeous, Ava. Stunning, actually. Call me sometime...I promise I don't bite.
Unless, of course, you want me to.
Lochie

The corners of my mouth turn up as I reread his text. My fingers type profusely, but then I erase my response, trying to keep it simple and not come across like some needy chick.

Me: *Cocky Aussie, but you do have a way with words. I'll call you tomorrow xx*

And with a rush of excitement, something I haven't felt in a while, I exit the elevator and leave the building to hail a cab.

Tomorrow can't come fast enough.

SIX

AVA

My phone lays on the plush white carpeted floor while I sit cross-legged in my closet, listening to my sister ramble on about work. It's not unusual for me to be on the receiving end of these conversations since we speak almost every day.

"I mean, these men are pigs," Amelia proclaims, her tone heightened with frustration. "You cheat on your wife for someone half your age and then demand your kids call her mom?"

"Men are pigs," I concur, struggling to move from the spot I find myself in. "But this is your job, right? You've got to fight for justice."

"Geez, Ava. I'm not wonder woman."

"You do have that costume, though." I chuckle while eyeing a pair of hot pink pumps in my closet, which Olivier once said made me look like a drag queen. Clearly, he'd been around them enough to know. I pull them off the shelf with the intent to wear them sometime this week. "I'm sure your husband enjoys the role-playing."

"Will is away for work. It's been two days. Meanwhile,

I'm like some horny teenage boy. You know that part of your cycle when all you can think about is sex?"

I'm never one to track cycles, so the concept is foreign. All I know is that when I turn into a hot-headed bitch, it's time to get the tampons ready. And of late, sex hasn't been on my mind until last night.

"Speaking of sex, I met someone last night."

"Hold up," Amelia raises her voice. "We've talked for almost an hour in which I complained about a funny noise my washer was making, and you only bring this up now?"

"You were rambling on about it. Considering your husband is a billionaire, I don't know why you just don't buy a new one?"

"Stop distracting!" Amelia then follows with a groan. "What happened last night?"

I begin with my encounter at the bar, to the woman I saw him with, then the moment while waiting for the elevator. This is followed by describing precisely what he looked like, though, for a moment, my memory fails.

"So, I'm going to text him soon, and I know about the stupid bet..." I mention with annoyance.

"Screw the bet. Sparks don't just fly with anyone," Amelia informs me. "And an Aussie? Give me his name, so I can stalk him online."

I laugh, then wonder why I haven't done the same. This is the first point of call after I meet someone as good-looking as Lochie.

"Look, let me text him first and see what happens. After the start to this year, I just want to be cautious."

"Uh, hello? Am I talking to Ava Edwards? When have you ever been cautious?"

My sister knows me well. After all—she is my best friend. But, then, it flashes before me, the night with Austin.

I try to suppress the guilt, knowing it will fade away eventually, and some other man will be my focus.

Amelia sighs heavily. "What's going on with you, Ava? You haven't been the same since Olivier left you."

I swallow the lump inside my throat, never one to be consumed by emotions. Life has thrown me a curveball, tested me more than I care to admit. Mom pointed it out, reminding me of how fortunate I've been, and it may not always be that way. Yet even though I know I'm resilient, something isn't right. The problem is, I don't know what's causing this unsettled feeling.

"I'm just tired," I confess, taking a breath. "It's been a shit start to the year."

"Maybe you need a girls' weekend? We can organize a nice resort just for you, me, Mom, and Addy. We might be able to drag Alexa if I can convince her it's cool to hang out with us."

Perhaps that's all I need—a break from life with the women who mean the most to me. It's been a few months since we've all been together.

"Ava? Did you hear me?"

"Yeah," I mumble, breaking my thoughts. "It sounds like a plan."

"Okay, something is very wrong because normally you would be all over this idea, take over, then plan something epic. What's really going on with you?"

"Honestly, Millie, I just don't know, and that's the truth. But if you're too busy, I'm sure Eric can plan something for us."

"I've got a meeting in an hour, and then when I pick up Ashton from Mom's this afternoon, I'll talk to her," Amelia tells me, then falling quiet for a moment. "You'll get through this, Ava bear, I promise."

I laugh softly. "You haven't called me that since elementary school."

"I mean it, okay? You know I'm always here. You're my sister. No judgment from me, no matter what you're going through."

Since Amelia married Will and became a mother, she has changed for the better, if I'm honest. She's a lot calmer, always nurturing the closest to her, and it's almost like she became our mom. She often worries about me by regularly checking in to make sure I'm okay. According to Addy, who sees her more than I do, it's like someone took our hot-headed sister and replaced her with someone the complete opposite.

Yet moments like earlier in our call remind me that Millie will always be passionate about what matters the most. She's just become more patient when it comes to family.

"I know you'll always be there, Millie. But you do have a demanding husband and a two-year-old."

"Will knows how important my sisters are to me."

We speak for a few more minutes before Eric texts me with a reminder to be at the photoshoot at three o'clock sharp. He then continues to send me images of the gown, suggesting I wear a white strapless bra to suit the design.

Pulling open the drawer with all my lingerie, I take out my white satin strapless bra. As I unclasp the bra and put it on, the cups are too tight, and my fingers fidget with difficulty. My patience wears thin until I let out a frustrated growl with dead arms, throwing my bra across the closet. I close my eyes, take a deep breath, open them, and place my hands on my breasts. My skin feels tender, and the swells of my breasts are slightly larger than usual. What the fuck? These stupid diet pills are working in reverse. Why I agreed to be a guinea pig again highlights my poor judgment.

The diet pills are next to the basin inside my bathroom. Still topless, I walk inside and read the back of the bottle so I can google the ingredients. I type into my phone tender breasts, hoping for some medical advice and connection to the pills. But as I click on the top results, my stomach churns. The A/C is on, yet the room is stifling hot as my eyes read across the page. There's mention of breast cancer, and although we don't have a history of that in our family, anything is possible. I try not to let my mind exaggerate and conjure up crazy scenarios. But then, the website delves into hormonal changes resulting from menstrual cycles to pregnancy.

My period.

Shaking my head, I stare blankly at the shower while trying to calculate my last period. It was about a month ago, or maybe a little bit longer. It was lighter than usual, but I'm not a heavy bleeder like my sister. Instead, I'm fortunate enough to have light cycles.

And as for pregnancy, you have to have sex to fall pregnant.

I continue to read, noting some of the other symptoms I've had of late, including fatigue. When I finish reading, I'm no closer to a self-diagnosis and decide to call my doctor to see if she can squeeze me in.

Dr. Taylor's receptionist informs me of a last-minute cancellation, which doesn't leave me much time to get ready and head downtown. Just as I'm about to go charge my phone, it pings with a text.

Millie: *Three weeks from now, clear your schedule.*

We're going to Cancun! Mom is in, Addy is in, and I even got Alexa. You can't say no!

When Millie puts her mind to something, she makes it happen. I just didn't expect it to be this quick.

Me: *I'm in.*

The afternoon schedule is tight, no thanks to my last-minute doctor's visit. Dr. Taylor goes through the usual questions. How I've been feeling, what I've been doing, and then requests I take a blood test. Not wanting to come across as rude, I try to get out of there fast to avoid the wrath of Eric.

I make it with only a few minutes to spare, which is very unprofessional of me, given tardiness is my biggest pet peeve when it comes to working. Eric rushes me to hair and make-up without a hello.

The dress is elegant yet simplistic. The purpose is to focus on the hotel's surroundings, therefore not distract with a gown that demands attention. My hair is styled in mermaid waves with natural tones for my makeup. The make-up artist does a fantastic job of bringing out the emerald color of my eyes.

I pose around The Four Seasons for the rest of the afternoon while the photographer takes what feels like a million shots. By the end of it, I'm utterly exhausted, drinking a whole bottle of water in one sitting and narrowing the fatigue down to dehydration.

"You were fabulous, honey." Eric claps his hands while the photographer packs up his equipment. "I have some amazing news for you."

"You're Donatella Versace's long-lost son?"

"Don't you tease me, Miss Edwards." Eric points his finger with a playful grin. "Victoria's Secret has decided to switch up their new campaign and wants influencers. They specifically requested you."

"Me?" I touch the base of my neck with a confused stare. "When, where?"

"Well, here's the catch..." Eric trails off, which is never a good sign when it comes to him. "It's tomorrow in the Bahamas. Before you get all worked up, I can reschedule your week to make it work. It's only three days."

I cross my arms, smelling a rat. "That's last minute. I'd assume they'd have this planned for months, not days?"

"They did, but the venue they chose was wiped out by that hurricane last week. So, they had to find another location in the Bahamas to suit the shoot, but it means they had to bring it forward. A few models aren't able to travel right now, and so they decided to switch up the campaign."

My eyes scan Eric's face, studying his expressions to make sure he's telling the truth. Of late, he has tip-toed around me because of Miami. I don't blame him, given my mood swings and shattered confidence.

I let out a loud breath. "You know what, I'm in. Leaving Manhattan is very appealing right now."

"Fantastic!" Eric pulls his phone out then draws his attention back onto me. "I see big things in your future, Ava. My tarot reader even said so."

"Your tarot reader read my future?" I repeat, raising my brows.

"Anyone in my life who I bring up. I knew you were having a tough time of late, so I asked, and she delivered."

I shake my head in disbelief. "What else did she say?"

"Big things are coming your way. Life-changing. It's this trip, I know it."

Suddenly, Lochie comes to mind. Maybe it isn't the trip, but rather my love life. I pull my phone out, half-listening to Eric, and send Lochie the text I'd been putting off.

Me: *Are you free this Friday for dinner?*

Lochie: *So, you are alive? It depends...my pick?*

Me: *Demanding but sure.*

Lochie: *Some call it demanding. I call it being a gentleman taking charge.*
Let me confirm reservations.

Lochie: *And by the way, I'm glad you reached out.*

Lifting my head, I see Eric still rambling on about auras and energies. To be polite, I nod a few times, unable to hide my smile from reading Lochie's text.

"Are you even listening to me?"

"A little bit yes, and partially no," I drag, bored with his talking. "Look, I'm beat and need to pack for tomorrow."

"We're leaving at midday, sharp."

"We?"

"Yes, we," he announces, crossing his arms while minutely shaking his head. "Me and you. I'm your publicist and need to make sure nothing goes wrong."

"Well then, I'll pack the Xanax. You on an island with pool boys, something tells me I'll need it with all the high-pitched fangirling."

Eric pouts his lips then follows with a malicious laugh.

"Honey, it's like we're two beautiful peas in a glamorous pod. You know me too well."

I'm unable to hold back my grin. "You're hard work, Eric Kennedy. How you're still married is beyond me."

~

The obnoxious ring of my phone wakes me. The morning sun is shining through the drapes while I answer the call with a croak in my voice.

Dr. Taylor informs me my results have returned and requests to see me immediately. Over the phone, her tone is cold, making me break out into a panic. I beg her to tell me, but she insists on face-to-face contact but assures me it's not life-threatening, so to calm down.

I crashed early last night, tired again from the day and hoping Dr. Taylor has solutions to fix whatever the hell is wrong with me. Lochie responded with an address for dinner, and after a few flirty text messages, I fell asleep with my phone on my face.

After a quick shower and dressing into a pair of jeans with a black bodysuit, I answer the door and motion for Dr. Taylor to come in. She keeps her greeting short and simple, not looking me in the eye, which causes me concern.

Dr. Taylor sits on the sofa across from me.

I'm waiting for her lecture on how the diet pills I've been consuming is what's causing me to be so ill over the last month or two. Perhaps, in hindsight, I should have listened to Millie when she warned me of the damage they can do to my body. But stubborn me just continued, and now I'm paying the price.

"Miss Edwards, I have your results here."

Dr. Taylor procrastinates in the most annoying way

possible. She's pushing close to a hundred— okay, exaggerating a little—but doesn't she know that time is of the essence? In less than two hours, I need to board a flight to the Bahamas for a photoshoot. Just give me the pep talk, and I'll be on my merry way.

"You're pregnant, and the blood work shows you're about four months along."

Frozen on the spot, Dr. Taylor hands me a piece of paper with the results. I barely make out the words, all of them jumbled and blurry. My skin tingles in discomfort as my chest tightens, restricting my ability to breathe so effortlessly.

This. Cannot. Be. Happening.

I gasp for air, my eyes twitch, followed by the room spinning. Dr. Taylor is concerned, calling my name in the distance. I focus on her face, mumbling the question that is bursting to come out.

"So, when you say four months, I fell pregnant around…"

"January," she confirms.

My breaths come hard and fast, the panic crippling my ability to even talk.

"But it was only one time," I beg, almost in tears. "I had my shot back then, and we used a condom…I think."

"Miss Edwards, I always advise my patients that the birth control shot is not one hundred percent effective. You did the right thing using a condom if you did, but even condoms aren't one hundred percent."

"Why does everyone say that?" I raise my voice, the cushions falling off the sofa as I pace the area in front of it. "I can't be pregnant! If nothing's one hundred percent, then why are people having sex?"

"Abstinence is your one hundred percent," she reminds me.

What a stupid remark. No one is going to abstain from having sex.

My life is a fucking mess.

This will *ruin* me.

"I was with the same man before that night for nearly two years. How come I didn't fall pregnant with him?"

"It could be several things. Perhaps you weren't having intercourse during ovulation, but most likely, you've found a male partner with strong sperm that's extremely compatible with your eggs."

"And if I don't want this kid?" I ask in a strangled voice.

"I'm afraid it's a little too late if that's what you're asking me. However, there is always placing the baby up for adoption." Dr. Taylor keeps her gaze fixated on me. "So, I take it you're not in a relationship with the father?"

"Three words for you, Doc. One. Night. Stand."

I see pity or maybe even a little bit of judgment in her eyes. She carries on about prenatal appointments, supplements, and other things that are flying in one ear and out the other. In my head, I only see the look on my family's face when I tell them.

Chances are—this will destroy them.

And it's all because of one night.

A night when my entire life came crashing down, and the only person able to comfort me was a man completely forbidden.

SEVEN

AVA

D r. Taylor leaves my apartment but not before referring me to an OBGYN.

This can't be happening.

I don't even hear the sound of the door closing, fixated on the sofa in a catatonic state.

All noise drowns out, from the sound of the sirens outside the apartment block to the sudden burst of thunder from the predicted storm.

Breathe, Ava.

My head drops between my legs to shut out all the incessant noise inside my mind, which refuses to shut the hell up. The tips of my fingers run through my hair while I intake shallow breaths. Then, suddenly, my head snaps up, my hands gravitating toward the paper Dr. Taylor left on the coffee table.

Pregnant—positive.

I continue to sit in silence, not even to blink as I watch, hoping for a miracle that the word 'positive' disappears. Closing my eyes, I pray that this is an awful dream, and at any moment, I'll wake up, and everything will be back to normal. I will go back to being the fabulous Ava Edwards who will take the world by storm.

But denial is a curse for the weak.

Minutes later, I open my eyes as reality slaps me in the face—hard, forceful, and unapologetic. Thoughts run rampant, from everything I assumed I knew about pregnancy to reality. There's supposed to be morning sickness, but aside from a few questionable moments, not once have I thrown up in the past few months.

I hop on my feet, scurrying to the bathroom. The damn bodysuit I'm wearing doesn't help, so I strip off in a rush to stand naked in front of the mirror. Slowly, I turn to the side and gaze upon my stomach. There is a slight bulge the closer I look. Yet nothing alarming and it can easily be passed off as bloating.

My hands move on their own accord, falling flat against my skin to see if anything feels different. Nothing at all feels unusual aside from my breasts.

And then reality hits like a wrecking ball. This time, knocking the wind out of me.

Austin is the father.

Barely managing to cover my mouth with my palm, I race to the basin before throwing up repeatedly. My breaths come hard and fast until I slow my breathing down enough to coordinate turning the faucet on to splash cold water on my face. With my hands resting on the edge of the countertop, my eyes close from exhaustion, incapable of moving from this very spot.

In less than an hour, a car service will take me to the airport to board a plane to the Bahamas. A trip where I'm expected to dress in a swimsuit and pretend nothing is wrong.

When in fact—everything is wrong.

If I call Eric to cancel, I'll never hear the end of it. It's unprofessional, and the last thing I need is people speculating. But right now, no one else knows because who can I tell? If I tell Mom, it will be impossible for her to keep it from Dad, and the last thing I want is to burden her with a secret this big.

And if Dad knows, I'm sure Austin will be hunted down and fed to a den of lions.

Yet as horrible as that all sounds, nothing in the world compares to the gut-wrenching feeling of having to admit the truth to my sister. Every time I think of it, a wave of nausea hits laced with guilt.

The more I go over this in my head, the clearer my need to keep this a secret for as long as possible. Maybe, if I'm fortunate, there will be a few more weeks before my body changes, and everyone will know. If I dress in baggier clothes, I highly doubt anyone will notice.

Inside the living room, my phone rings. I run to quickly grab it until I see Millie's name on the screen. Without a second thought, my finger hits reject. There's no way I can speak to Millie right now, so to avoid her, a quick text to explain I'm busy should suffice.

Me: *Sorry, just heading to the airport. Last-minute photoshoot in the Bahamas.*

I suck in my stomach, taking the deepest of breaths. All I need to do is get through the next three days. My suitcase is already packed and sitting beside the door. Moving quickly around the apartment, I fill the smaller items into my carry-on to distract my thoughts until my phone alerts me of a text message.

Millie: *Sorry, I was just having a moment. I got my period.*

My knees turn weak, forcing me to sit down on the sofa before they give way. A thickness forms in my throat as I mentally curse myself for being so stupid. Not only did I sleep with Austin, but I also have the one thing Millie is so desperate for.

And the worst part is, I would trade places in a heartbeat. Being pregnant was not part of my life plan. It's not that I disliked kids, I'm just selfish and will admit it. I enjoy luxurious holidays, spending money on designer clothes, and drinking martinis on private islands while being pampered.

Now, not only am I going to raise another human being, but I have to do it all alone.

There's no response worthy of forgiveness. So, I quickly think of the only thing which comes to mind.

Me: *I'm sorry. Maybe next month xx*

The door buzzes with the doorman informing me of the arrival of the car service. I grab my things, ignoring the constant heaviness inside my chest, and try my best to forget I'm pregnant with my sister's ex-fiancés baby.

The Bahamas photoshoot is nonstop. Eric chose the entire flight to map out this year's business goals from the moment we boarded the plane. The irony is that I participated like nothing at all in my life will change. A few times, I opened my mouth to admit the truth but retreated with fear each time. Thankfully, many of the things scheduled aren't photoshoots as we are focusing on my product line for loungewear and jewelry.

The shoot itself begins in the early hours of the morning on a gorgeous beach with pristine blue skies above us. The sun burns my skin, more so than usual, leaving me extra sensitive. I make a conscious effort to suck in my stomach when needed, scared someone will notice.

When the shoot is over, I breathe a sigh of relief. The swimsuit part is complete, and tomorrow is less revealing with the attire being photographed.

Thankfully, there's time to stop for anything. Even though we're in the Bahamas, this trip is far from relaxing. The other influencers are demanding with my time, all wanting to talk business. Eric schedules video conferences and meetings, which were initially planned for this week. Then there are the dinners which are like mixers with liquor served. I politely take a cocktail but end up throwing it in the bushes hoping no one sees it.

While there are moments that distract me from reality, the pregnancy makes sure to fight for attention every second I'm alone.

And the most critical thought is telling Austin.

The three days intended for this trip extend to six through no fault of my own. When a reminder comes up on my phone about my dinner with Lochie, I have no choice but to cancel. I send him a text, stating I'm caught up with work and now isn't a good time for anything. It sounds cold, but what else can I possibly say to let him down? He never responds, and frankly, I don't blame him.

I'm sure I'll never date again.

Who the hell wants a single mother with a baby?

Back in Manhattan, reality is unavoidable. I toy back

and forth with the idea of not telling Austin, but when my thoughts become too much, I run to the only person who, at this moment, I can trust entirely.

"Hey, short stuff, haven't seen you in a while?"

Andy extends his arms as I fall into his embrace. Against his muscular chest, I close my eyes while he squeezes me tight. I wrap my arms around him, not wanting to let him go, desperate for the comfort he provides me.

"Is everything okay?" he asks, kissing the top of my head. Andy towers over me, so it isn't unusual for him to do that. "You're kind of not letting go of me."

I shake my head without a word, then pull away slowly.

"Can we talk?"

Andy draws his eyebrows together, extending his arm to motion for me to come in. "Always available for you."

There's something about Andy's studio that feels like home. The exposed brick wall is the feature of the small space, rustic yet appealing to the eyes. Hanging on the wall are framed black and white photos which Andy has taken over the years. Beneath it sits a tanned leather sofa with a plush white rug and a coffee table with a stack of books. Andy has always been a reader, his love for books inherited from Uncle Julian.

The color palette is earth tones with an artistic vibe which sums up Andy perfectly.

I take a seat on the sofa, allowing my body to sink in while I grab a cushion and hug it for comfort.

Andy sits beside me, watching with a curious gaze. For my entire life, Andy has been a big brother to me. Our families did everything together, and there isn't one memory without him being a part of it. Dad has a special bond with him, treating Andy like his own son. It's why I consider him a brother more so than a cousin.

When he moved to Manhattan along with Millie, it felt like I lost my entire world. I'm two years younger than them, always falling behind as they moved on with life. Yet over the years, the tides shifted. Millie moved back to LA, and Andy stayed in Manhattan. After graduating from NYU, he began traveling the world. I admire him for following his passion, and just like his father, he's always trying to do good in the world.

Andy Evans-Baker isn't like any other man I know. It's one of the many reasons why girls have always lusted over him. He is a good-looking man who is just happy doing his thing and doesn't get caught up in the drama.

"How have you been?" I ask, caressing the faux fur of the cushion with my palm.

"Good. Great, actually. I've got an assignment in London which I'm excited about."

"Photographing the Queen's Corgis?"

Andy's mouth curves upward, a loose chuckle escaping him. "Close, but not quite. It does involve a celebrity."

"Hmm, nice. You going to visit Jessa?"

Andy shuffles uncomfortably, making it obvious I've struck a nerve.

"Not likely..."

I shift my gaze back onto Andy, knowing the last time they spoke was months ago before she moved to London. With everything going on in my life, I haven't had the chance to catch up with her either.

"What's going on? I haven't spoken to her in months."

"Nothing's going on, Ava," he tells me firmly. "She's in London living her life."

I sense more, but Andy being a typical guy, doesn't give me much.

"So, why aren't you there with her? Cut the bullshit, Andy. You're in love with her. You have been for years."

"You cut the crap, Ava. What the hell is wrong with you?"

"I'm pregnant," I blurt out.

I almost feel relieved as it leaves my mouth, my shoulders falling as I let out a breath and throw my head back against the sofa.

"Congratulations?" Andy quips, unsure. "Is that what I'm supposed to say?"

"You might want to reconsider when you know the whole story," I profess, sucking my stomach in then exhaling. "I need you to not judge me."

"When have I ever judged you? I'm not Millie."

I nod in agreement, then fall quiet.

"Ava, c'mon, it's me. You can't do anything wrong in my eyes."

My mouth opens, but then it falls shut. I must tell him because I need a male perspective, and keeping this secret is killing me.

"It was New Year's Eve. I was a mess after Miami. Then I walked in on Olivier. In my entire life, I've never felt as insecure and insignificant as I did that night." I swallow the lump in my throat, finding the courage to continue. "I went to this Irish pub because, well, I don't know why. I just didn't want to be around the same usual crowd. So, I drank, and then Austin walked in..."

"Austin?" Andy tilts his head. His blue eyes fixate on me. "Millie's Austin?"

"Thanks for the reference."

"Sorry," he quickly mutters. "So, Austin walked in?"

"He was having a bad night at work, and well, we drank, then one thing led to another..."

As my words trail off, Andy lets out a huge breath then rubs his face with his hands. "Ava... " he murmurs, "... are you telling me Austin is the father?"

"It was just one night, Andy." I almost choke."I haven't seen him since."

"He doesn't know?"

I shake my head, keeping quiet.

"And Millie? Does she know about that night?"

My eyes fall to the floor as I shake my head again. "I fucked up, Andy. I don't know what to do."

Andy places his arm on my shoulder, bringing me in for an embrace. My chest hitches, the wave of nausea rearing its ugly head again. I practice my breathing, not wanting to hug the toilet bowl since I can't think of anything worse.

"I don't have any advice for you," Andy confesses, his voice low. "The truth is, this baby will come whether you accept it or not."

"I know, but, Andy? If you were a guy in this situation, would you want to know?"

Andy takes a moment to ponder my question. Given the complexity of the situation, I don't push him while he thinks.

"Honestly? Yes. This isn't the child's fault, and every child deserves to have a father."

His answer is nothing less than what I expected from him, especially since he lost his biological father so early on in life.

"But Austin has this great career," I argue softly. "He worked so hard to become a doctor, and I don't want to ruin it for him."

"Ruin it for him or you?"

I narrow my eyes, distancing myself while turning to face him. "What does that mean?"

"You've always been independent, and if we're getting real here, you struggle with factoring men into your life. You do what you want when you want. If you were to raise this baby on your own, you could do things your way. But if Austin knows, I'm certain he will want to be a part of the child's life. That means you'll need to factor in his needs too."

I'm offended Andy says such a thing even though I considered moving to LA for a split second to be closer to Mom and Dad, yet quickly squashed the idea. My life is here. My work is here.

And Austin is here.

"What about Millie?" I can barely say her name without the guilt riddling me. "Or even Will. They're going to know."

"Ava, this isn't going to be easy. The quicker you swallow that, the quicker you move on and rip the band-aid off."

"I'm terrified it will tear my family apart," I choke, barely able to admit the truth.

"Family is for life. Sure, at first, there may be some battles, but never forget the power of love. You know, if you want more advice, maybe talk to Mom? She went through this when she started seeing Dad."

From the bits we knew, Aunt Adriana's relationship with Uncle Julian caused major conflict when they came out as a couple. Dad was on the warpath, disowning his sister and blaming Mom. But according to Mom, Uncle Julian saved my life. There was no elaboration to that story, so that's the extent to what I know.

"I think I might," I agree. Aunt Adriana knows Mom and Dad well enough to help guide me through this.

Andy's phone rings, and in sheer coincidence, he lifts

the phone, so I can see the video call coming in from Aunt Adriana. Even he looks surprised.

Wow, Universe, you're on some roll.

"Hey, Mom."

'Hey, kid," Aunt Adriana greets, all cheery as usual. "Dad just reminded me to remind you about the phone conference in an hour. He had to step out because Willow's damn dog ate something in the garden and started throwing up all green."

"Thanks for the reminder, Mom, and gross about the dog." Andy glances my way. "Actually, I'm here with Ava."

Andy moves the screen over as Aunt Adriana waves.

"Look at you. You're gorgeous as ever!"

"I'm pregnant."

Aunt Adriana's mouth falls open as her facial muscles turn slack. "Well, I didn't expect that... "

"Austin is the father," I reveal.

"Austin?" she repeats in a high-pitched voice. "As in Millie's Austin?"

I clench my jaw, annoyed at the reference, then nod. Just because they were once engaged doesn't make him hers.

"Okay, you need to talk me through everything."

Andy excuses himself, giving me a chance to speak in private. I begin with exactly what I told Andy, starting from Miami but reveal more about the morning after. Aunt Adriana and I have always been close, and at times when I felt I couldn't share something with Mom, she has always been someone I can be honest with. When I finish, she lets out a long-winded breath.

"I need help," I plead, trying to remain calm. "I don't know how to tell my parents, let alone Millie."

"In my experience, if you can control how it comes out, the better. Don't let it slip through the grapevine."

I nod with a deep breath. It makes sense. "Right, okay. Anything else?"

"We love you, honey. Your parents love you. Sure, Lex might act like an asshole, but you know him... let him cool off, and he'll come around. We're all here to support you, and you don't need to do this alone."

"*But Millie...*" I barely whisper.

"She'll be angry. But she's your sister, and if Lex can forgive me for marrying his worst enemy, Millie can forgive you."

"Uncle Julian is Dad's worst enemy?"

"Not anymore, but at one point, he was," she confesses. "He had everything Lex wanted."

Perhaps this situation is different. After all, we're sisters. We share the same blood. We came from the same womb.

But there are so many band-aids to rip off, and which is worse is yet to be determined.

All I know is that Andy is right. Austin deserves to know. I'm about to change his life forever.

Though no matter how hard I try to find the courage to call him, it's never enough to reveal the truth. I need to see him, and time is of the essence.

This baby isn't going to stop growing.

And soon, the whole world will know exactly what I've done.

What *we* have done.

EIGHT

AVA

The automated doors open upon walking toward them, and a deep breath escapes me.

Stepping inside the main entrance, I'm immediately confronted by the sterile environment. The pungent smell of cleaning supplies or possibly sanitizer engulfs my senses, but I do my best to ignore it despite my queasy stomach.

As I walk to the reception desk, a few people are waiting in line. It moves quickly, and when it becomes my turn, I smile politely at the older lady behind the Perspex glass.

"I'm here to see Dr. Austin Carter," I say, trying to remain calm. "Could you please tell me which ward I can find him in?"

The lady types in her computer, barely acknowledging me.

"Dr. Carter is in ER. You're best to head over there. Turn left, then follow the signs down the hall."

I thank her before turning left to follow her directions. Without even realizing it, I lower my head to avoid making eye contact with people. I'm not fond of hospitals, and then it hits me—five months until I am here pushing a baby out of my vagina.

My breathing falters, the air surrounding me becomes stifling hot. Finally, I stop in my tracks, retrieving a water bottle from my bag to take a long sip. Instantly, my temperature stabilizes, allowing me to continue my hunt for Austin.

The ER has a completely different vibe. Everything is fast-paced with First Responders in and out of the large doors. A woman lying on a stretcher is brought in with what appears to be some sort of neck or back injury if her neck brace is anything to go by. I thank my lucky stars she isn't covered in blood because I would have fainted on the spot.

The waiting room is full, though I try my hardest not to stare at patients sitting miserably in plastic chairs. No one is waiting at the reception, so I quickly make my way over and ask for Austin.

"If you walk down this corridor, there's a small desk on the right. Jennifer can help you locate him."

"Thank you," I tell her.

The corridor isn't as long as the other one. I continue to walk down, and just when I spot the desk, my attention is drawn to laughter ahead of me.

My glance shifts toward Austin conversing with a woman. They are both wearing scrubs, laughing at something together. I suspect it's his colleague until he raises his hand to brush a loose strand of hair away from her face before whispering something in her ear.

Avert my eyes momentarily, I try to ignore the tightness in my chest while struggling to find the courage to go through with this. But unfortunately, the temptation to run in the opposite direction sounds more and more like the easiest thing to do until it becomes too late.

His deep hazel eyes have locked onto mine.

And something inside of me shifts, almost freezing me on the spot.

"Hey, Austin."

Forcing a smile, I place my hands in the pockets of my jeans. The waist is a bit too tight, and I'm certain this will be the last time I wear them. I chose to wear a loose white blouse to be more comfortable with a pair of yellow Manolo Blahniks I'd only bought last month. Soon, gorgeous heels like this will mock me from my closet.

Austin raises his brow as the woman beside him glances at me. "Ava? What are you doing here?"

"I need to talk to you in private. Is there somewhere we can go?"

"Yes, of course," he responds, still perplexed as to my visit. Then, after a few awkward seconds, Austin shakes his head as if he forgot something. "Sorry, I should've introduced you to Lane. Lane, this is Ava, an old friend of mine."

Lane extends her hand. "Nice to meet you, Ava."

There's nothing at all bitchy nor stuck-up about her. Her ginger hair, and chocolate-colored eyes, make her look simple, but not in a bad way. In a natural, there's-nothing-fake-about-me way. Although I've requested to speak to Austin—who appears to be her boyfriend—in private, her smile doesn't waver.

"How about we take a walk outside?" Austin suggests, his smile still lingering. "I was just about to go on a break."

"Sure."

He kisses Lane goodbye on the cheek as I purposely glance at the wall. Then, we slowly walk down the corridor in silence until the brisk air meets us. Although it's spring now, which means we would usually be privy to the sun shining and warm air, today is unusually cold, quite like my mood.

"Sit." He motions at an empty bench. "How have you been?"

"*Pregnant,*" I blurt out, instantly regretting my outburst. I should've warned him gently. After all, this will change his life forever.

Austin rubs his freshly shaven jaw, pausing momentarily to shift his gaze onto me.

"I guess congratulations are in order?"

"It's yours."

The second it leaves my mouth, his smile wavers, and slowly, his eyes widen in disbelief. Even the color of his skin pales, almost as if he's seen a ghost.

"Mine? Are you sure?" he stammers, shaking his head unknowingly. "We used protection. We weren't that stupid."

I shrug, unsure how to explain how it happened. Austin is the doctor here. Surely, he must know more than me. Yet he's looking at me to answer him.

"We did, but maybe there was a hole in the condom, or you were drunk, and it wasn't placed right. I don't know how to answer that, Austin."

He stands up, pacing the area in front of me. "How do you know it's mine?"

Folding my arms beneath my chest, I raise my brow with an icy stare.

"Because I'm four months along," I snap in frustration from his assumption. "And you have been the only man I've slept with in six whole months."

"So, you've only had sex with me in the last six months?"

"Yes," I concur, my annoyance quickly morphing to anger. My nostrils flare on their own accord as my pulse begins to race. "You know what, Austin? I came here to tell you the truth, and understandably you're upset just as I was when I found out. But right now, I don't appreciate being called a whore."

"I'm not calling you a whore, Ava," he proclaims, his tone low. "You were single and had every right to do what you wanted. But, I'm sorry, I shouldn't have interrogated and made you feel that way. This is a lot to take in. I'm just about to start my second year in residency, we're not together, and I'm with someone."

"Lane?"

"Yes, Lane."

"She's nice, real cute."

"She doesn't deserve this," he tells me.

The bouncing emotions exhaust me, and when I'm tired, my patience wears thin. It sounds like he cares more about her feelings than mine, and I'm the one carrying his baby!

"You're right, she doesn't deserve this, but you know who has it even harder? Me. She doesn't have to be pregnant for another five months then give birth. She doesn't have to be a single mother and hey, let's not forget about the biggest issue here," I fume, knowing my face has turned bright red from my unflattering temper. "She doesn't have to tell her family, especially her sister that she's knocked up by her ex-fiancé, who she slept with on New Year's Eve."

Austin remains silent, burying his face in his hands. Then, after minutes of no communication between us, he finally lifts his head. "How is this going to work?"

"Look, like you said, you're almost a second-year resident. I don't need your help, Austin. I can do this on my own."

"You don't need my help?" he exasperates, drawing

back with an unrelenting glare. "So, what? I'm supposed to have a kid and never see it?"

"See it, don't see it. All I'm saying is that I can do this on my own."

"And all I'm hearing is that you don't want me around."

Austin turns his gaze toward the building, refusing to look at me. "I need to go back."

And just like that, he walks away. Out of sight, but definitely not out of mind.

This turned out to be a disaster. But what did he expect me to say or do? Beg him to be a father to a child he never asked for? Demand he supports me, or worst yet—be in a relationship with me? No matter what I say, it all sounds wrong.

Right now, I'm the woman who has ruined his life.

And nothing will change that.

I take the long route home, walking in a daze up Madison Avenue. People walk past, going about their business as usual. There's a group of young girls in front of me, laughing while carrying designer shopping bags. I envy the life I once had before my insecurities ate away at me, which ultimately led to making wrong decisions. But then, I remember what Mom said, how I'd been fortunate in life. I expected bumps, but this is a next-level dark hole ditch with no chance of climbing out.

Before I know it, I turn right and head in a different direction until I find myself in Eric's office. Without a greeting or a single word, I take a seat and just stare at his desk. Eric is a minimalist, and he can't get enough when it comes to diaries and planners. He refuses to get with the times and go electronic, but I don't care what he does as long as he gets the job done.

"You look like rat shit." He cringes, eyeing my hair to then scan my face.

"Thanks, I don't know what rat shit looks like, but it can't be pleasant."

"Ava, what's wrong? You're scaring a very fragile Eric. During my Pilates class this morning, I split my pants, and it was laundry day. The hot blond behind me caught a glimpse of my no branded underwear."

"Well, there's no easy way to say it, so here's the trigger warning." I take a deep breath as Eric bites his lip. "I'm going to tell you something, and you'll need to sit down. In the risk of aging you a few years, which we know you've worked hard to stay wrinkle-free, I suggest you serve yourself a wine or something stiff to process all I'm about to tell you."

"It's eleven in the morning, and the only drink I have in here is some fairy cocktail stuff someone assumed I'd love because it's pink."

"I suggest you start pouring."

Eric walks to his shelf and removes the bottle to pour a glass. He sniffs the liquor, with a slight dry heave following.

"Okay, I'm ready, and I'm sitting. Shock me."

"I'm pregnant," I tell him, then rush, "Austin is the father. We slept together on New Year's Eve after I found Olivier in bed with another man. Only Andy and Adriana know. But I just told Austin, who frankly, didn't take the news well. I'm going to answer the list of questions circulating inside your brain right now. We used protection. We were both drunk. From what I remember, it was really good, and yes, he's well-hung. The end. Should you have that drink now?"

Eric takes a long drink, not stopping until the champagne flute is empty. When he pulls it away, he lets out a raspy groan and begins to cough.

"Ava, honey, you've just aged me to my golden years." He fans his face, then pours himself another glass. Without a second thought, he drinks it straight. "You're pregnant to Austin? This is scandalous, and I'm talking worse than all the stuff Lex and Charlie went through."

I nod in silence. How can I argue that? This is the beginning of what will be a media scandal, more so than my relationship with Olivier. To everyone's knowledge, we broke up. There was some talk about it, but for the most part, people were sad to see the split because their social media feeds weren't as aesthetically pleasing without the two of us together.

"Eric..." I trail off, twisting my hands together. "I'm terrified to tell Millie."

"Amelia? What about Daddy Dearest?"

"My father will be angry," I admit, trying not to have a panic attack for the hundredth time today. "Him, I can handle. I'm just worried Millie will—"

"What?"

"Disown me. Is that even a thing with sisterhood?"

Eric releases a sigh. "Amelia would never do that. She loves you, and besides, she's married to a man she loves. It's not like she can get jealous. So, when are you telling them?"

"I'm thinking about flying out tomorrow. I can't hide this for much longer."

"Oh, to be a fly on the wall," Eric gasps. "Wait, what about Lochie?"

I purse my lips, glancing out the window. "Nothing, I stood him up. I can't deal with anything else, Eric."

"Could've been something great."

"Yeah, well, now I'm pregnant to another man. The Universe sure has a way of fucking up my life for me."

"Ava, sweetie, you need to breathe, and we'll get through this." Eric places his hand on mine, his breath close enough that I can smell the potent pink whatever the hell it is. "I'm here, and so is Tristan. You've got our support always, no matter what happens from here.

I have no idea what will happen.

But I know my sister better than anyone else. My gut is telling me the worst is yet to come.

I can't afford to lose her, but deep down inside—I know it is inevitable.

NINE

AVA

After my pity stop at Eric's office, I change my mind and head back to work instead of wallowing at home.

Inside the sanctity of my own office, workaholic Ava comes back to life. To say I miss her would be an understatement. In the space of six hours, I schedule several meetings and even approve the final touches on our fall loungewear line. Ideas are flowing, so I make sure to write them down, ready to explore when I have more time.

Powering through emails, I even respond to Dad, who sent me an article he read on manufacturing locally and incentives for business owners. It was an interesting read. Given my company has grown over the last twelve months, it makes sense to source a factory space and maybe even a shopfront. Aunt Adriana had been pushing me for years, but it didn't make sense financially to establish a brick-and-mortar business when most people preferred online shopping.

When night falls, I drag myself home but make a quick stop at McDonald's for a cheeseburger and strawberry shake. It had been on my mind all day long, and I've never been one to crave cheap junk food, unable to recall the last time I ate such a thing. Yet the greasy burger and sugary drink are oddly satisfying.

It's barely eight when I let out a yawn. My limbs feel heavy as I lazily make my way to the closet to grab a tank and bed shorts, ready to hit the shower and sleep. Today felt like it dragged on forever, especially after this morning with Austin. I haven't heard from him, nor do I want to make contact. I figure, being a guy, he needs to let off steam and me pushing this pregnancy in his face won't do any good.

Besides, there's another pressing situation fighting for attention—my family.

My flight for LA leaves at midday tomorrow. Then, suddenly, I remember I forgot to tell Mom. Quickly, I pull out my phone to text Mom, praying my impromptu trip won't alarm her.

Me: *Hey, Mom, just letting you know I'm flying over tomorrow. I should be there late afternoon. Sorry for the late notice, last-minute trip.*

Mom: *You've made your Mama happy. Any reason for the trip?*

Me: *Just need to sort some things out.*

Mom: *Love you, Ava. Can't wait to see you xx*

My stomach flips, but I blame the cheeseburger and do not succumb to the nerves of visiting my family.

I grab my things to head to the bathroom. When I strip

off my clothes, my glance shifts toward the mirror, turning sideways to examine my body.

The swell has become more evident over the last week, but it feels like it popped overnight. Slowly, I glide my hands across to try to connect with this unborn child inside of me.

Motherhood.

I have no idea how to be a mother despite being raised by the most perfect woman ever to exist. Charlotte 'Charlie' Edwards set the bar so high, setting gold standards. I don't think my sisters or I can ever compare.

When it came to raising us, we were never without anything. Mom cooked delicious dinners, making all of us eat together every night at the same time. She would make each one of us talk about our day, encouraging us to be communicative. Often, it resulted in dramatic arguments, but what did my parents expect with four girls? When Millie left for college, it eased, making it obvious that she caused most of it.

Then, during my sporting phase, Mom drove me around to practice. It wasn't just me, but my sisters too. Each one of us played different sports which made it all the more time-consuming.

Although Mom worked too, it never felt like we missed out. She tried to work when we were at school or asleep, and when she had deadlines, Dad took over.

How she juggled it all with a husband who ran an empire is beyond me. To add to that, Mom didn't believe in nannies or full-time maids. We did have a house cleaner and gardener—an old married couple whom Mom met through work, but they only came once a week.

All in all, Mom ran a tight ship and still managed to look unbelievably beautiful.

As for me, I have a cleaner who comes twice a week, and I still can barely take care of myself. At what point will I be able to take care of a baby? I'm not sure how I feel about nannies, but something about another woman raising my child doesn't sit well with me.

Stepping into the shower, I'm desperate to slow down my thoughts. The hot water and steam are so relaxing I wish I could stay here forever. I use all the fancy body washes, basking in the smell of vanilla and lavender.

When my skin begins to wrinkle, I climb out only to hear the door buzzer ring. I'm not expecting anyone, so I quickly throw on my tank and shorts, my skin still damp, then run to the door.

I press my finger on the intercom.

"Miss Edwards, I have an Austin Carter here to see you."

Oh, shit.

"Send him up."

The second I let go of the button, I bolt to the kitchen basin to throw up. My chest heaves until I control myself and splash cold water on my face. Then, taking a deep breath, I head to the door and open it to Austin standing on the other side. He's leaning against the door frame, looking handsome in just a pair of jeans and a white tee. His hair is a wild mess, but I narrow it down to the wind picking up until I see him run his finger through his hair in a nervous panic.

"Come in," I tell him.

He enters the apartment as I close the door. I motion for him to take a seat on the sofa as I purposely sit on the other end to distance myself. Upon sitting down, my gaze shifts toward my breasts. Shit, I forgot to wear a bra. Swiftly, I grab a cushion and cover my chest though chances are he already saw.

"I want to apologize for my reaction earlier. It was uncalled for."

"It was perfectly called for, Austin. I spring this on you, and your whole world changed," I admit, then continue, "You woke up this morning intending to go to work, and I pretty much changed your entire life all in one conversation."

Austin scratches his cheek, looking irritable. "It wasn't how I was raised to treat a woman, especially one who's carrying my baby."

"Screw that," I respond, raising my voice. "You're human. Your emotions are valid. I have no idea how to raise a child for the rest of my life. I'm terrified of failing. When you have the perfect parents who never once made me feel any less loved than I needed to feel, it puts a whole lot of pressure to get this parenting thing right."

"I was caught off guard, that I'll admit." He takes a deep breath, though his tone is much calmer than mine. "Ava, how are we going to make this work? We aren't together."

I shrug. "It would be presumptuous of me to give you an answer now. I don't know what it's going to be like when the baby arrives. It will be hard work. I'm not a kid person. I am not Millie."

The moment I say her name, his eyes snap up, almost looking tortured by the sound of it.

"God, Ava." Austin sighs heavily. "You know Millie is going to be hurt?"

"Yes, but I can't lie to her," I mumble, unable to look at him while consumed by my guilt. "Even if I did lie, that's not fair to the baby. You're the father, and why should our kid feel ashamed?"

Twisting my hands, I wish my hormones would take a god damn seat because my eyes begin to well up. I'm not a crier, spared for the few moments in my life which called for it. But lately, the smallest things will set me off.

"When do you tell them? I can be there with you," Austin offers.

I'm grateful Austin is stepping up when truthfully, I had my doubts earlier today. But this family affair needs to be a solo event. We need to air our grievances right there and then, knowing it will be unpleasant and confronting. I can almost hear Dad falling radio silent. His hopes and dreams for me shattered in a heartbeat.

My mother will be torn between comforting me, then trying to settle an upset Millie. Addy and Alexa will sit there in silence, shocked but keeping their opinions to themselves. Granted, Alexa will probably record it and upload it to some site with a hashtag 'when your sister screwed with her older sister's fiancé,' combined with some dramatic music hoping for likes or shares.

And then there's Will and Millie. I know Will enough that his jealous streak will get the better of him. He'll be eerily quiet, but you'll see the veins protruding and hands clenched into tight fists if you look close enough.

Millie will vocalize her opinion of me without a single care in the world.

She'll call me names, everyone will be stunned, and it goes without saying she will storm out without an apology.

"I need to do this alone, Austin. If Millie weren't in this equation, then I'd want you there. Will might be there, too, making it all the harder. I don't want any extra drama."

Austin rests his elbows on his knees, staring blankly in front of him.

"The offer is there, Ava. You don't need to do any of this

alone. We can make this work, this co-parenting thing," he says, continuing to ramble. "I mean, I was saving to buy a place closer to the hospital, but I can look for one now. It might not be close but two bedrooms—one for me, and then the baby's room. I'll need a crib, but maybe my mom can help with all that."

I breathe a sigh of relief, knowing Austin is panicking about all the things I had too. Stupid things which aren't a big deal but in the heat of the moment, where to position a crib seems like the end of the world.

But all of this could be worse. I could be pregnant with a man who I don't even know.

"Austin, what about Lane?" I raise the topic with curiosity. "Does she know yet?"

"We're together, and no, she doesn't know. After you left, we had a trauma case come in, so there wasn't a chance to think about this. Besides, I needed to process this myself before I could tell her."

"Look, Austin. I don't want to get in the way of things for you."

"Ava," he breathes, his voice instantly calming me. His hand moves to sit on top of mine, a small gesture I welcome. "You're the mother of my child. You and this child will be my number one priority from now. My relationship with Lane is new. Yes, she's great, but I don't want anyone to feel less important; therefore, ending things would be the sensible thing to do. Maybe, in the future, people can come into our lives. But it doesn't make sense to hold onto my relationship with her right now."

To hear Austin say these words makes me think, can we do this forever? Co-parent a child yet have separate lives with other partners. Uncle Noah and Kate did it, plus they made it look easy. At least, to me, it did. If boundaries are established, why would it be a problem?

But do I really want another woman playing mother to my child?

A burning sensation spreads across my chest, forcing me to clench my teeth. God, how can I be jealous of someone who doesn't even exist? *Calm the fuck down, Ava.*

I lean back into the sofa, raising my hands to my face. "We screwed up."

Austin glances at my stomach as my tank pulls up, exposing my skin.

"You're showing," is all he says.

My eyes drop to my stomach. Then, in a rush, I pull my tank down.

"Yes, only this week."

"You look beautiful, Ava," he murmurs. "You have that pregnancy glow."

"It's called vomiting."

Austin dips his head with a smirk. "Have you been taking any folic acid supplements?"

"Uh, Dr. Taylor mentioned something, but I was kind of in shock."

"Folic acid helps form the neural tube," he asserts with a straight face. "It's also very important because it can help prevent some major birth defects of the baby's brain."

"Okay, you're freaking me out," I confess while rubbing my stomach. "Birth defects?"

"Sorry." He cringes then relaxes enough to smile. "It's the doctor in me."

"It's okay. It's good to have a doctor around, and it doesn't hurt that you're not bad looking," I muse.

Austin chuckles softly. "You're a tease, Ava. Always have been."

And then it all begins to shift, a moment, a few simple words which question whether I have it in me to last a lifetime not falling in love with the father of my child.

Austin is a great guy. He will be in my life forever.

Yet, in so many ways, it feels like he has always been in my life.

Taking a breath, I ignore my racing heart and blame my unstable hormones. Then, I remember my scan tomorrow morning before I fly out.

"My first scan is tomorrow morning," I mention, not wanting to push him. "Sorry, I'm only just telling you. My brain is scattered and—"

"I'll be there, Ava." He smiles, then moves my hair away from my shoulder, causing my breath to hitch. "I wouldn't miss it for the world."

I tilt my head, finally allowing myself to look at him properly and not through a side-eye. Austin has beautiful eyes and one of those faces which light up when he smiles. His perfectly straight teeth are white, making his smile endearing. Our child will be beautiful if he or she is anything like him.

"I hope our baby has your smile," I profess softly.

"Hmm..." He rubs his chin, then breaks out into a relaxed grin. "And your eyes."

"My eyes?"

"Emerald."

Pursing my lips, I silently cuss myself for having a blonde moment.

"The Edwards' gene is strong that way," I muse.

Austin stares at me wistfully. He raises his finger to touch my cheek softly. "We can do this, Ava, okay? I meant it when I said you aren't alone."

His reassurance is exactly what I need. I rest my face in his hand, allowing his comforting gesture.

"You don't know how much I needed to hear that," I whisper.

This is far from perfect and not how I ever imagined my life to turn out. But as I stare into the eyes of the man who is the father of my baby, I can't help but wonder if this was always in the cards.

The Universe has a fucked-up way of aligning the stars and dealing cards.

Just how far it will test me will soon be revealed.

TEN

AUSTIN

Ava's pregnant.

My head rests against the wall until a page goes off calling all available staff to the ER.

A multi-trauma case is on its way. A woman in her mid-twenties and two young children—a boy aged six and a girl aged four—hit at a pedestrian stop by an out-of-control driver.

There's no time to stop and think of anything else. The team prepares the equipment with all trained staff on standby. First, we will need to examine the patients to get a better understanding of their conditions.

When the first responders arrive, each patient is rushed to a separate team. The little girl is brought to where I stand, and simultaneously while we start examining her, the first responder is informing us of her condition.

We work busily, following protocol. The child is conscious but in obvious pain as she begins to cry. The nurse administers some pain relief, then begins the x-raying of various parts of her body.

The rush continues however, at this stage, we can see

she hasn't sustained any internal bleeding. Instead, the pain she's experiencing is from a broken leg.

Her brother is in a similar condition, only with a broken arm. According to the report, they landed close to one another as their mother tried to shield them seconds before impact.

Across the room, the team rushes the mother into emergency surgery. There is a commotion when the nurse brings in the father and what appears to be the grandmother. The two of them weep, calling out in a panic while Dr. Hanson —who is in charge today—tries to update them on the condition of the children. Both are stable but will remain in ICU for observation. As for the mother, it is too early to tell.

Hours pass with more patients admitted but thankfully —not as serious as earlier today. Before my shift ends, a nurse updates me on the mother. She has been stabilized, and they managed to stop the internal bleeding. After seeing those two children injured, I'm grateful the mother has pulled through. I can't even imagine being a parent and going through that.

And then, the wrecking ball swings past and knocks the wind out of me, forceful with its nature and leaving me entirely breathless.

You're going to be a father.

My feet drag as I walk to the breakout room, time lost on me though I'm aware my shift has ended. Only an hour over scheduled time today, a record if I'm not mistaken. Inside the small area, a few colleagues have also clocked off, chatting away animatedly but stop for a moment to say hello. I'm not in the mood to converse, keeping my smile to a bare minimum.

I open my locker in a daze, grabbing my things, then close the door to see Lane beside me.

"Hey, handsome, you look beat."

I'm unable to look her in the eye, my limbs numb and unable to move. Multiple thoughts are running through my mind, only catching up now. How will it even work with Ava and me? We aren't together, and I barely have time to take care of myself, let alone a baby. The roster at work is so hectic, and for the last few weeks, I've worked seven days because we are short-staffed.

Then there is the huge matter of her family. I'm dead certain Lex will hunt me down and kill me. But more pressing than that is Millie's reaction.

After all, she is the Edwards daughter I once loved and wanted to marry.

Aside from New Year's Eve, I hadn't thought about the Edwards family in a long while. It was a memory I buried, and it felt like so long ago.

But then my mind wanders to the night we fucked so carelessly. I swear I placed the condom right. It wasn't my first god damn time. I just don't understand how we defied all odds. From a medical standpoint, how the hell was she ovulating the one time we screwed around and with a condom? I didn't even go in bareback, not for one second.

Yeah, sure, at first, I thought it was someone else's. Ava is beautiful, and men had always bowed down to her. But I also knew she would never make up such a lie. Ava never cared for kids, not ever voicing she wanted to settle down. Quite the opposite, she repelled commitment because she wanted to do things her way. It was a joke Millie and I often teased her about—a spinster with a vast collection of cats.

And why would Ava tell me I'm the father knowing full well it will tear her family apart?

But, I reacted prematurely and doubted her. It was wrong of me, yet all of it rendered me speechless. Never in my wildest dreams did I think she'd tell me such a thing when I saw her.

"Austin?" Lane calls, her hand gently falling on my arm. "Austin?"

I shake my head, then turn to look at her. "Sorry."

"Is everything okay?"

"Uh, no. Not really."

"Do you want to talk now? Or over dinner?"

I forgot she organized dinner at this restaurant a few blocks over. It wouldn't be fair to continue this charade, not when I need to sort things out and process my thoughts.

"I need to take care of something."

"Uh, sure." Lane forces a smile, despite my cold tone. "Do what you need to do."

Kissing her cheek, I distance myself quickly because the guilt begins to weigh on me. There's no way I can continue my relationship with her. It just wouldn't be fair.

But that wasn't front and center on my mind.

Ava deserves an apology.

I acted like a fucking jerk earlier, and she shouldn't have been in the firing line.

The easiest route to her apartment is via the subway. It's late and not overly crowded. There are a few questionable people, but like always, I ignore them.

When I arrive at her apartment, Ava opens the door dressed in a white tank and pink boxers. As she stands in front of me with bare feet, her stature appears much shorter. I'm quite tall, but usually when I'm with her, she's wearing heels.

Though, that isn't what is catching my attention.

She's obviously not wearing a bra, so I do my best to turn away, ignoring the slight stir in my pants. Now isn't the time to start thinking with my dick.

Ava invites me in, motioning for me to take a seat on the sofa. Her penthouse is simplistic yet warm and cozy, with her scent lingering everywhere. It clouds my thoughts, but I take a deep breath and begin with an apology. My behavior was uncalled for, and I'm ashamed I took my anger out on her.

The famous saying 'it takes two to tango' couldn't ring any more true.

We both played with fire to end up right here in *Hell*.

The more we speak, the more I see in her eyes just how terrified she is, thinking she will have to do this alone.

Then, there's the matter of her family.

I've been around the Edwards enough to know it won't go down well. Lex is highly protective of his daughters, Ava being his favorite, but Charlie will be understanding. She always is the person you can run to for anything.

As for Millie, I honestly don't know. I suspect her husband will have more of an issue than her. And then I think, can I handle being back in that family? They weren't an ordinary family, not when the patriarch is a billionaire who runs an empire.

In comparison, my family is super low-key. Dad is an architect, and Mom owns a furniture store. My oldest sister, Ivy, lives in Sacramento with her husband. My younger sister, Ella, is studying at Berkeley.

We meet for holidays if convenient for everyone but still keep in contact regularly.

I'm sure once I tell them, they'll be more excited than disappointed. My parents are never ones to voice their opinions on our relationships. When Millie and I split, they expressed their apologies but didn't involve themselves. They knew well enough to leave the situation alone. If anything, they were more worried about my studies.

I reassure Ava it will be okay because what else can I say? The last thing she needs is me projecting my fears onto her. Then, as she vents openly, her tank rises, and I see the swell of her stomach.

Fuck, this is going to happen.

It's staring me in the face.

The fear gnaws at me until I ignore its desperation to hold me hostage and focus on Ava's face. She appears worn out with slight bags under her usually vibrant eyes, but her skin still has that pregnancy glow.

Just admit it, she's fucking stunning and always has been.

When I look back at the times we hung out with each other, there were often moments when I spent more time with Ava than Millie. Perhaps, in hindsight, we'd always had some sort of connection. With Ava, it's just easy. She always said her mind, never once holding back. Millie was different. There was always this hesitation with her. Rather than speak her mind, she bottled things up between us or deflected. To look back now, a lot of it had to do with Romano.

We never had a conversation on exactly how they ended because frankly—I couldn't care less at the time. I was naïve to think he wouldn't come back, and when he did—it was probably the worst time of my life. The only thing which got me through it was studying. I'm glad I persisted, never once giving up all because Amelia Edwards couldn't admit the truth.

Ava quickly informs me of the sonogram tomorrow, apologizing for telling me last minute. Thankfully, it's my rostered day off.

"It's late," I say, though my own exhaustion starts to creep in. "You look like you need sleep."

She nods with a half-smile. "I should probably get some before I never get sleep for the rest of my life."

I chuckle softly. "We may get lucky. A child who sleeps through the night."

"Austin, there are so many things we need to sort out."

"We will, but you need rest. It's not just about you now."

"I'm so tired I can't even move." She yawns, resting her head on the cushion.

It only takes a matter of seconds before her eyelids close. I grab the cream throw blanket and place it on top of her, covering her shoulders. Her face looks angelic, the natural long lashes accentuating her closed eyes. The color of her cheeks is pink, and as I watch her sleep, I quietly count the few freckles scattered across her nose.

Like deja vu, the memory comes roaring back.

I'd done this, once, before.

And I remember telling myself to stop. Only last time, we were waiting inside the cabin at Lake Tahoe for Millie and her parents to arrive.

We laughed until our stomachs hurt, threw peanuts in each other's mouths when we realized we had no phone coverage, and tore our hair out from boredom.

Then, Ava fell asleep.

And I watched when I shouldn't have.

This time is different. There's to be no watching, no looking at each other differently. We have a kid to raise, and that's all that matters.

Rising from the sofa with an odd feeling settling in my stomach, my body stiffens, and my muscles tense from the stress.

All I need to do is get out of here.

The sooner, the better, to avoid my mind from wandering any further.

"Are you ready, Ava?"

The sonographer, Melinda, smears the gel across Ava's abdomen. Then, with the probe in hand, she presses it gently in waves with her focus on the monitor.

My gaze is glued to the monitor, instantly noticing the baby on the screen. It's small but enough to see its shape and body which has formed. Each time Melinda moves the probe, the image fades in and out.

There's a burst of warmth inside my chest. A surreal feeling I've never experienced before. So many emotions run wild, from the urge to protect this baby I'm yet to meet to an overwhelming amount of love. This kind of love brings happiness of a different kind, but in the same breath—I'm terrified of failing and causing more harm than good.

Ava turns her head to face me. "Can you see the baby?"

"I sure can." I point to the screen, waiting for Melinda to steady the image and welcoming the distraction from my overbearing thoughts. "See that circle on the right. That's the baby's head. If you follow it left, you'll see the body and legs."

Melinda raises her brows with a slow smile that builds.

"Austin is a second-year resident."

"Almost," I correct Ava. "In about two months."

"I didn't realize and now feel self-conscious," Melinda muses, almost looking flustered. She turns to both of us. "Are you ready?"

Ava glances at me nervously.

And then, like music to anyone's ears, the heartbeat echoes in the room.

Several times in the ER, there have been instances when we'd wait for a sign of life, the greatest gift possible. But this is different—this is my baby.

"Is that the heartbeat?" Ava chokes.

"Yes," Melinda confirms, then continues to take measurements. "Perfectly healthy and happy. Now, you measure eighteen weeks along, almost halfway. Everything looks good. Did you want to find out the sex of the baby?"

"You can do that now?" Ava questions in a high-pitched voice.

"Yes, you're far enough along."

Ava raises her eyes to the ceiling, only to shift her gaze to me moments later. "I don't know."

"You don't have to decide now," I tell her.

"But do you want to know?"

"A surprise would be nice. As long as the baby is healthy."

Ava remains quiet but shortly lets out a sigh. "I agree, please don't tell us."

Melinda continues with measurements, going through the various parts of the body. Her focus is fixated on me like she has something to prove. A few times she batts her eyes, possibly unaware she has done so. Soon after, she grabs some tissues to wipe the gel off Ava.

"Here is the photo to take home. You're free to leave whenever you're ready." Melinda glances at me with a knowing smile. "It was nice meeting you, Dr?"

"Dr. Carter," I respond politely.

"You can call him Austin," Ava mumbles beneath her breath.

"And, of course, Ava. Good luck with the pregnancy."

When Melinda exits the room and closes the door behind her, Ava lets out a groan.

"She was so flirting with you."

"That's what you took from all of this?" I question her, still in awe from seeing the baby.

"I'm trying to forget that in four months from now, I'm going to have to push this baby out of my vagina."

"Okay, if we're playing the game of denial, then no, I didn't notice."

"Everywhere we go, women are trying to flirt with you."

I grab her hand to help her up. "How would you like me to respond to that?"

"What are we supposed to tell people, you know, when we're together?"

To give Ava some privacy, I turn around so she can change.

"The truth? Ava, I don't know, okay? We aren't the first couple to raise a child without being together. Let people judge. At the end of the day, what does it matter?"

"I guess," she mutters. "You can turn around now."

"Is this really about people or your family?"

Ava lowers her eyes, fidgeting with the ring on her index finger.

"One minute, I'm like, I can do this. I'm twenty-five and have my own money. It's not like I have to live with my parents or anything." Ava's ramble causes her breath to hitch. "Then the next moment, I literally can't breathe. A heartbeat? This baby is alive inside of me, and it's only going to grow bigger."

Placing my hand on hers, I try to calm her down. "The offer still stands if you want me to come."

She shakes her head. "No, as I said, I think it will make it worse. But can I call you afterward?"

"Of course, you know you can call me anytime."

"Even when it's two in the morning, and I'm craving ice cream and pickles?"

"Chances are I'm on call. So, sure."

Ava removes her hand but shifts her gaze back onto the floor. With the number of times she's done that, you would think something interesting is on there.

"Did you tell Lane yet?"

"No," I admit, slightly annoyed she brought it up. "I was going to tell her tonight."

"Oh, okay," Ava trails off, then takes her phone out of her purse to check the time. "Listen, I should go, or I'll miss my flight."

With her purse in hand, she remembers the photo on the table beside the bed. She retrieves it, falling into a deep stare. "I think it's a girl."

I chuckle softly. "Funny, me too."

"Shut up, liar," Ava blurts out with a grin. "You saw, didn't you?"

I place my hand on my heart. "Swear, I didn't."

"You swear on that tattered Lakers jersey you always used to wear, which you swore you'd be buried with?"

"You remember that?" I tilt my head, surprised by her memory. "And yes, I still have it and swear on it."

Ava lets out a heavy sigh, keeping her smile fixed. "Goodbye, Austin."

"Ava, just breathe. Lex and Charlie love you no matter what. Just give Lex time to process."

"And Millie?"

"It'll work out. Everyone just needs time."

Inside the small café, I sit across from Lane after asking her to meet me. There's no point delaying the inevitable, and just like a band-aid—I need to rip it off now to clear my conscience.

"Lane, can we talk?"

"Sure," she responds slowly, with a grimace. "Is everything okay?"

"There is no easy way to say this..."

"You're breaking up with me?"

"Yes, but it's more complicated than that," I quickly inform her.

Lane bows her head, hiding her pained expression. "I don't understand."

"The woman who visited me yesterday—"

"Ava?" she interrupts, lifting her gaze simultaneously.

"Yes, Ava," I repeat while rubbing the back of my neck. "Well, she, um, a few months back, we kind of had a one-night thing, and she's kind of pregnant."

Lane's face falls blank, to the point her stare is fixed, and it doesn't look like she is breathing. "I didn't see that coming."

"Neither did I."

"Look, Austin. I get it. I really do."

Lane stands up, throwing her purse strap over her shoulder. Unexpectedly, she drops her lips to plant a soft kiss on my cheek. I close my eyes in an attempt to stay strong and not allow the guilt to consume me.

None of this is fair, and Lane didn't deserve this.

"For what it's worth, Ava is really beautiful. When you saw her the other day, I could see how happy you were to see her."

"Lane, it's not like that between us. It was one night."

"Maybe." She shrugs half-heartedly with a glazed stare.

"But that doesn't mean the feelings aren't valid."

And with that said, she walks out of the café.

Breaking up with someone is never easy, but of all the breakups I've endured, this probably was the easiest. Lane is a no drama, uncomplicated woman, which is why I was attracted to her. In addition, we had medicine in common, and having a relationship at work was easy because we got to spend more time with one another.

That is until now.

Working with an ex isn't quite ideal.

I pull out my phone and look at the time, noting Ava would be in the air.

Me: *I told Lane. She took it well, considering.*

I'm not sure why I felt compelled to tell Ava, but I tuck my phone back into my pocket to head home.

In only a matter of hours, the Edwards family will know the truth.

The persistent lead weight on my chest onsets a headache, so the minute I get home, I pop some Advil to alleviate the stress.

But nothing works because I can't seem to get Ava out of my head, worried as she walks into the lion's den and I'm standing here doing absolutely nothing.

It's no good for me to stay here, waiting on edge, knowing I'll get no sleep.

I knock on Jonah's door. "Hey, buddy, you up for a drink tonight?"

Jonah opens the door, dressed in a pair of white jocks. It should shock me, but I've seen it too many times that I've stopped caring.

"Name the place, bro. I'm coming."

ELEVEN

AVA

.

The foyer inside my parents' home appears grander than I remember.

My penthouse apartment in the city isn't even a quarter in size compared to this house. Although they also own a penthouse in the city, that too is double the size of mine.

Just like an old movie, memories play on a reel. The time I fell down the grand staircase because Amelia dared me to use the laundry basket as a sled. It was all smooth sailing until three steps from the bottom, gravity intervened, and my body flew in the air. To this day, I still have the scar on my knee from when I hit the floor.

And then there was Millie's prom moment when she stood at the top of the stairs in the most beautiful gown to ever exist. I still remember exactly what it looked like. It was a burgundy silk strapless gown with a mermaid hem and high split in the middle of the dress. Her hair was styled with soft curls, parted to the side, showcasing the diamond choker around her neck which belonged to Mom.

I stared in awe, thinking I will never be as beautiful as her.

Then, at the bottom of the stairs with a proud smile on his face, was her prince charming.

Austin Carter.

My gaze falls upon the floor, willing the unwanted feeling of jealousy to dissipate. The dark oak floors are cleaned to perfection since Mom is crazy obsessed with them. As I breathe in the intoxicating smell of something cooking in the kitchen, Mom walks out of the kitchen and down the hallway to greet me.

My suitcase stands beside me at the door when my eyes steadily shift toward her. I swear, this woman never ages, always looking eternally young with flawless and wrinkle-free skin. It doesn't surprise me why Dad is still irrevocably in love with her even after all these years.

A genuine smile sweeps across Mom's face. She extends her arms until I fall into her embrace yet keep my distance so she doesn't notice the swell in my stomach. Inside her warm hug, everything feels right in the world again, if only for this moment.

"Look at you, just as beautiful as your pictures online," Mom teases while pulling away.

"Mom, you saw me at Christmas. Nothing has changed." The moment it slips, I mentally scold myself. Everything has changed, you idiot. "Aside from my hair growing longer."

Mom holds her gaze long enough to make me feel like she can see right through me. I smile, willing she be distracted, and when I choose to keep my mouth shut, she wipes her hands together and asks me to join her in the kitchen.

Leaving my suitcase in the foyer, I follow her through to the kitchen.

"Where is everyone?"

"Your father is at the office but promised he'll be home for dinner. Addy has a class today and will be home soon. As for Alexa, school, I hope."

"And Millie?"

"Ashton stays home on Fridays, but she has an activity group with some other mothers down at Venice Beach."

I can't think of anything worse than a mothers' group. No one wants to talk about babies all day long. Was this even compulsory? I make a mental note to google it as soon as I am free.

"She's really fit into the mom life," I say with a hard swallow.

Mom smiles proudly. "She has, but you know, she's always been very nurturing, much like yourself."

"Me?" I raise my hand to my chest, curious as to how she has come to that conclusion. "You think I'm nurturing?"

"You're always taking care of others, Ava. It's how we raised all four of you," she affirms while placing a plate of sandwiches in front of me. "I didn't come from a large family. In fact, my family was quite dysfunctional. Your father, though, I envied what he had. It's why I spent so much time over there with Adriana. I used to imagine what it would be like to live in a house where parents loved each other and didn't fight. I wondered what it would be like to have a sibling who was around, not one who took off on some backpacking adventure the moment things got tough. I craved stability."

"You have it, now, though," I remind her.

As Mom pours a glass of homemade lemonade for me, her eyes turn soft, filled with an inner glow.

"I couldn't have asked for a more perfect family," she admits with a beaming smile. "So, tell me, what's been happening with you aside from the Olivier situation?"

I clear my throat and my mind, trying to come up with anything which isn't about the pregnancy. As tempting as it is to tell Mom now, I don't want to put her in a position where she feels compelled to hide it from Dad.

"Eric is doing amazing things as my new publicist. I wish I hired him sooner than wasting my time on Elle Harrison. I should've gone with my gut, just like Dad taught me."

"Eric definitely found his calling. I'm glad he's doing great things for you. He knows branding and how to leverage from that, plus his legal knowledge is a bonus."

My hands reach for the sandwiches in front of me. They look so delicious, so I can't help but grab two even though Mom is watching me.

"The summer launch went well. I'm really excited about the pieces for that. I've tried to stay away from skimpy and catered to all women, no matter the sizing. There's something for everyone this summer."

"And how are the orders going?"

"We've sold out on most of the swimwear, and that's on pre-order only. The team is trying to see if we can increase manufacturing speed to fulfill orders, especially because we're only at the beginning of summer. We didn't expect it to take off. The loungewear and jewelry are what we're working on now. Dad is really pushing me to produce locally."

"It always was going to take off, honey." Mom beams then places her hand on mine. "You understand what women want. You make them feel empowered. By doing that, they feel confident in your product."

So then, why all of a sudden do I feel like an imposter? An empowered woman wouldn't sleep with her sister's ex-fiancé because she felt worthless.

"Perception, it's powerful in its own right." My feet touch the floor as I hop off the stool with one sandwich in hand. "I'm going to unpack and catch up on some emails."

"Ava, is everything all right?"

I let out a sigh. "I hope so, Mom."

There is always a nostalgic feeling when I lay on my childhood bed and stare at the ceiling. I've done it so many times I've lost count. From the time I first got my period, wondering if I looked any different because I had officially become a woman. To when I lost my virginity for the first time, questioning why having sex was so hyped since my experience was less than desirable.

The wallpaper is blush-colored. It's subtle enough not to come across as overly girly and was my favorite color growing up. Against the back wall is the king-sized bed which I lay on. The plain white duvet, along with perfectly positioned pillows, style the bed nicely. In the middle of the two large pillows is my stuffed cow—Petunia. I dragged this thing around everywhere from the moment I began crawling, according to Mom, which is why it's tattered and covered in stains.

Removing my shoes, I toss them to the floor, then grab Petunia to inhale her scent. Just like I remember—she smells of fabric softener. Mom tried her damned hardest to clean her up, but nothing will bring Petunia back to her original condition. The corners of my lips curve upward at the scent of the stuffed childhood toy, and gradually, I find my shoulders relaxing.

Petunia continues to sit on my chest as I roll over to my side and reach for my phone in my purse. When I disembarked the plane earlier this afternoon, a text from Austin came through. He had told Lane the truth and broke it off. I'm not sure why a simple text brought this unknown wave of satisfaction. What did I have to be jealous about? We weren't together, and I don't harbor romantic feelings for Austin.

Nevertheless, I muster up the courage to respond.

Me: *Sorry, I know it wouldn't have been easy.*

I guess, if I'm honest with myself, a huge part of me was worried they would stay together, and she would be a step-mother to my child.

Just as my thoughts spiral into uncharted territory, my phone pings.

Austin: *Good luck tonight. Not sure if that's the right sentiment. I'm working tonight but just text me if you need me.*

Me: *I don't think there is such a thing as luck. Though maybe I should say that to you? My dad is ruthless.*

Austin: *Believe it or not, I've stopped worrying about Lex. I may not have the gold star from him, but that's cool.*

Me: *I forgot that you were his golden star once upon a time. The doctor extraordinaire. Maybe this won't be that bad.*

There's a knock on my door. It opens as Addy pops her head in.

"Hey, sis. Glad to have you back."

Out of all us siblings, Addy is the most level-headed. She never creates drama, always focuses on her studies, and does her own thing. Addy rarely dates guys, or at least—she never mentions anyone. Hands down, she lives the most uneventful life out of all of us. Plus, she's incredibly smart studying psychology.

She throws herself on the end of my bed, leaning on her elbow. So many people say we look alike. The same goes for Alexa. The shading of our hair is the same as Dad's, and of course—the emerald eyes. Addy has Mom's nose if I must point out something that's slightly different to me. Oh, and she's taller—another trait from Dad.

Millie is the only one who is the spitting image of Mom except for the eyes. We used to joke that she came from a different father, but of course, Dad never saw the humor in that.

As Addy grew older, we became close, but our relationship is a lot different from Millie's and mine. We're not as explosive together which many people agree on, including my parents.

And if there's anyone I can confide in, it's the person lying on my bed twisting her long braid between her fingers.

"Addy..." I begin with, only to pick Petunia up for comfort. "I need your help."

"What's wrong?" Addy immediately sits up, her eyes broadening with concern. "Are you sick? Because, no offense, you look tired."

"Yes, no, I'm pregnant."

Addy jerks her head. Her eyes are still wide, and I swear she hasn't blinked.

"Um, wow, congratulations?"

"There's more."

"More?"

"You need to promise me you won't judge."

"I never judge."

"We all judge...it's what we do as sisters."

"You, Millie, and Alexa judge," Addy corrects me. "I don't judge."

"Before I tell you this, I need you to know that I was upset. I just caught Olivier in bed. Plus, the Miami event fell through."

"So, you were feeling sorry for yourself and screwed someone you shouldn't have on a one-night stand?"

"How did you know that?"

"I study psychology."

I take a deep breath, then swallow the lump inside my throat. "It's Austin's."

"Austin? As in Millie's Austin?"

"He's not hers," I fire back in annoyance.

Silence falls between us. Addy releases a heavy sigh but keeps her thoughts at bay.

"I feel you judging me."

"I'm shocked," she admits while shaking her head. "I would say there's a curiosity more than judgment."

I go ahead and explain exactly what happened that night so she knows the full story with the hope she can maybe give me some advice on how to handle tonight.

"I think you'll need to prepare yourself for the outcome. Of course, Dad will be quiet, fester his anger, but let's get honest here. It is you, so maybe you might be spared the storm."

"I highly doubt it, but continue... "

"Mom will be worried about your condition, yet also

trying to deal with Dad at the same time. They'll do that secret eye thing where they're staring at each other but not saying a word." Addy is so accurate, knowing our family too well. "Alexa will congratulate you because she's too busy thinking about her social life to understand the enormity of the situation. As for Millie, she'll be vocal and angry. She will think you did this on purpose, and chances are, Will's going to be just as livid. That whole jealous alpha trait will come out because Austin will be part of our family."

"But Austin isn't part of our family. We're not in a relationship," I tell her adamantly. "We will co-parent. That's it."

"Yes, but you know Will, it means Austin is around you. You're around Millie. Seven degrees of separation right there."

I throw my pillow over my face. "I'm fucked. No matter how I look at it, Millie will be angry."

"C'mon, Ava. She won't stay angry forever."

"Oh really? Once, she didn't talk to me for two weeks straight because I borrowed her favorite cardigan and stained it."

"The cream one that looked like something from a grandmother's closet?" Addy cringes.

"So beside the point, Addy."

"Yes, it is. But I'm trying to distract the part of your brain which is focusing on what you can't change. You cannot change how our family will react, especially Millie."

Addy jumps off the bed to walk toward the window. She pulls the drape aside to get a better glance of outside. "They're here."

Nausea consumes me, forcing my hands to clutch my stomach. Addy is right. I need to remind myself that I can't change how they will react no matter what I say. Each one of my family members is stubborn at the best of times.

Addy moves toward the door but waits for me.

"Are you ready?"

I purse my lips, then inhale deeply with a nod.

We both head downstairs to the foyer, where Will, Millie, and Ashton are lingering. Mom has already found them, scooping Ashton into her arms while smothering him with kisses. He has grown so much since I saw him at Christmas, but nevertheless—still cute with his bronze hair and big blue eyes.

Millie catches a glimpse of me walking down the stairs. I pull my buttoned shirt out, conscious of my stomach. Her face lights up, and I'm quick to dig her cute denim jacket and sundress beneath it.

When I reach the bottom step, Millie reaches out her arms as I fall into her embrace, careful not to press my body against hers.

"I missed you, Ava," she says, holding onto me. "We need a catch-up, just you and me."

Forcing a smile, I pull away. "Sure, whenever you're free. I'm here for a few days."

"How about lunch at our favorite restaurant in Malibu tomorrow?"

"Sounds like a perfect plan."

Millie tilts her head, watching me furtively but doesn't say another word.

Ashton runs over to hug me, with Will following him. His small arms wrap around me, prompting me to lean down and hug him. I'm not great with kids, not like Millie.

"You look different," Will points out, followed by an obligatory hug.

I pull back in paranoia. "I do?"

"Yeah, you do."

Mom requests everyone to head to the dining room. Moments later, Dad walks through the doorway. Out of everyone in my family, I spend the most time with him. He flies to the East Coast often, which means his visits are regular.

Dad turns his head in my direction with a warm smile the second he lays his eyes on me. I stop in my tracks to take a moment to say hello.

"Ava," he calls softly. "Always good to have you home."

I throw my arms around him as he kisses the top of my head. The thing which terrifies me the most is losing him. I may be an adult and one who runs a successful business, but what if he doesn't talk to me? Or worse yet, he disowns me. I watched what happened with Millie. Their relationship was strained for a while after her affair with Will was revealed.

Inside his embrace, I linger a bit longer and bask in his aftershave—its scent bringing back so many memories of my childhood. He senses my reluctance to let go, holding onto me tight. When I pull away, his smile is fixed, but worry comes over him.

"Is everything okay, Ava?"

"I'm hoping so," I tell him firmly, trying not to break down. "But let's eat dinner, please."

He doesn't press further as we make our way to the dining room.

As always, Mom has cooked up a storm. I choose to sit next to her, knowing I will need her to support me the moment it comes out. Addy sits on the other side of me, and after a few minutes, Alexa joins us with her head buried in her phone which Dad tells her to put away.

Millie sits across from me with Will by her side. Ashton demands to sit next to Dad.

Mom calls for a moment to say grace, then encourages us to all begin eating.

I choose to tell everyone after dinner, not wanting to ruin Mom's delicious food. Thankfully, Ashton takes center stage most of the time. He is incredibly attached to Dad, and the feeling is mutual. I can't help but watch how Dad softens when talking to Ashton. I wonder how he will feel when I have the baby. Living across the other side of the country will make it difficult, but I'm torn between staying in the city and moving back home.

Addy nudges my arm with her elbow, then subtly lowers her head while mumbling, "Do it now."

Everyone has finished their meal, although the conversations are still continuing. I place my hands beneath the table, wringing them together while riddled with nerves. Then, Addy places her hand on mine and squeezes it tight. No matter what happens, at least I have her by my side. Not everyone will hate me.

"Um, I have some news to tell everyone."

Everyone stops what they're doing with all eyes focused on me. All but Ashton, his time is spent with two Hot Wheel cars running across the table.

With every single person waiting with bated breath for me to speak, the temperature in the room becomes increasingly hot. Beneath my clothes, sweat builds, and my heart races, making it difficult to breathe, let alone speak. Underneath the table, Addy squeezes my hand tight again.

"Good news, I hope?" Dad asks.

"Uh, it depends on which way you look at it," I begin, then stall, my breaths becoming shallow. *I'm pregnant.*

I drop my head, refusing to look at anyone, and focus on the empty plate in front of me.

"Pregnant?" Millie chokes, her voice unsteady. "But you aren't with anyone?"

My muscles tense, making it challenging to move. I'm unable to look Millie in the face, averting my gaze to Mom. As predicted, she draws her brows together with worry but remains silent, assuming she is trying to process this information.

Then, I quickly glance at Dad. He is staring blankly at the glass of wine in front of him.

"Congratulations," Alexa blurts out, her tone upbeat. "I thought you looked different."

Addy watches with a sympathetic gaze, also keeping quiet.

"Who is the father?" Dad finally speaks in a low, controlled yet angered tone.

"Um, this guy. It was one night, but I've known him forever, so it's not like he's a stranger and..."

I cut myself off before I make this even worse.

Mom clears her throat. "This is a surprise, but nonetheless, you have our support. How far along are you, honey?"

This is it, the final moment.

The straw to break the camel's back.

"Four months..." I murmur, only to fall into a digestive silence.

Slowly, I inch my gaze toward Millie. In a matter of seconds, her confused expression morphs into a look of contempt.

The damage is done.

And the raging storm is about to make landfall.

TWELVE

AVA

Across the dinner table, Millie bares her teeth with an unrelenting stare.

The shade of her skin turns pink, yet despite the bright shade—her eyes are stone cold. Suddenly, the chair she sits on screeches across the floor from the force of her standing up. Crossing her arms, she stands in defiance.

"Four months?" she barks unapologetically. "So, what? Early January, late December?"

I lower my eyes to the table again. "Around there."

"New Year's Eve?"

"Millie, please," I beg quietly.

Millie points her finger, keeping her chin high and lips flat. "Don't you dare ask me for sympathy! I can't believe you would stoop that low. I know you're jealous of my life, but I didn't expect you to hurt me like that."

"I didn't do this on purpose!" I shout in return. "You don't understand."

"I understand very well. You can't get a guy of your own, so what, you go for your sister's ex. What's next? You want to make a move on my husband too?"

I bow my head, swallowing hard to fight back the tears.

A disturbing laugh escapes her. "Yeah, I guess the real Ava comes out."

Millie throws her napkin on the table, storming out of the room. Will doesn't look my way, his pinched mouth and tightness in his eyes make him appear hostile. Without a word, he leaves the table, to which I assume he is looking for Millie.

Mom places her hand on my back, rubbing it softly while I bury my face into my hands.

"Austin is the father?" she questions softly.

Unable to speak, I nod, but Mom's gentle back rub starts to calm me down enough to breathe normally again.

"It's nothing at all like she said. I just was so upset that night after Miami and then catching Olivier with another man. Austin walked into this bar I was drowning my sorrows in. He had a rough day, too, lost a kid in ER. We were hurting and drunk so much. Neither one of us remembers the night clearly, and here we are. I would never purposely hurt Millie.

"Of course, you wouldn't, honey," Mom soothes. "She's upset, understandably. But, Ava, please, you need to calm down right now. This isn't good for you or the baby. And nothing changes what I said earlier. We will support you no matter what."

As I glance over at Dad, I sense his disappointment. He hasn't said a word since asking me who the father is, nor has he made eye contact. When I turn away, guilty for causing him this pain, he excuses himself, then walks away in silence.

"He hates me," I utter.

"Your father will never hate you. Let him process the news. His little girl just told him she's pregnant, and the circumstances may not exactly have been what he envisioned for you."

Mom has a point. I need to give him space even though a small part of me prayed for some miracle, hoping everyone would be happy with the news.

"How did Austin take the news?" Alexa asks, only realizing now the severity of the situation. "I always liked him. He was a nice guy."

"Angry, upset, denial. How many more emotions can I describe?"

Mom places her hand on mine. "I'm sorry you felt you needed to go through this alone. I wish you'd told me earlier."

Addy offers to clear the table and wash up, to give Mom and me some alone time. When Alexa doesn't get the hint, Addy raises her voice at Alexa to get off her ass. Addy encourages Ashton to join them, and he happily does so, too little to understand what just happened.

When the two of us are alone, I let it all go.

"Honestly, Mom. I don't know who I am anymore. The last few months have been this blur, and I don't even know how I got here."

"One day at a time, that's all you should worry about now," Mom assures me. Her concern for my well-being is not lost on me. I should have told her earlier rather than go through this alone.

"Austin wanted to be here, but I thought it was best to keep him out of this."

"We would love to see him again when you're both ready."

"How am I going to do this, Mom?" I sputter, momentarily beyond words. "Be a single mother? Austin wants to help, and I know he's going to be a great dad, but this is for a lifetime."

"You will do it because you have no choice. No matter what I say, it can't prepare you for motherhood, but just know we're here to help."

I fall into her embrace at the same time Addy comes back in and tells me Millie is leaving.

The slam of the front door startles us. I push my chair out, then run to the front to hear the engine start. Mom joins me when Will walks back in, unable to look me in the face.

"I think it's best we leave, Charlie."

"I understand," Mom responds accordingly. "Please, call me tonight. I'd like to talk to Amelia."

As Will turns around to leave, I call his name.

"You have to believe me when I say this wasn't done on purpose."

He stops in his tracks, his head fallen and back still facing me.

"I believe you, Ava," he answers coldly. "But the damage to my family is done. Now, I need to go home and console a very broken wife."

I clutch my stomach as he walks away, the sick feeling causing me to dry heave. Mom notices my body language, suggesting I sit down and drink something.

"Mom, I just want to be alone right now."

"Take your time, Ava." She runs her finger along my cheek. "Go rest, and I'll check on you later tonight."

Staring at the ceiling, I try to clear my thoughts, but all they do is run rampant. Millie's face haunts me, the pure anger raging through her when she figured out the truth.

With my phone beside me, I contemplate texting her but decide against it. Instead, I hop off my bed and walk toward my father's study.

I knock on the door, yet he doesn't say a word. I draw in a deep breath, then turn the knob to open the door to let myself in.

Inside, the room is dark aside from the small desk lamp. Surprisingly, there is no drink in front of him, just a man looking solemn as he stares blankly at his desk. I move toward his shelf and pour his favorite scotch into a glass, the exact portion he always drinks. Then, I place it in front of him.

"I know you're angry, Dad... " I begin with, then continue, "... but please know I'm just as angry with myself. This isn't how I envisioned my life to turn out. I made this stupid decision because I let my emotions take control. Me, someone who always thinks with my head and not my goddamn heart."

My shoulders slump as a deep sigh escapes me. "I had all these hopes and dreams to make something of myself, and in just a heartbeat, it's been taken away from me."

I bow my head, to be distracted by the movement of Dad taking a sip of his drink.

"Having a baby doesn't stop you from achieving, Ava. Of course, there will be challenges, but you don't stop dreaming. If anything, you dream bigger."

"I screwed up, Dad," I croak, my emotions turning raw. "I've hurt Millie so much."

Across from me, Dad presses his lips into a slight grimace. Much like Mom, I assume he is torn between Millie and me.

"This isn't ideal, Ava. But now, you pull your shoulders back and gain the confidence to be the best mother you can be."

"I'm so sorry, Dad."

"Come here."

I fall into Dad's embrace, clutching onto his shirt, allowing myself to sob.

"Fuck the Universe. I don't even know where to begin rebuilding my life and the relationships I've destroyed."

"This is why you have family, why you have a team." He pulls away but keeps me within reach. "Firstly, you sit down with Eric to put together a plan of how you will announce this. This will change nothing in your brand, but you do need to start thinking about expanding in areas that don't require you to be young, fit, and pressured. Do you understand what I'm saying?"

"Yes, I need to be smart with my next moves," I mutter, too tired to even think about anything but sleep right now. "Let the funnels of income derive from sources which can effectively push to the market without the connection of my body."

I pull away to ask him a serious question. "Are you upset Austin is the father?"

He sits back down, then takes a long sip of his drink.

"It could have been worse. How is he, anyway?"

"Second-year resident. He's busy, of course."

"I think it's only right we have dinner with him soon. He is now a part of our family."

I nod, taken aback to hear this from my father.

"Yes, he is. But we're not together, Dad." I tug on the bottom of my shirt, fumbling on my thoughts. "Do you think Millie will forgive me?"

"Give her time. She's your sister. This is complicated, but she will never stop loving you."

"I guess this is like the whole Uncle Julian and Aunt Adriana saga," I dare to raise, cautiously glancing at him.

Dad shakes his head. "Oh, sweetheart. That was much worse."

"But everyone eventually reconciled and moved on?"

"Sometimes, Ava, there is no choice. Unfortunately, this is the hand we are dealt, and nothing we say nor do will change how someone feels about another person."

If Dad and Mom forgave Aunt Adriana, then eventually Millie will forgive me. But for now, I agree with him—she needs time. And so that's what I will give her.

Letting out a yawn, I stretch my arms in the air. "I'm going to head to bed, it's been a long day, and I'm still on East Coast time."

"Of course, get some rest, Ava."

As I stand up to leave his office, I stop to say one more thing. "I'm sorry if I disappointed you, Dad."

His gaze falls upon me, and even though this is not what he wanted for me, his soft expression reassures me that I have his support.

"Ava, I love you. Nothing will ever change that. Now get some rest, please."

I head up to my room, shower, dress in my pajamas, and climb into my bed. There's a gentle tap on the door the moment I get comfortable.

"Come in."

Mom enters the room, carrying a grilled cheese sandwich and a glass of milk.

"Under different circumstances, I would have come up with vodka."

The corners of my mouth curve upward into a smile as she places the items on the nightstand beside me.

"Thanks, Mom."

"I noticed you didn't eat much at dinner," she tells me honestly. "Have you been experiencing much morning sickness?"

I shake my head. "I think it's been more stress-induced nausea."

"With all four of you, the first trimester was terrible. I had morning sickness all day long."

My hands move behind me to adjust the pillows so I can sit upright and eat. Then, not wanting to get crumbs on the blanket, I move it off me. I'm about to reach for the glass of milk, but instead, I lift my top so Mom can see, followed by pulling the photo up on my phone from the ultrasound.

"Here's my baby, Mom."

Mom's eyes glass over with a smile gracing her entire face, then slowly, she reaches out. "May I?"

I nod, allowing Mom to place her hands on my stomach.

"I can't believe my baby has a baby inside of her."

There is another knock on the door, but without even getting a word out, Addy and Alexa come in. The two of them lay on the other side of me, and just like Mom, they place their hands on my belly.

As we all laugh softly, Dad walks past. He stops at the door, surprised to see us all in bed together.

"I think this baby will be so loved," he mentions with a smile, then sits beside Mom.

As I look at my family and relish at this moment, I can't ignore the heaviness inside my chest from the one person missing.

It's not the same without Millie, but just like Will said, I've torn his wife apart.

It wasn't just about Austin, but because she's trying her damn hardest to fall pregnant, and it happened to me on a one-night stand.

And only a few minutes away in their own home, I know my sister is crying herself to sleep.

The thought alone pains me, but nothing I can say or do right now will change how she feels.

I'm the evil sister who just ruined her life.

THIRTEEN

AMELIA

"*I'm pregnant.*"

Ava drops her head, refusing to look at anyone, then focuses on the empty plate in front of her. The words hit like dynamite, every part of me exploding into tiny pieces, shattering beyond repair.

This doesn't make sense. How can she be pregnant? It must be a joke, a sick twisted joke she's playing on the family.

But her silence speaks a thousand words.

Beside her, Addy leans in with a thoughtful expression, her brows pulling down in concentration. *Did Addy know this and not tell me?* Like I'd been purposely kept in the dark.

A sharp pain runs across my chest as I begin to grow hot, trying to fight my emotions.

"Pregnant?" I choke, unable to swallow the lump inside my throat, stopping my ability to breathe at a normal pace. "But you aren't with anyone?"

I rack my brain to replay all our recent conversations. We often spoke daily, at least via text. But the last few months, we communicated less. Ava often used the excuse of being busy with her work, or she kept her responses closed. So, I narrowed it down to the stress of her breakup with Olivier, or maybe a quarter-life crisis.

Olivier—it must be his baby.

But then I recall her mentioning she hadn't slept with him for months, not before the night she found him in bed with another man.

The only thing which stands out is the Aussie guy. Maybe she lied and slept with him.

But the lie isn't what's bothering me. It's the fact she fell pregnant.

The one thing I am unable to do.

"Congratulations," Alexa blurts out, overly cheery. A slight growl escapes my throat at my younger sister's disregard for my feelings, like she's taking Ava's side. "I thought you looked different."

Still in shock, my gaze shifts toward my father. His silence is deafening. As someone who has fallen under his wrath, I know first-hand just how intimidating he can be. But, I've done my time, and Ava is an adult who has clearly made a poor decision and now must face the consequences.

"Who is the father?" Dad grits, barely able to open his mouth to speak.

"Um, this guy. It was one night, but I've known him forever, so it's not like he's a stranger and..."

One night.

That's all it took.

Meanwhile, I've been fucking my husband in certain positions while using ovulation kits and tracking my basal temperature. I've even watched my diet, consuming certain foods to better increase fertility. This has been going on for months, and for what? To see one blue line greet me every month with the ever-so-gut-wrenching 'negative' in the small window.

Mom clears her throat. "This is a surprise, but you have our support. How far along are you, honey?"

Beneath the table, Will places his hand on my thigh and rubs it softly. I can't look at him, the overwhelming feeling of being a failure consumes me.

"Four months..." Ava murmurs, only to fall into a pensive silence.

Slowly, her gaze lifts and fixates on me. I watch her, thinking back to four months ago. December? January? Ava's gaze doesn't falter. Her emerald eyes are distressed as her chin quivers. So, what, she fucked someone around the holidays?

Christmas? Or New Year's Eve?

Then, our video call flashes before my eyes like a bolt of lightning. My hand is resting on the table, yet it begins to shake unwillingly.

The phone call with Austin.

Austin.

Austin.

The name repeats like a broken record inside my head.

And the remorseful expression of my sister across the table confirms my suspicion. She's not looking at Mom or my father.

She's staring right at me.

My lips pull back, baring my teeth as my heart beats uncontrollably like the sound of a loud drum. The hand that rests on the table clenches into a tight fist as my entire core is consumed with animosity. Finally, I stand up, and the words I sputter are hurtful and the truth. She lied, hid everything from me, and to top it off, she slept with my ex-fiancé.

Throwing my napkin on the table in a fit of rage, I storm out to the yard for fresh air. Alone, with my anger intensifying as the minutes pass, I question how she could do such a thing? Okay, fine, Austin is a guy, though a dick for doing this to seek revenge on me. It's been two fucking years. Surely, he has moved on and has better things to do with his life.

As for Ava, I wish she wasn't *born*.

Behind me, the door makes a creaking sound. I don't turn around, sensing Will beside me. He doesn't say a word, assuming he is trying to process this. Over the years, he has never hidden the fact that my engagement to Austin tore him apart. And now what? Is Austin my brother-in-law?

"Did you know they had slept together?" Will questions in an arctic voice.

My head swivels slowly to glance at him. "You think this is my fault?"

"I never said that, Amelia."

"No, I didn't know they slept together, okay?" I declare with anger lacing my tone. "I knew they were together on New Year's Eve. She lied and told me she ran into him."

Will's eyes blaze as the muscles on his face tighten. I've seen this expression many times before. Jealousy is something he has long battled with, and once again—his stubborn self can't see the truth. "You never told me this."

"I didn't say anything because it wasn't worth the argument, Will. Every time someone raises Austin's name, you have a very strong opinion, and that somehow becomes all my fault."

"Do you blame me?" he shouts, then drops his gaze. "You were going to fucking marry him!"

"Oh, so all of this is my fault? Ava sleeping with Austin is my fault? Her falling pregnant is my fault? And me not falling pregnant is my fault?" I sputter, the resentment running through my veins like deadly poison.

"Stop twisting my words," Will demands with a hard edge to his voice. "I never said that."

"You didn't need to. Your body language said it all." My glance shifts toward the evening sky. It's pink and beautiful, but it might as well be pitch black. "I want to go home."

I turn around to head back to the house. Inside the kitchen, Alexa is handing Ashton a piece of chocolate. My lips press together as I cross my arms in annoyance.

"Alexa, he didn't finish his dinner," I almost bark.

"Sorry." She retreats with a shrug of the shoulders. "I didn't think it was a big deal."

I grab his hand, allowing him to have the chocolate and praying he doesn't burst into a sugar rush later. Addy and Alexa quickly glance at each other, but I turn away, not wanting to converse with either of them.

Ashton doesn't say a word or ask why we're leaving, too busy devouring the sugary treat. So when we get to the car, I work in silence while buckling him into the car seat.

Will is standing at the driver's side when I realize we left Ashton's backpack inside.

"His bag is still inside," I mumble, unable to look at him.

"I'll go get it."

Sitting inside the car in the passenger seat, my head falls back against the headrest while I close my eyes to stop the impending headache. The moment I take a deep breath, Ashton calls out, "Momma, why are we leaving Grandpa-pa's house?"

"Dinner is finished, baby. That's why you got chocolate."

"But I don't want to go." I hear the tremble in his voice, and just when my patience begins to wear thin because all I want to do is be alone, Will enters the car and distracts Ashton with a story about dinosaurs.

The drive back home is short, less than ten minutes, but it feels like an eternity. When we arrive home, I change Ashton into his favorite pajamas and clean the chocolate off his face. His night routine is followed by brushing his little teeth.

Tucking him in, I kiss his forehead when Will follows, ready to read him a story.

Usually, I stick around, but I desperately want to be alone.

I head to the bathroom, and the first thing I do is pull out the draw with the ovulation and pregnancy tests. Throwing them in the trash, I'm tired of being stuck in this vicious cycle of infertility.

Without a second thought, I take the trash outside then strip my clothes to take a hot shower, hoping to relax my tense muscles.

The shower proves to be problematic—my mind refusing to shut the fuck up.

Is Ava still fucking Austin? Are they going to get married?

Frustrated with my thoughts, I hop out of the shower, dry myself off, and place my old Yale tee and robe on.

When I step inside our bedroom, I stare at the bed. Sleep is the last thing on my mind. I head back to the kitchen, assuming Will is in his office avoiding me after our fight.

With a bottle of red wine, I take a glass and go outside to the pool area and sit on one of the cabana chairs. We have an amazing view of downtown LA, so I pour myself a tall glass to admire it, drinking the wine in one sitting and unapologetic for doing this alone.

After my second glass, my limbs begin to relax. But my moment of solitude ends when Will sits on the chair beside me. He reaches out for the bottle, and instead of using a glass, he drinks straight from it.

"Amelia, you can't keep doing this to yourself. This blame is uncalled for."

I stare up at the stars trying not to cry. Will can't possibly understand the guilt I carry for miscarrying the first time, to now being the problem. It's my body doing this, and I'm supposed to be young and fertile.

He will never feel the same guilt I do.

After all, he's just a *man*.

"I'm going to bed," I tell him, avoiding his gaze.

"Amelia, please look at me?"

Slowly, my eyes shift toward him, but I stare with a cold stance because I am not worthy inside.

"Those things I said earlier—"

I drop my eyes again to cut him off. "I'm tired."

And without another word, I walk away toward the house and to our bedroom.

Inside our bed, I sleep on my side, right at the very edge. Will never comes to our room, and for the first time in what feels like forever, I cry myself to sleep.

My eyes fall heavy like a lead weight.

Barely able to open them, I glance at the clock. It's just after eight, which is late for Ashton to wake up.

Panicked, I sit up, my head spinning, forcing me to shut my eyes for a second to stop the dizzy spell. Beside me, my phone buzzes with a text message from Will.

Will: *I took Ashton to Adriana's. They're going to the beach today. I'll be in the office if you need me.*

Releasing a breath, my shoulders relax, knowing Ashton is safe. My fingers go to type a message back, but instead, I hit delete.

On my screen are several notifications of text messages received overnight. I don't have the energy for this, lazily opening each message.

Mom: *Amelia, call me when you're ready to talk, please. I love you xx*

Addy: *I'm not on anyone's side. I'm Switzerland, always have been. Here if you need me.*

Alexa: *OMG, Millie! I couldn't say it last night but WTF?*

Andy: *Millie, I heard what happened last night. I know you're hurting, but Ava is hurting just as much. Anyways, I miss you, cuz.*

So now Andy knows? The anger returns, though this time—I'm too exhausted to react, unable to move my body at all. But, I need coffee.

Slowly, I get out of bed and contemplate a shower, but my entire being is screaming for caffeine.

With my robe on, I walk barefoot to the kitchen. My movements are slow, from the pod being placed in the machine to retrieving a mug with a loud yawn escaping me.

I watch the brown liquid spurt, the smell intoxicating and awakening my senses.

There is a soft knock on the door. I pray it isn't Ava, as I can't stand the thought of seeing her right now. Dad is standing outside, dressed in a white polo shirt and khaki shorts.

"Oh, hey, Dad," I say, surprised to see him. "Will went to the office if you're after him."

Dad closes the door behind him as I go to retrieve my mug, which is now full of coffee.

"Actually, I came to see you," he mentions softly.

My hands wrap around the mug, my lips purse to softly blow the steam so I can take a sip. After my first glorious taste, I take a deep breath.

"I don't want to talk about last night."

"You can't run away forever, Amelia."

"Is that what you think I'm doing? Running away?"

"You're upset, and I understand why."

I vigorously shake my head, then tuck in my upper lip. "It's all my fault, right? Ava is so perfect. She can do no wrong in your eyes. Never could."

Dad masters a poker face, a trait he always says helps him in the boardroom. But as I briefly glance at him, his furrowed brows and the lowered head is anything but a poker face. My comment hurt but doesn't make it less true.

"Amelia, none of this is easy for me. You think I like the fact that my daughter had a one-night stand and is pregnant?" he questions, with a struggle in his voice. "I feel like I failed as a parent. The same when your relationship with Will first came to light, but this baby isn't to feel less loved because the situation doesn't fit the perfect scenario in my head."

I forgot, there's a *baby*.

"I'm not asking you for anything, Amelia. Your sister has her own cross to bear. Both of you are my daughters, and both of you have done things you're not proud of. That doesn't make me love you any less."

"Dad," I croak, then wipe away the lonesome tear which escapes. "I can't do this right now."

"I know," he assures me, then places his hand on my cheek. "In ways, you are much like me, although your mother will argue that in a heartbeat."

"Tell Mom I will call her. I just need time."

He nods, then kisses my forehead before letting himself out.

My chest rises, sucking in a breath, to let it all out moments later. Then, with my coffee finished, I head upstairs to take a shower. As I turn on the faucet, my phone pings again.

Will: *I don't want to lose you.*

The words constrict my lungs, making it hard even to take the smallest of breaths. I never want to hurt Will, and that's exactly what I am doing—pushing away because of my insecurities.

I don't linger in the shower, quickly washing then changing into the first dress my hands reach out for. It's a white backless dress with spaghetti straps and a patchwork design. My hair is wet, but I leave it out to wait for the warm air to dry it naturally.

Outside, the sound of an engine catches my attention.

With my sandals on, I walk downstairs to an empty foyer. Then, slowly, my feet move toward Will's office. I choose not to knock but push the door open slowly.

Will is sitting behind his desk, dressed in a pale blue

business shirt and dark pants. He mentioned yesterday afternoon he had an important video conference early today, which explains why he is dressed in business attire on a Saturday morning.

I don't say a word, moving closer to him. My hands reach out without a second thought, grazing his cheek with my palm. He releases a sigh, resting his face in my hand.

"You will never lose me," I tell him faintly. "Impossible."

"Amelia, I meant what I said last night. You need to stop blaming yourself." His voice is low but etched in pain. "Our time will come when it comes."

I nod. "I know, but this just hurts."

Will motions for me to sit on his lap. With his arms around me, I bury myself in the crook of his neck and inhale his scent.

"Don't think for one second I don't feel what you feel. As for Ava, I don't understand what she was thinking."

"Me neither." I sigh dejectedly. "But for now, I don't want to know. I just don't want us to fall apart over something she has done."

Will grazes my bottom lip with his thumb. My chest begins to hitch, the simple touch evoking so many emotions from me.

He shifts my hips, so I'm straddling him. My hands wrap around his neck as I kiss him deeply. A soft moan escapes me when I taste him on my lips.

"I missed sleeping next to you last night," he murmurs. "The spare room is torture."

I laugh softly. "I bet you that's not all you missed."

Will's eyes tease me as he smirks while sliding his hands beneath my dress, then behind me to cup my ass.

"You know me too well, Mrs. Romano."

And with his mouth on mine, the passion between us ignites. Just two people—husband and wife—finding their way back to each other.

But despite his feverish kisses consuming my thoughts, a part of me knows this isn't over.

For the rest of our lives, Austin will be a part of our family.

Nothing will change that.

And I can't help but worry that the storm is far from passing.

Not when the hurricane looms on the horizon, threatening to destroy everything we've fought so hard to build together.

FOURTEEN

AVA

After a disastrous night at my parents' house, I want nothing more than to flee back to Manhattan.

The following day, I wake up with what feels like a cold of some sort. My body aches, and my legs and arms are painfully sore. A lingering headache onset a wave of nausea, forcing me to rush to the bathroom repeatedly.

Mom begins to worry, rushing to my aid with medication safe to take during pregnancy and plain toast for me to try to eat. I manage to take a few bites, but it proves to be exhausting, and my eyelids barely stay open.

When I awake again, Mom is still on the bed beside me. When my eyes fall upon her, I hear another sound and slowly turn to see Dad on the other side. He moves closer to me, then places his palm on my forehead as he examines me with a worried expression.

It isn't unusual for Dad to worry about our health, and given he studied medicine though never followed it through, he has enough knowledge to diagnose certain ailments.

"How are you feeling?" he asks, sitting beside me and next to Mom.

"Tired," I yawn, then my stomach grumbles. "Hungry."

Mom rubs my hand with a hopeful gaze. "How about some soup?"

I nod with a smile. "Sounds good, Mom."

There's a struggle to sit up, but I manage to do so as Mom leaves the room to fetch the soup. Then, with my father beside me, I glance at him, looking for answers.

"What's wrong with me? I'm not losing the baby, am I?"

"Ava, no," he reassures me. "You're under a lot of stress and very run down. It makes you more susceptible to the common cold."

"Dealing with this privately has been difficult. Having to admit firstly to myself that this was happening, to having to tell Austin. Then coming here to tell you and Mom, and of course..." I trail off, unable to say her name.

Dad tips his head back, staring at the ceiling. I know this isn't easy for him, and I hate myself for putting him through this. "Dad, I'm s—"

"No, Ava. Don't apologize. You have nothing to be sorry about. There is a baby inside of you, a human being who will grace us with his or her presence in a few short months. I know the circumstances are far from ideal, but I cannot stress enough that I need you to take care of yourself and this baby. You understand me?"

I answer with a slight nod.

Mom returns with soup, water, and some crackers. We talk with Dad for a short while in which I tell them my desire to go back home tomorrow, mainly because I need to work. They keep their opinions at bay, but I can see the worry over my well-being in their expressions.

"Ava, have you considered moving back to LA?" Dad

asks, then continues, "It would make sense to have us close to you to help with the baby."

"Honestly, Dad? It crossed my mind for a fleeting moment. But my life is in Manhattan, and so is Austin."

Mom is unusually quiet, not putting her two cents in. When it comes to babies, she has baby fever. I'm surprised she isn't agreeing with Dad and making it heard.

"Well, if you must fly out tomorrow, I insist you take the private jet."

I smile, relaxing my shoulders. "If you insist, Father."

My parents leave me to get some rest, noting I look and sound better. I still don't want to get out of bed, so I grab my phone and text Austin.

Me: *It went as expected with my parents. As for Millie, let's say she is not talking to me.*

Austin: *Talk about timing. I just finished my shift. That bad?*

Me: *That bad. I'm pretty sure somewhere during her raging fit, she called me a whore.*

Austin: *You're not a whore, Ava.*

Me: *Right? Because a whore sleeps around, and the last time I checked, I've been revirginized.*

Austin: *I heard that's called cobwebs.*

Me: *Have you been hanging out with Eric?*

Austin: *Oh, yeah, maybe that's where I heard it from. It's been years since I saw him last, but some things stick.*

Me: *That's Eric. Anyways, I'm flying back tomorrow.*

Austin: *Take it easy and keep our baby safe.*

My head falls back against the pillow with Austin's words echoing around me. How can something so simple, and possibly innocent, evoke so much emotion from me. It's easy to blame the pregnancy hormones because everything I do or think is the opposite of what I usually feel in certain situations.

As I continue to sit here, contemplating a text to acknowledge what he said, it becomes clear that my desire to go back home is not just about work.

And then, Millie's voice plays on repeat.

I'm second best, picking up her so-called scraps, as she so bluntly implied.

What hurts the most is she couldn't be further from the truth. I was there for her entire relationship with Austin, and what they had was different. Of course, it's nothing like what she has with Will, but I guess none of it matters if she can't forgive me.

And what Austin and I have is very different.

We are going to have a bond for the rest of our life.

Inside my office, Eric is sitting across from me. It's the first time we've been able to catch up since Eric was held up in Chicago for meetings the last week.

Being back in Manhattan is a relief, a part of me feeling somewhat normal again. The cold I'd caught back in LA was a twenty-four hour thing, and by the next day, I was perfectly fine to travel back home.

"And then what happened?"

"She flat out called me a whore, or close to it."

Eric cringes, throwing his hand to his neck. "If I could pitch your family to the *E* network, I'd be a millionaire."

"You are a millionaire, Eric," I point out, with a faint eye roll. "Didn't your grandmother leave her estate to you?"

"Perhaps." Eric shrugs, then focuses his attention back onto me. "My point is, this drama is next-level crazy. I literally have no words."

"Good, because I'm done talking about it."

"I'm not done," Eric counters.

"What else is there to say?" I ask with exasperation. "It's been a week. She has nothing to say to me. In fact, she even blocked me on social media."

Eric's eyes widen in visible shock. "A block on social media is a powerful statement."

"Yeah, the statement being she hates me."

"She doesn't hate you, darling Ava. No one can hate you."

I let out a long-winded sigh, so over worrying about this. I can apologize a thousand times, but nothing will change the outcome. Unless, of course, I attempt through Will.

"Can we get back to work? I only have four months before I'm supposed to slow down before the baby comes. That's not a long time, not when we have to finalize the new lines, and look at a space to buy to manufacture. And who will feature in photos for our social media content when I'm too big?"

Eric leans over and places his hand on mine. "Breathe, Ava, just breathe. That's why I'm here."

"You're my publicist," I remind him with a soft smile. "Your job is to make me look good, not source real estate for me."

"I know, but I'm a man of many talents. Once, I picked up an orange with my butt cheeks and held it for a solid minute."

I shake my head, then burst out in laughter. "I want to ask, but at the same time, I think some things are best left as a mystery."

My phone pings with a text from Dad.

Dad: *Your mother and I will be in Manhattan in two weeks. Please organize a dinner with Austin in attendance.*

"Fuck," I voice loudly, then show Eric the text.

Eric covers his face then lets out a groan. "It's just one shitshow after another."

"It'll be fine," I tell myself, then exhale. "Austin has done this before with my parents."

Then, the realization of Austin's ties with my family again reminds me that I am second best. Millie is right. I'm walking in her shadows. Suddenly, a burning sensation inside my chest makes me question my entire life.

And this only leads to one thing—anger.

"Yes, he has. He's even asked Lex for his daughter's hand in marriage," Eric carelessly reminds me.

The muscles on my face tighten as I adopt a sullen look.

"Right? Austin has done this all before. Lucky him," I sneer.

My anger shifts toward Austin now, the blame game very real in my head.

"C'mon, Ava." Eric laughs softly. "Even you must admit this situation looks, how shall I say it, contrived."

My chest thrusts out, but I try to control my breathing and not tear Eric apart as the anger festers within me.

"Have you thought about how we should tell people? I can't hide this anymore, Eric."

"The issue is not your bump. It's who stuck their weenie in you and made that bump happen."

I throw my hands in the air. "I can't win!"

"Ava, sweetheart, calm down."

"No, Eric. I am the one who's labeled a whore. I'm the one who is supposedly after my sister's scraps. I'm the one who will always be second best!"

"Nobody is saying that," he assures me.

"But everyone is thinking it?" I snap, my eyes wide while waiting for Eric to argue my point. When he chooses to remain quiet, I laugh faintly. "That's right. Ava is the evil sister."

"What the hell is happening here? I've heard of hormones, but Jesus Christ, Ava. You're giving me heart palpitations."

I stand up, then grab my purse, unable to look Eric in the face.

"I'm going home," I inform him with a low voice. "I honestly don't care how you announce it. Either way, I'm to blame."

With my head fallen, I leave my office with the intent of going home, but during my walk, the anger only intensifies, and there is only one person with a target straight in the middle of their chest.

"Ava?" Austin calls upon opening the door to my loud knock. "What are you doing here?"

He is dressed in jeans and a nice shirt, with hair styled in casual disarray. The scent of his aftershave lingers, and he seems to be freshly showered like he is going out on a date.

"Are you going out on a date?" I blurt out.

Austin tilts his head. "No, I am going out with some friends."

"Girlfriends?"

"Yes, there are women in my group of friends."

My lips press flat, the jealousy consuming my rational thoughts. "Will Lane be there?"

Austin's head flinches back slightly. "What the hell is going on?"

"You're not answering me."

"Because you're not explaining why you've shown up, unannounced, and are questioning me on my whereabouts or who I will hang out with?"

My pulse quickens as my muscles begin to quiver. Austin standing there, ready to go out with God knows who, reiterates how his life has not changed at all. I'm the one who has paid the price for our indiscretion and will continue to do so for the rest of my life.

His family was excited to learn of the baby, according to him. Mine is at war with me, at least—Millie is. Austin can continue his career, his dating, and all the things he does without having to carry a baby.

And he doesn't have to give birth in a few short months.

"You know what? I can't even speak to you."

As I turn away, Austin grabs my arm to stop me. "What the hell is wrong with you?"

Lowering my eyes, I gaze at the concrete floor. "You've got it easy. You're not the villain. It's me. I'm the one who must suffer for my mistakes."

Austin lets out a sigh, and just as he's about to open his mouth, my phone beeps with a text message. I pull it out of my pocket to glance at it.

Eric: *Too late,* TMZ *just posted this article. Sorry honey. Call me when you're ready to talk.*

I click on the link, and there is the headline—Influencer and Daughter of Lex Edwards Pregnant with an Unknown Man.

The article is three paragraphs about me being pregnant, my father's reaction, and how my family has shunned me. According to them, Lex Edwards has completely cut me off. Then, in paragraph two, it says, *Ava is known to frequent the party scene, so we're not surprised this has happened given her long list of lovers.*

Along with the article are several photos of me. The angles they photographed me make me look pregnant, or I've purposely concealed my stomach with a bag, making it look more pronounced.

My body collapses in on itself as my chest begins to hitch. Then, without a single word, I hand Austin the phone for him to read. Moments later, he releases a sigh, only for my phone to ping again.

"There's a message on your screen from Millie," he warns me softly.

I swallow the lump inside my throat. "What does it say?"

Austin's hesitation is enough for me to figure out it isn't pleasant, nor an 'I'm sorry'.

"Ava, look—"

"Just tell me!"

He doesn't tell me. Instead, he hands the phone back.

Millie: *It's only a matter of time until* TMZ *finds out who the father is, and you've destroyed us all. Thanks again, sis.*

My arms fall to my sides, causing the phone to almost slip out of my hand. The pain inside my chest and throat makes it difficult even to think or move. I'm humiliated, and soon everyone will know the truth. No matter what I say or do, they'll judge me on my actions, and I will forever be labeled a *whore*.

"Ava, come in, please."

I shake my head. "I want to be alone."

"Okay, but I'm always here if you need me. You know that, right?"

I knew that. Just like I know Austin will never understand what it's like to walk a mile in my shoes.

Without another word, I walk away.

It's easier than trying to explain to him why my life has fallen apart.

How even with a life jacket of him wanting to support me and be part of this child's life...

I am forever drowning.

FIFTEEN

AVA

The moment my pregnancy leaks, the media outlets hound me relentlessly.

I'm forced to stay home for two weeks as Eric deals with the media storm. Of course, the biggest question on everyone's mind is the father, and the lengths reporters go to is downright disgusting.

It's expected of Olivier to be presumed the father. But that isn't enough for them, and speculations include a list of men I've never even met.

Once again, I'm labeled the party girl who enjoys her men. They couldn't be further from the truth.

My parents worry over my well-being, insisting I fly home and stay with them until things settle. Both of them, more notably my father, have had their share of media scrutiny. I recall being in middle school when curiosity got the better of me, and I googled our family. At the time, Millie wanted no part of my nosy findings, preferring to keep the perfect image of our family in her head exactly that —perfect.

Not me, though. I read article after article, fascinated

with the media's depiction of my parents' marriage. So it didn't surprise me that Dad was always dragged into some cheating scandal. Though from memory, there was one story about Mom having an affair with our pool boy. That was funny because we didn't have a pool boy. Our gardener, John, was like sixty at the time and happily married. He occasionally cleaned the pool, but Dad had one of those expensive cleaning systems which cleaned it automatically.

Yet I've spent enough time in the spotlight over the years to know this will blow over, eventually. The media will get bored of me, and they are looking for any story to make a dime at the end of the day.

I choose to stay in Manhattan since this is my mess to clean up, and I can't run to my parents every time something goes wrong. However, I did ask them to postpone dinner with myself and Austin for a few more weeks, just until the air settles and the paparazzi lose interest in me.

In my own forced isolation, I manage to keep busy, spending my days working. It's incredible how much you can get done when you're not distracted by lunches and social outings, or even Eric inside your office complaining his back is sore from yoga because he was too busy staring at the yoga instructor's ass and bent the wrong way.

Beyond working, I spend a lot of time online shopping, figuring out what I need for the baby. I text Mom often, asking for advice. Between her and Aunt Adriana, they give me a list that I need to make sure is ticked off before the baby comes.

As for Austin, he is busy with work as usual. After my argument with him, things are dicey between us. He didn't press further, and when TMZ revealed I am pregnant, I suggested he stay away from me so that he doesn't get dragged into this right now.

But this circus show can only go so far.

When I woke up this morning, I decided to take matters into my own hands and take a selfie. I'm sitting on my sofa, opting not to glam up with my hair in a messy bun. The outfit I'm wearing is a white boho dress with spaghetti straps, cute yet simplistic. With my legs crossed, I cradle my bump, gazing lovingly at my stomach while my phone clicks, taking snaps.

Without telling anyone, including Eric, I post it on my social media channels with the caption 'Baby.'

I turn my phone off, willing the impending calls to go to voicemail, then take my tea and a book out onto my terrace. I miss coffee so much, and tea can never compare to the glorious taste of caffeine. Out of everything, more than alcohol, coffee has been the hardest thing to give up.

Oh, and sex.

Lately, I've fallen into this habit lately of reading romance, which doesn't help me since I have no partner to ravage. The steamier the book, the more sexually charged I become. It's so frustrating, like an itch I can't scratch. I'm sure this is why you should be married when pregnant. It has gotten to the point that I'm too scared to take matters into my own hands or use my trusty toys, worried I'll hurt the baby. It's all weird but doesn't stop the damn ache below, which refuses to subside.

As I get comfortable on the lounge chair, a slight sensation taps on my stomach. I place my hands on my belly for the flutter to happen again though it is bizarre as I can't feel it with my hands. I thought I felt something a few days ago but narrowed it down to gas.

Quickly retrieving my phone, I turn it on, ignoring the constant pinging from messages, including a shouty capitals text from Eric saying CALL ME NOW!, to dial Austin's number.

"Hey," is all he says.

"How do you know when the baby moves?"

"The kicks? I've heard patients tell me it's like a flutter. Then, as you progress, they become real kicks."

"I think the baby moved."

"It did?"

"I think so. I don't know. It should be moving by now, right?"

"You're what?" he asks, then stalls, "Twenty-four weeks? So, yes."

"It's surreal," I breathe, my eyes glancing up at the perfectly blue sky. "It's kicking and doing its little thing in there."

"Ava?"

"Yeah?"

"I just saw your post. For what it's worth, you look beautiful. I don't want you to feel you have to hide that I'm the father."

"I just want to protect you, for now. Once the media know, they will follow you, and they can be brutal. I just want us to enjoy this time in the pregnancy without all this unnecessary stress."

Silence falls between us when it dawns on me that my honesty was perhaps too raw. I'd insinuated there is an 'us.' *Blame the romance novels.*

"So, anyway, are you up for dinner with my parents? Dad asked a few weeks ago, but with everything going on, I kept pushing it back."

"It's fine, Ava. I can have dinner with Lex and Charlie."

Breathing a sigh of relief, I shuffle uncomfortably. "I'm

sorry about my outburst the last time I saw you. You can date whoever you want. I was just having a bad day."

"Happens to the best of us," he assures me, though his tone is slightly off. "Listen, I have to go, about to clock in. Send me when and where you need me. I'll be there with bells on."

"Actual bells?" I tease.

"Just to annoy you, yes." He chuckles heartily. "Bye, Ava."

My parents were unable to fly over for a few weeks, but I didn't mind, given I had been busy with work.

"Where are the bells?" I ask Austin as he pulls my chair out for me to take a seat. "I'm quite disappointed."

"They don't make designer ones, and I know you judge when someone isn't wearing designer clothes."

Austin looks sexy in his dark blue suit with a white shirt beneath it. He opted not to wear a tie, keeping it less formal. The top of his chest is slightly exposed, and sitting beside him—I can't help but squirm.

Calm down. It's just a chest.

"I can't recall the last time I saw you wear a suit."

"Let me see." He raises his finger to his lips while thinking, and stupid me focuses on his lips. "The unfortunate night at the Hamptons?"

I bow my head. "Oh, sorry. Forgot."

Austin laughs softly. "It's okay, Ava. Life has moved on. I don't have any ill feelings toward either of them."

"But how?" I question abruptly. "I'm still pissed with the girl who tried to steal my prom date."

"Because... " he mouths, then leans in closer to me. "I'm

sitting next to a beautiful woman who is pregnant with my baby."

My parents walking through the entrance of the restaurant is the distraction my goddamn vagina needs—the so-called splash of cold water. Although, it's more of an ice bucket, hard enough to dwindle the heat level to below zero.

Austin and I both stand up to greet them. As always, they're both looking as stylish as ever. Dad is dressed in a charcoal suit with a black-collared shirt beneath it sans the tie. It's slightly unbuttoned, just like Austin's, and it's obvious to see the women in the restaurant have turned to look at him.

What's new?

Mom is holding his hand, wearing a lantern green tunic dress with a short black blazer to compliment the outfit. Naturally, my eyes instantly gravitate to her Manolo Blahniks—they're new from the latest line, if I'm not mistaken.

Austin politely extends his hand to Dad in which he shakes. Mom, on the other hand, hugs him. There doesn't appear to be any animosity, allowing me to breathe a sigh of relief, for now.

Mom places her hands on my stomach with a warm smile. "Ava, honey. Look at you. You've really popped."

"Yeah, I know. Though I've had cravings for creamy pasta, so the carbs could also be the reason."

"Lex... " Mom calls softly, "... look at her. You wouldn't even know she was pregnant from the back. It's all at the front like a round basketball."

Dad extends his arms as I fall into his embrace. Then, as we pull away, he gazes at me lovingly. "You're glowing, Ava. Just like your mother when she was pregnant with all four of you."

Mom winces. "Except Alexa. That pregnancy was a nine-month glow of morning sickness."

We all take a seat when a waiter appears at our table to take our order. Dad takes it upon himself to order wine for him, Mom, and Austin while I'm forced to nurse a glass of water. This restaurant is one of Dad's favorites, and from memory, he's a co-owner or something like that.

"Dad, do you own this place?"

"It is part of a chain in which I'm a stakeholder," he confirms, then raises his chin. "I expect only the best service tonight."

We all briefly turn quiet, and I wonder at what point Dad's interrogation begins.

"So, Austin... " Dad starts with, then takes a sip of wine before continuing, "... Ava tells me you're almost a second-year resident?"

"Yes, in a few weeks, actually. It's flown by really quickly."

"And you're in the ER?" Mom intercepts with a fond smile. "That must be challenging."

"It is, Charlie. The days just become a big blur. Even today, we had a multi-car pile-up on the I-78. Thankfully, no fatalities."

"And have you considered transferring to Cedars-Sinai if the two of you move back to LA?" Dad questions, his expression serious.

"Um, Dad, there's no we." I turn to look at Mom for a lifejacket. She reassures me with her eyes to calm down. "Austin and I aren't together."

"I'm aware of that, Ava. But don't you think moving closer to us will be beneficial? Having a child is not easy."

"Actually, Lex," Austin intervenes. "I have looked into it."

Turning to face Austin, my mouth almost falls open. "Since when? I never mentioned moving back."

"I just want to explore all options because your father is right. Having a child isn't easy, and having family around will help. My parents moved to Thousand Oaks, but it's not too far from Hidden Hills.

"We have Eric," I remind everyone at the same time the food is served.

Mom purses her lips with her fork in hand. "Eric once threw up in your room when he had to change your diaper. You had just started solids, and it wasn't pleasant.

At this stage, I wasn't sure whether to be mortified or worried. It's not like I'm immune to all this baby stuff either. Aside from my younger sisters, I've never taken care of a baby, let alone an actual newborn.

"Maybe," I tell my parents, then glance at Austin. "Austin and I can have a serious conversation about this once the baby is born, but for now, I'm happy to stay where I am. Manhattan is where my life is, and also Austin's life."

Thankfully, the subject is dropped.

Most of the dinner is Dad asking Austin about work. It doesn't surprise me since Dad still has a keen interest in medicine even though his career led him elsewhere. Beside him, Mom watches with a relaxed gaze. It's almost as if she enjoys watching Dad immersed in these discussions. I recall many years ago, she mentioned to me that she sometimes wished Dad continued his medical career. Though in the same breath, she said that passions can shift when life leads us elsewhere.

Our conversations alter between Austin and me. Dad reminds me once again to get on top of my manufacturing. He even offers his time, willing to do most of the leg work for me. How can I say no? I can barely fit in going to the bathroom these days with my work piling up as we lead closer to the end of this pregnancy.

"Austin, I was thinking of contacting your mother, Kristen, to organize a lunch," Mom says while nursing her wine in the tall glass it's served in. "It's been years, but I would love to catch up with her."

"I'm sure Mom would love that." He grins, then turns to me as I lower my head. "She was thinking of flying over to meet Ava properly finally."

I lift my gaze, then blink slowly. "Your Mom?"

"Relax, Ava. You've met her several times."

"Under different circumstances."

"How do your parents feel about the impending arrival?" Mom asks, keeping her smile fixed. "Ava must have told you that we were shocked, but nevertheless, any child is a blessing."

Austin finishes his wine, then wipes his lips with the napkin. "Actually, they were excited. They've wanted a grandchild for a while."

"I'm glad to hear that, Austin," Dad concludes, then nods. "Ava doesn't need any more stress while pregnant."

"Yeah, well, too bad Millie can't see that," I blurt out.

Everyone at the table falls quiet as the elephant stands beside us, twirling in her pink tutu, yelling, 'look at me!.'

Austin is the first to speak. "Give her time, Ava. You know what Millie is like."

My parents choose not to comment. I assume, by the look on their faces, something has happened back in LA with Millie. If I know my sister well, she has mouthed off about what a terrible sister I am and probably wishes I was never born.

We continue to enjoy our dinner, though we leave little room for dessert. When we finish our meals, my parents call it a night. They plan to stay in the city for another day as Mom has a meeting with Aunt Nikki, and Dad has a day trip to D.C.

All four of us say goodbye, but Mom pulls me aside.

"Ava, a little advice?"

"Sure, Mom."

"Remember when I said let the chips fall where they may?"

I nod, unsure where she's leading with this.

"Austin is a good man. Always has been. Don't let his past with our family stop you from building a future with your new family."

And with those parting words, she kisses my cheek then steps aside for Dad to do the same. Instead, he uses the opportunity to remind me of the factory space we need to look at. I assure him that I'll start scheduling some time over the next week.

"So that wasn't too bad?" I breathe a sigh of relief while Austin grabs my purse for me. "I'm just going to use the restroom."

"No worries, I'll wait by the front entrance."

I head toward the restroom and quickly relieve myself. This pregnancy is doing a number on my bladder. Between all the water I'm consuming and the baby pressing down, I might as well set up my office next to the toilet.

After I wash my hands and exit, I walk past the bar where my eyes fall upon those which look familiar.

"Lochie?"

"Well, if it isn't the ever-elusive Ava Edwards," he responds with a smirk.

Lochie Fletcher, the sexy Aussie who caught my eye months ago, looks just as handsome tonight. He's dressed all in black, standing in front of a motorcycle helmet perched on the bar's countertop.

"I'm sorry for having to cancel dinner months ago," I mention, keeping my tone neutral to avoid any conflict.

Lochie's gaze falls upon my stomach. "I can see you've been busy."

I place my hands on my belly, then tilt my head with a smile. "You could say that. But, look, it's not what you think. I found out after I met you, and the situation wasn't ideal."

"Some things aren't meant to be," he murmurs while staring intensely into my eyes.

Swallowing the lump inside my throat, I will my nerves to calm down. The moment a hand settles into my own, my heart slows until I realize the hand belongs to Austin.

"Are you ready to go?" Austin asks, though his tone comes off more like a demand.

Nodding, I then turn back to Lochie. "It was nice seeing you again, Lochie. All the best with the bar."

"You too, Ava. All the best with the baby."

As I leave the restaurant with Austin still holding my hand, he remains quiet as we wait on the sidewalk for a cab. When one pulls over, he ushers us in before giving my address to the driver.

"I'm taking you home."

"Uh, okay, sure."

The cab ride is quiet, and I distract myself with my phone until we exit and take the elevator up to my apartment.

"Who was that guy?"

"Which guy? The one at the bar?"

Austin doesn't say anything, keeping his gaze fixed on me.

"Lochie is just someone I know."

"Someone you know, or someone you've been with?" Austin questions with a hard stare.

"I haven't been with Lochie," I tell him honestly. "We met a few months ago before I found out I was pregnant."

"Is that it?"

My head flinches back, confused as to where this sudden outburst has come from. Maybe I'm not the only one with pregnancy hormones here.

"We exchanged numbers and were going to have dinner, but then this happened." I point to my stomach.

"So what if I wasn't there tonight?"

"Wouldn't change anything. I'm pregnant with your baby, and I'm not exactly looking to date anyone."

I open the door to my apartment and motion for Austin to follow. My feet ache from the heels I wore, making each step unbearable.

Austin removes his jacket, then takes a seat on the sofa beside me. With his hands shrouding his face, I assume tonight has caused him more stress which explains this bizarre interrogation of my personal life.

"Tonight was a lot. I'm sorry, you know what my dad is like."

"It was fine. I've gone through worse with Lex."

Now, it's my turn to fall into a funk. But as I watch Austin beside me, leaning back with his shirt slightly unbutton and sleeves now rolled up. I try to ignore the fluttering sensation in my chest and beg my heart to stop racing. Then, I shuffle uncomfortably beside him, ignoring my raging hormones that turn my mind into a pornographic parade.

"Do you still think about Millie?"

Austin shifts his glance. "Ava, c'mon, really?"

"You guys were together for a long time, and she was your first."

"That she was. There have also been many women after her."

"But still."

"Still what?"

"Never mind."

The past will always be the baggage we carry wherever we go. But as I sit here next to a man who will be the father to my child, I can't help but wonder just how we'll get through this because right now, my thoughts are impure.

Austin looks deliciously sexy.

And that's exactly how I landed myself in this mess, to begin with.

SIXTEEN

AUSTIN

Ava removes her heels while recoiling in pain.

She managed to shift the energy between us after my interrogation over the guy at the bar. The moment I saw the way his eyes feasted upon her, I knew they had been more than just friends.

I'm not fucking stupid. I know Ava has a past. I just didn't expect it to hit me the way it did when I saw this jerk with her. The burning sensation inside my chest made it difficult to think straight, especially when his gaze lingered too long.

When Ava confirmed they weren't anything, it only mildly calmed my jealousy. The truth is—there will be other men.

Something I'd been grappling with of late. Ava is carrying *my* baby, and selfishly—no one else can touch her.

Not if I have any say in it.

These vicious thoughts came and went, which is why I've distanced myself of late and kept myself busy with work.

Until tonight, seeing her for the first time in weeks since

the news broke to the public of her pregnancy and after her outburst at my apartment over my social life.

Her outburst caught me off guard, but Ava apologized and admitted she was stressed out, taking out her frustration on me. I didn't blame her, so I let it go.

But tonight, my eyes fell upon her at the restaurant, which only solidified my thoughts. I did my best to keep things platonic, especially in front of Lex and Charlie.

We both sit on her sofa while Ava raises Millie again and the past, making it clear we both have our struggles. There is no easy answer to any of this. The situation is far from ideal, no matter how you spin it.

"I can't do this walking thing anymore." Ava switches the topic, which I'm grateful for. The last thing I want to discuss is Millie again.

I let out a soft chuckle. "How about you don't wear heels. Besides, you're starting to grow bigger, so it's not as safe to do so."

"The joys of having a baby with a doctor." She cringes as she rubs her feet. "Next, you'll tell me I can't eat cheese."

"Avoid soft-vein blue cheeses," I lecture her, then motion for her to shuffle. "Give me your feet."

With a joyous smile on her face, she places them on my lap while I massage them, kneading where she claims it aches.

"Oh, God," she half-moans, closing her eyes. "That feels so good."

"A trade-off. I'll massage, you give birth. Deal?"

Ava opens her eyes with a grin lighting up her face, then smacks my chest with a cushion. "That's not fair. It's not like I have a choice. Have you ever seen a woman give birth?"

I nod. "Several times."

"And?"

"And what?"

"How bad was it?"

"It's beautiful," I tell her, rubbing her ankle. "It's almost like the moment a baby is in a mother's arms, all the pain goes away, and nothing else in the world matters."

Ava throws her head back, letting out a huff. "You make it sound so easy. This pregnancy is killing me."

I glance at her as my pulse picks up. "You never mentioned experiencing pains? Have you had an OBGYN look at you?"

Ava purses her lips, glancing at the wall in a notably avoidable stare. "Um, no, it's something else."

"What is it?"

"I'd rather not say."

"C'mon, Ava. It's me, plus I'm trained in medicine, so if there's anything I can do..."

"I'm not comfortable discussing this with you."

Now, she has me worried, and my brain starts to conjure up all these scenarios. I'm not a specialist in prenatal care, but I know enough to diagnose if something is incorrect.

"Don't give me that worried look," she's quick to accuse me, playing with the ends of her dark brown hair. "It's not like that."

"If it's not a big deal, then just tell me?"

Ava releases a groan, then crosses her arms. "Fine, you asked. I'm horny all the fucking time."

I bite my lip, wishing I didn't push so hard. At the same time, my dick stirs in my pants. Fuck, don't go there. For the love of God, don't go there.

My throat makes an unflattering raspy sound. "Okay, so I didn't see that coming."

"Yes, well, there it is. The truth. Now, if we can go back to talking about anything else, I'd greatly appreciate it."

Yes, we need to talk about something else, pronto...

"So, your dad mentioning LA?"

"I'm sorry, that caught me off guard."

"You honestly haven't thought about it?" I question, grateful my dick has calmed down enough so I can think straight again.

"Our lives are here. It's a big decision."

"It is, but it's not just about us anymore," I remind her.

"I guess, maybe in a way, it would be easier with my family. But I don't want it to disrupt your life. You already gave up, Lane."

Ava has this weird obsession with Lane. Her name comes up regularly, even though I've ended things. I don't understand why Ava can't understand that and let it go, especially since I have.

"Breaking up with Lane was the right thing to do," I assure her, not regretting my actions though, at work, it is awkward whenever I am in the same room as Lane now. "It's not giving up something when it was never right, to begin with."

Ava curls her lip. Then her shoulders push back with a stare challenging me.

"But how do you know?" Ava persists with her questions. "How do you know she's not the love of your life?"

"Because if she were, I wouldn't have done it so easily."

"But you'll date again someday, right?"

"It's not something I think about, Ava."

"You're a man." She points out with a slight eye roll. "A man who has needs."

Deliberately raising my brows, I cock my head with a smirk. "Believe it or not, I'm rather proficient in taking care of that situation. I have been since I was fifteen, maybe?"

Ava shakes her head with a grin, then throws her hands on her face. "You should go before I maul you."

My hand continues to rub her leg, inching closer to the edge of her dress. Her skin is soft with an intoxicating vanilla scent, luring me in like an animal in the wild. I bite my lip, begging myself not to succumb, but then I think, who fucking cares? Who has to know besides us?

"Ava, I'm here if you need me. And I mean in any way you need me."

"Austin," she breathes, then follows with a hard swallow. "Don't play with me right now."

"Well, it's not like I'd allow anyone else to touch you while you're pregnant with my baby."

Her eyes turn wild with fire, the emerald penetrating with its intensity, but then she lowers her gaze. "I mean it, Austin. I'm this close to not caring about anything because you look damn good, and I don't know if it's the warm air or the full moon, or because you smell so good..."

I lean over and continue running my hand up her thigh beneath her dress. Ava has always been hot, and yes, it has been hard to ignore on many occasions. But tonight, in the dusty rose silk dress she wears—she looks irresistible.

Her tits have grown so much, making it impossible to look away. Yet my conscience is torn because she is pregnant. I've never looked at a pregnant woman and thought, 'oh, she's sexy, and I'd like to fuck her'.

It's completely forbidden territory.

But Ava has blurred the line, allowing my thoughts of exactly what I'd like to do to her, run rampant. My memories of the night we were together are hazy, but I do remember how intense it was because I couldn't get enough in the moment.

Slowly, she tilts her head back and exposes the veins on her neck. I close my eyes for a brief moment, struggling with my thoughts. But upon opening them, her body is beside me like a temple waiting to be worshipped.

Angling my body across and placing my lips against her skin, I taste the heat spread all over her, then gently inch my hands between her thighs. She lets out a gasp, then grabs my face with her hands and brings my lips to hers.

Ava's passion is raw and charged, not allowing me a moment to breathe. Our kisses are rushed, only fueling this sexual tension between us.

Then, before I can say anything, she shuffles to climb on top to straddle me.

Fuck, now there's no chance I can resist.

"You don't have to do this," she repeats, barely above a whisper.

"Ava," I breathe, watching her lips part. "I haven't had sex with anyone since you told me you were pregnant."

Her mouth crashes onto mine, feverish and demanding with every twist and turn. Then, slowly, she pulls away but etches her lips close to my ear. "If I'm honest, that makes me happy. The thought of another woman touching you drives me crazy."

I pull her back so I can stare into her eyes. But as our gazes fall under a spell, something odd passes between us. This connection runs deeper than two people bringing a baby into this world after a one-night stand.

My hand moves around to the back of her neck, drawing her closer while she pulls the straps of her dress down, exposing her chest. A white lace bra is covering her engorged breasts, although the lace is transparent enough for me to catch a glimpse of her nipples.

Beneath her, my cock is so damn hard to the point it aches. My entire body is drowning in different sensations, all heightened by the beautiful woman on top of me.

Without even asking, I raise my hands to caress her tits, watching her reaction with a delicious stare. My chest is pounding. The desperation to take her is at its peak. The wait is killing me. My patience is growing thin by the sheer desire running through my veins as her back arches while she expels a moan. My lips fall upon the middle of her chest with soft kisses, slowly inching toward the edge of her bra as I tear it out of the way with my teeth.

My hands move toward her back, unclasping her bra until she's completely topless. *Fuck, they're huge.* My urges become challenging to control, worried I will hurt her.

With care, I run my tongue at a slow and agonizing pace, tasting her nipples as she cries my name softly while running her fingers through my hair, demanding more.

"Austin," she barely manages to breathe. "Will it hurt the baby if we..."

"No," I tell her faintly. "I'm big, but the baby is nowhere near where I enter."

She places her hand beneath my chin, guiding my face, so we're staring intensely into each other's eyes.

"Then fuck me. Now, please."

I'm barely able to think as Ava shuffles out of her panties while I remove my pants, allowing my cock to spring free. The moment her eyes lay on my engorged cock, her body flushes, and she's quick to go back to the way she was positioned. I grab my shaft and slowly guide myself, basking in how incredibly wet she is. I'm careful not to hurt her, easing myself in and relishing in being bareback.

Fuck, I can't even remember when I'd done this last.

Conscious of my movements, I'm careful not to hurt Ava and allow her to ride me at a comfortable pace.

Ava's fucking beautiful. The way she arches back with her chest out, to when her eyes open and close as strangled moans escape her. I don't need to fantasize anymore. She's living and breathing, consuming me with her entire being.

"I'm close," she warns me.

My fingers move on their own accord, pinching her erect nipples as she groans for me to go harder. Her confidence is a goddamn turn-on, commanding I do things to her and unapologetic with her demands. I study her body, having never seen something so beautiful.

And that includes her sister.

I bite down hard again, willing to last the distance myself. But it only takes a few seconds for me to feel her contract all over, and I'm unable to hold back any longer, letting myself spill inside her while a groan escapes me.

I'm seeing stars, my eyes blinking rapidly as my vision goes in and out of this blurry haze.

Our breaths come hard and fast, the high slowly coming down as the minutes pass.

"Ava," I whisper, still keeping myself inside her because I feel a second wind coming on. "I don't want anyone else touching you."

"I don't want anyone else touching you," she counters, though she closes her eyes with a slight wince.

"Am I hurting you?"

Her body moves slowly, again, causing my dick to remain hard. "God, no, Austin. Fuck me again, please."

Pulling her mouth onto mine, I taste her lips before demanding she ride me until she comes.

What we're doing is breaking all the rules.

It's a recipe for disaster.

But she's the mother of my child.

And her body is an addiction I have no intent to recover from.

I want to taste Ava Edwards and only her, but this isn't a game. The stakes are too high. I've known Ava my entire adult life. She's not one to commit and doesn't believe in falling in love.

Yet, in the throes of passion, we've both committed to remaining exclusive with each other.

It's just sex.

Falling in love is another story altogether.

SEVENTEEN

AVA

I scratched an itch.

And now there's no turning back.

Austin satisfied me in more ways than I ever imagined possible. It got to the point I came so quickly, embarrassing on my behalf. He didn't seem to care and followed through just as quickly, probably to take the heat off me.

But just as I thought it was all over, we did it again.

I'm not sure how my body even managed to do that. I've been with a few men, but no one has ever made me orgasm twice and within the space of five minutes.

It has to be all the pregnancy hormones swirling inside of me—that's it.

Nothing more.

I mean, Austin is sexy and incredibly ripped but not overly muscly where he belongs in some body-building contest with an awful tan and shimmery gold thong.

His arms are, let's say, perfectly veined. When he flexes to grab something, I find myself staring in awe. It's not like I haven't seen him in swim shorts before with a bare torso—

we've spent a lot of time at the beach and in the pool back in the day—but now he is all man.

A man I should not be having these wicked thoughts about.

And I especially need to stop thinking of his cock. It's just so *hard*.

As we sit here, out of breath, an awkward silence falls between us. I adjust my dress, pulling my straps up as my bra lies on the floor near the coffee table. When Austin slides his pants back on, I gaze in the opposite direction.

"I should probably go," he mumbles, unable to look me in the eye. "I have an early start tomorrow."

"Oh yeah, sure."

He runs his hands through his hair, making him look even more delicious. Geez, he makes you come twice, and now you want more? I cross my arms beneath my chest, aware I have no bra on, and my nipples are hard again. This is ridiculous, and I'm sure some sexual demon has possessed my body. Usually, after one fuck with a guy, I'm fine for him to leave so I can carry on with my day. Olivier had been the only exception, though sex with him was nothing compared to Austin. Then, I remember Austin was previously intimate with my sister.

Like a splash of cold water, my thoughts dissipate, and I'm brought back to reality.

"So," he drags, scratching his chin. "I'll call you soon."

I nod, averting my gaze to the wall.

The moment the door closes, I fall back onto the sofa and let out a huge breath. *What the hell did I just do?* I grab my phone to dial Millie's number only to remember she's not talking to me.

Throwing my phone on the opposite end of the sofa, I realize my past habit of always running to Millie when I need advice or clarity on a situation involving a guy. Unfortunately, when it comes to men, I second-guess myself, which is why I rely on her to either talk me off the ledge or make me jump ship because red flags are waving in the distance.

For all of my life, she's been my security blanket. Always by my side, and even though she dared me to do dangerous things when we were kids, she was always there to catch me when I fell.

She is part of who I am, and without her, there's a void I can't shake.

Needing her more than ever, I know this ache inside with her gone will never subside. But this isn't one of those times to run to her, even if I could.

I just screwed her ex-fiancé twice.

It's just me and my thoughts, all of which are confused by what just happened. In the throes of passion, who the hell was I? Demanding he take me this way, that no one else can touch him. Everything slipped out, and in the heat of the moment, I had no concern for the consequences of my actions.

Then, he echoed my sentiment. No man is to touch me. The fire in his eyes only cemented his demands, but at the time, it turned me on more than anything.

But now the moment is over.

I drag my tired self to my room to shower and change for bed. But, when I eventually climb in, my body isn't in sync with my mind. I can barely move a limb, but my mind refuses to shut down.

Tonight was a big deal, and I can't get out of my head how it ended. Austin isn't a man I can ghost, even though I'm notorious for doing this when something doesn't go my way. He's is the father of my baby. No matter what, I'll have to face him at some point.

I yank my phone off the bedside table, only to put it back moments later. My hands move toward the lampshade, switching it off with the hope that the darkness will put me to sleep.

My eyes are open wide, staring at the pitch-black ceiling with no chance at all of falling asleep.

A long-winded sigh escapes me as I lean over, turn the lamp back on, and grab my phone once again. *Just do it, just text him.* I must find a way to move on from tonight.

Me: *Sorry if that made it weird between us. I shouldn't have brought up my predicament.*

I don't expect him to respond straight away, but the bubble on the screen taunts me until his text appears.

Austin: *Is that what you think happened?*

Me: *There was a lot of silence afterward.*

My phone begins to ring with Austin's number calling through. Shit, I can't ignore it, given I had just texted him. I suck in my stomach, inhaling a deep breath, then quickly press accept.

"Hey," is all I say.

"Ava, what happened tonight..."

"I know, I know. It can't happen again."

"That's not what I was going to say."

"Oh really? What were you going to say?"

The line goes quiet, forcing me to check to see if we're still connected.

"I meant what I said earlier," his voice is low, almost strained. "I don't want anyone touching you while you're pregnant with my child."

"No one has, Austin. I mean, it's not like I can go out and find someone the way I look right now. Kinda obvious I'm with child."

Austin sighs, appearing more relaxed. "You're kidding me, right? You're stunning. You could walk out onto the street right now in your tattered Lakers shirt, and every man would still turn to look at you."

My lips curve upward into a smile. "Hey, how did you know I still have that shirt?"

"Intuition," is all he says. "Ava, I'm serious about the other men."

"Austin, there's no other man or men. So, it's not a problem."

"Good."

My fingers tug at the blanket, unsure whether I should say how I feel, given our conversation has turned a corner I didn't see coming. But, if we're honest, maybe I owe Austin that too.

"Well, if we're honest here, then the same should be said for you. I'm not exactly thrilled you're a single sexy doctor."

"There is no one else, Ava," he assures me.

"There can be, at any time. You have the whole package, and you're still around Lane, right?"

"Yes, I work with her."

"So..." I drag, hoping he figures out the obvious without me having to spell it out.

"So what?"

"What if the temptation is too hard to resist?"

Austin chuckles softly. "It's doubtful."

"Why?" I question, failing to see the humor in this.

"Because, Ava, once you've had amazing sex with some-one, it's hard to go back to subpar."

It takes a moment for my brain to register. The truth is, amazing sex is hard to come by, but no matter how much I try to deny it, sex with Austin is *mind-blowing*. I don't know why, but I let all my inhibitions go with him and allow myself to succumb to my own fantasies.

"I have to agree with that." I sigh, then continue, "I should probably sleep. Tonight took it out of me."

"Get some rest, Ava."

"You too."

We end the call, but now I'm even more confused than before. What just happened? And what did we agree to? Not sleeping with other people, but does that mean we sleep with each other?

Without Millie to dissect the situation, I go to the next best thing—Addy.

"Hey, what's happening?"

"I slept with Austin."

"Well, duh. Cat's out of the bag, baby."

"No, I meant tonight and twice."

"Twice?" she blurts out over the speaker. "Tonight? As in now?"

"Keep your voice down!" I warn her, worried Alexa will hear since they're alone together. With my parents here in Manhattan, Dad instructed Addy to make sure Alexa doesn't get up to anything. "An hour ago. Addy, what do I do?"

"Did you want this to happen? Who initiated?"

I quickly bring her up to speed with tonight's events, leaving certain details out which she doesn't need to know.

"You aren't going to like what I'm about to say," Addy proclaims in a confident tone.

"Just say it. I'm a big girl."

"You're falling in love with him."

"Addison Kate Edwards!" I shout, startling even my tired self. "I'm not falling in love with Austin."

"Quite some reaction, dear sister."

I throw my head back against the headboard of my bed. "You're messing with my mind."

"Look, Ava... " Addy resigns, then continues, "... you've blurred the line and crossed the boundary. I don't think you're in a position to be fuck buddies. There's too much at stake, and despite you not wanting to acknowledge this, you guys have a past. This isn't some guy you picked up on the street."

"I know," I barely whisper. "It's just, sometimes, when we're together, it feels like I've known him my whole life. It's easy, you know?"

"You have known Austin for half your life, so I understand that feeling. But, Ava, there is a baby coming. The two of you need to work together to raise this child. This whole sleeping with each other just complicates things. Unless, as I mentioned, you're in love."

"When did you become so mature?"

Addy laughs, then releases a sigh. "When I decided not to follow in my older sisters' footsteps."

"Speaking of older sisters, um, how is Millie?"

"Truth?"

"Always."

"Not good..." Addy admits, then stalls. "She just needs time, Ava."

"It's been a while," I barely manage to say. "Should I reach out to her?"

"Millie has a lot on her plate. She's juggling her marriage, work, and a toddler. So give her some space to navigate through this."

"What's wrong with her marriage?" I ask, panicked.

"Nothing, Ava. Will is being Will. He's not exactly thrilled about Austin and has it in his head that Austin and Millie will be around each other all the time if the two of you reconcile."

"It's always the billionaires who act all jealous and unreasonable."

"Well, Lex Junior is known to be protective over his wife."

I think of Millie almost every day but admit I haven't really considered how this affects Will. Of course, he's a big boy who runs an empire just like Dad. But I guess I've forgotten just how alpha male Will is, especially when it involves Millie.

"Just tell her I miss her, okay?"

I say goodbye and end the call, possibly more confused after speaking to Addy. Yet maybe, it isn't confusion but denial.

I can't fall in love with Austin.

It will ruin everything.

When I wake up the following day, it all becomes clear. I need to distance myself from Austin, stop any feelings from growing into something uncontrollable.

The answer is to flee Manhattan, at least temporarily.

I call an emergency meeting with Eric. There is so much which needs to be done before the baby comes anyway, and there's not much time before I need clearance to fly. So, it makes sense to throw myself into work and travel as much as I can.

But, I'm a fugitive running from my own mistakes.

So, I send Austin a text out of courtesy to let him know I'll be traveling for work. I half expect a lecture on pregnancy and flying, but instead, I get a 'take care'.

The response comes with mixed feelings, but none of it matters—we both need a time out, and distance is the perfect solution.

∼

"Eric, I really don't have time for lunch. I know it's Saturday, but I need to go to the office to finish up some paperwork."

In the middle of the sidewalk, Eric stops me with his hand.

"Will you just not think about work for two seconds?"

Placing my hands on my hips, I'm tired from the short walk and outfit he insisted I wear today. Something about paparazzi scouring the streets this morning, so I need to look my best. He even picked out a Dolce & Gabbana strapless floral-print dress with a simple pair of blush-colored heels to match.

"Consider it lunch, and work. There, satisfied?"

We walk for another block until Eric stops at a familiar building. When he opens the door for me, I enter and wait for him to give further instructions. He tells me we're having lunch on the rooftop. When we enter the elevator, it becomes familiar—Bar Luna.

"Is this Lochie's bar?"

Eric nods, then the door pings open.

"Surprise!"

There is a big arch with the words 'baby shower' spelled out. My eyes immediately gravitate toward Mom standing beside it, and while still in shock, I see Adriana, Nikki, Kate, Alexa, and all my girl cousins besides Jessa.

I turn to face Eric, now understanding why he insisted I dress the way I did for what was supposed to be a business lunch.

"A baby shower?" I ask, unable to hold back my smile.

Mom comes up to me, extending her hands with a grin. "Every mother deserves a shower."

Nikki, Adriana, and Kate are carrying glasses of champagne. They all hug me, though all three of them look like they've had a few, their eyes glassing over and unwarranted giggles coming out of nowhere.

"This is amazing," I say in awe, admiring the beautifully decorated tables with white linen table cloths and flower arrangements in the middle. As I gaze around the space, the theme is white and mint green, my two favorite colors. I'm assuming it's also because it's gender-neutral. Finally, I turn to face Mom and Eric. "You guys did amazing."

"Oh, it wasn't us, honey," Mom quickly intercepts.

"Then who?"

"Me," the voice says behind me.

I quickly turn around to see Millie with her head tilted slightly to the side. She's wearing a twist peekaboo yellow dress which compliments her olive skin. Since I saw her last, she's cut her hair so it's sitting just above her shoulders.

"You planned this?"

"You deserve to be spoiled." Millie smiles, keeping her gaze fixated on me. Then, her eyes begin to glass over while she bites her bottom lip. "I'm sorry, Ava. I don't know what came over me to treat you that way."

I don't even think, throwing my arms around her. Inside the familiar embrace, I hold onto her tight as I fight back the tears.

"I missed you so much, Millie," I whisper in her ear, my words becoming strangled. "God, I'm so sorry for everything."

We both pull away, but Millie places her hands on my stomach with a grin spreading across her face.

"Missed you too, Ava bear. More than you can ever imagine."

EIGHTEEN

AVA

Millie stopped at nothing to make the baby shower spectacular.

There is nothing she didn't think of. Across the rooftop space are clusters of mint and white-colored balloons. The most prominent design is an arch hovering over a floral backdrop and a copper circle with *Baby Shower* in cursive plating.

In the corner, though large with its stature, are four wooden blocks stacked on top of each other with the letters spelled out to say, BABY.

Scattered around the floor are white rose petals, making the area a perfect backdrop for photographs. Not too far is a table covered in gifts. How the hell does a baby need so many things?

As I continue to take it all in, I'm rendered speechless at the small details Millie thought of. I lay my hand against my breastbone as my chest expands with an overwhelming feeling of gratitude. After all my sister and I have gone through over the past few months, I never expected her to shower my baby and me, especially since she's been trying so hard for her own.

There are small tables spaced evenly for guests to sit down, and of course, each table is decorated to perfection. I desperately search for the food at the same time my stomach grumbles.

The timing is perfect. Servers walk out of the bar area, which I assume leads to a kitchen.

It's hors d'oeuvres and small dishes, prepared and cooked by a well-known chef who works at one of the restaurants in the city which my father owns.

The servers walk around, offering each dish to the guests as well as champagne. As for me, I stick to the mocktail yet eye the champagne with jealousy, counting down the weeks until I can drink again.

Correction, months, according to Kate, who also chooses the opportunity to bring up breastfeeding.

"Ava, wait until you see how big your boobs get. They'll look like some engorged alien head," Kate mentions casually.

I slowly chew the food in my mouth, unsure whether to be excited about large breasts or terrified by her analogy. They have already grown, almost double my usual size, but I had no idea they will grow even bigger.

"When I was pregnant with Will, Rocky couldn't get enough of mine. If I told you what he did when I was lactating—"

"And there goes the crème brulee," Millie groans beside me, placing her small bowl on the table while scowling. "Please don't finish that sentence. Thank God Will isn't here."

I'm glad Millie kept the guest list small. Just our family and close friends. Back in high school, I had several girlfriends, but we drifted apart over time. I've found it hard to find good friends for most of my life when many girls just wanted to hang out with me because my family is wealthy.

In college, I became friends with a few people, but they ended up moving back to England. We keep in touch via social media, but that's it.

As for Gigi, who was my sidekick for many years, we had a falling out. I was sick of her getting into trouble, especially with men. She was a homewrecker, and I was always caught up in her scandalous affairs. Millie kept warning me about her, but I assumed she was just pissed because Gigi made a move on Will at the Hamptons all those years ago.

The guest who surprises me the most is Austin's mother, Kristen. She greets me hello when I walk in, but just like I remember, she's laid back—even looking excited about the impending arrival. I'm not sure whether she is my mother-in-law, or do you have to be married to garner the title by definition?

Married to Austin.

The word marriage onsets a string of emotions, all of which I need to suppress to get through the day. Now isn't the time to be having these ludicrous thoughts.

Addy stands beside me, and I realize I hadn't spotted her earlier.

"Hey, sis, sorry I'm late."

"I was wondering where you were." I wrap my arms around her, into a tight embrace, then slowly pull back. "Did you just fly in?"

"Yes, I had some stuff to finish and didn't fit into Millie's strict schedule." Addy clears her throat, placing her hand on my shoulder. "I told you it would work out."

I smile while reaching out to place my hand on hers. "Thank you."

"So, how's the Austin thing going?"

"There's no Austin thing," I answer defensively. "We're civil, and things have stayed the way they should have."

"Or did you coerce the journey to detour by escaping to travel the last few weeks?"

"I needed to work," I argue back.

Addy purses her lips with a judgmental stare. I know she doesn't believe a word I say, and frankly, I don't care. Things with Austin are back to normal after that one night, where apparently, I turned into some sex-crazed maniac.

"I'm going to get something to eat and drink," Addy informs me. "Enjoy yourself today. Remember this is all for you."

I take the deepest breaths, ignoring Addy's comments about Austin, and engage with those who come to chat with me. More than anything, I want a chance to sit down with Millie. Every moment I turn to search for her, she appears busy dealing with servers or Eric.

Then, when I think she's free, Millie announces it's time to have fun and play some games.

I don't want to dampen the fun, but baby shower games? My feet already ache, and a nap sounds so good.

"Now," Millie yells out, commanding everyone's attention. "Our first game is to guess how big Mama Ava is."

"Great," I utter, then force a smile. "Are we guessing my weight?"

Millie shakes her head with a grin. "Each guest will be handed a piece of string. The person whose string fits perfectly around Ava will be the winner."

Two men bring out a chair, replicating a throne, and I sit beside the floral wall like a guinea pig. Everyone um's and ahs, examining my body and making me highly self-conscious.

Millie collects all the strings, requesting I stand up so we can determine the winner. It is down to Mom being the closest until my cousin, Luna's string is close to perfect. Eric hands her a small Tiffany gift bag. Damn, maybe I should play if these are the prizes.

Considering Eric spends the most time with me out of everyone here, his string is so big, you can fit two of me in there.

"Sorry, hun." He cringes, then breaks out into an overbearing smile. "You still look fabulous, though."

"I'll remember that the next time you ask me how you look when we're in the change room of Prada."

Eric throws his hand to his neck with a dramatic gasp. "You wouldn't dare lie to me in the Holy land."

I glance sideways, purposely ignoring him.

Millie calls for order as she announces the rules for the next game.

"The game rules are that each person is given a baby bottle with champagne inside it. The first to finish wins," she informs everyone. "Now, don't think this is easy. It's quite a challenge, so don't be afraid to give it your all if you want to win."

Only a few come forward to play, so it doesn't surprise me when Adriana, Kate, Nikki, and Mom, decide to challenge each other.

"Ladies," Eric says confidently, "I shall join you. Let the games begin."

When Millie counts down, each of them begins sucking the bottle in hand. Apparently, it's more complicated than it looks since the teat is relatively small, so it comes down to your sucking skills.

"Why is this so disturbing?" Alexa complains.

Luna raises her hand to cover her mouth, attempting to control her laughter. "Because Aunt Charlie is winning."

"Why is my mom doing that thing with her tongue?" Sienna scowls, then closes her eyes. "Is it some British trick?"

I burst out laughing, knowing Uncle Noah and Kate are very active in the bedroom. Actually, not just the bedroom but everywhere. I'd overheard several conversations between Kate and Adriana because Mom didn't want to hear anything about her baby cousin Noah and his stallion ways.

"Is anyone wondering why Eric looks like he's deep-throating?" Millie pipes up, forcing us all to turn our attention on him.

We shudder upon watching, yet none of us can turn away.

"I think it's down to Mom and Nikki," I say out loud while wrinkling my nose. "I'm torn between wanting Mom to win but also not wanting to think about how she can suck on something so good."

"Lucky Uncle Lex," Luna snickers.

As the bottles start to empty, Nikki takes her final sip and raises her bottle as everyone cheers, prompting a satisfied grin.

"Rocky would be so proud of me right now," Nikki boasts.

"Will would die if he heard this," Millie mumbles, handing over a gift bag to Nikki with a forced smile. "I'm not so sure your son would be proud of you."

We erupt into laughter as the women who competed try to catch their breaths, each one complaining just how difficult the task was.

After we take a small break in which a three-tiered cake

is rolled out, we're each served a slice of what I'll call heaven. Like Mom, Millie knows just how much I love red velvet cake, making it easy to devour the piece in record time.

I greedily go in for seconds, unapologetic for wanting more.

"Are you ready to open your gifts?" Millie asks, ushering me back to my throne.

"I have to do that in front of everyone?"

She laughs, then releases a sigh. "Yes, part of the baby shower experience."

Millie is beside me to hand each gift as Eric sits beside her, noting the gifts and names.

There are onesies, stuffed toys, things for feeding, and this big plastic trash can-looking thing.

I stare at it in confusion.

"Ava, honey, it's a diaper genie," Mom mentions softly near me.

"Does it make them disappear?" I ask, still confused.

A few people laugh until Mom continues with, "It seals the dirty diapers and makes it easy to take it to the trash later."

"Oh," is all I say, then offer a thank you to Nikki, who purchased it for me along with other bits and pieces.

As I open each gift, everyone ooh's and ah's. The smaller the item, the louder their sounds. Although I have to admit, the outfits are cute, especially a onesie which looks like a little bunny suit.

The stroller is from Mom and my sisters, apparently the best stroller according to some parenting magazine. It's filled with so many things I never knew I needed, and it goes without saying they spoiled me rotten.

Standing up to hug Mom, I thank her for everything before taking a seat again to open the remaining presents.

Millie hands me a white box with a beautiful yellow bow on top. Slowly, I pull the card out and begin to read it.

Dear Ava,
To the beautiful memories this baby will bring us
soon.
Welcome to our family.
Love
Kristen

A warm sensation spreads across my chest as my eyes wander over Kristen's words again. Then, finally, I glance in her direction to be met with a gracious smile.

All these fears disappear, almost like a weight has been lifted from my shoulders. My parents have finally let go of their concerns, counting down the days until they can meet their grandchild. Kristen and Austin's father, Greg, are excited to meet the baby which also alleviates the stress because they easily could've not been so welcoming given the circumstances.

And now, Millie is talking to me again.

All feels right in the world again, and just maybe, this will all work out.

I pull the bow, then remove the lid. Under the tissue paper, there is a small blanket. It's yellow with colored stripes.

"That belonged to Austin," Kristen tells me, her tone subdued as she stares at the blanket fondly. "He was wrapped in it when he came home from the hospital. As he grew, Austin dragged it with him everywhere. When he went to preschool, he hid it in his bag every day. I even remember when we would travel, he insisted it be taken as carry-on."

Bringing the blanket to my nose, I inhale the scent. It smells like comfort and like happiness, everything Austin provides me when we're in each other's company. The soft texture feels nice in my hands, and soon our baby will be wrapped in the same blanket its daddy came home in.

"Thank you, Kristen," I choke, trying to fight back the tears.

Kristen stands up to offer me a hug, and in her embrace, I welcome the kindness and fight back the emotions which make me want to sob like a baby.

As we pull away, I intake a breath then turn to glance at Millie, hoping the mention of his name doesn't start something between us. Thankfully, she's busy with Eric arguing over what column Eric should've written the names and gifts in.

I take a moment to thank everyone for attending and for all the generous gifts, wanting to keep my speech short and simple. As much as I love events, the reality is my feet are numb, and my back is aching—the downside to being pregnant in your third trimester.

A few people say goodbye, and some, like Nikki, request the servers bring out more champagne. Upon closer inspection, Nikki, Kate, and Adriana are next-level obnoxious. They are big girls, and I'm sure Eric can handle them while drunk and talking smack about their husbands. But then I hear Adriana say something about anal and I swear, I move so fast, almost tripping over.

"Tired?"

Millie takes a seat beside me with champagne in hand. Finally, we're alone.

"Exhausted. Who would have thought baby showers could be so exhausting?"

She places her hand on my stomach as the corners of her lips curve up. "Do you think it's a boy or girl?"

"Everyone says it looks like a boy. But I think it's a girl."

"Ashton would love a boy cousin." Millie sighs wistfully. "Plus, Dad would be in heaven with all these boys around."

I place my palm on her hand. "Millie, I know this is hard."

She glances over at Mom, who offers a reassuring smile. "It's not easy if I'm honest, but my time will come when it comes. The doctors have said it's not uncommon to miscarry and then struggle with fertility. I have come to the realization that this is something I have no control over."

"And Austin?"

Millie takes a moment to collect her thoughts, something she is good at, whereas I blurt out the first thing which comes to mind.

"Austin is a great guy. He was always going to be a great father one day."

I twist my hands in my lap, not wanting to strain things between us even further. But there is so much more to this, and I pray with every fiber in my being we can pull through and go back to the way things were.

"I never did this to hurt you. I was just so fucked up that night, and Austin was just as bad. He lost a patient, a kid, out of all people. We got too drunk. I never expected this to happen, and I wanted to tell you, but I felt ashamed after I slept with him."

"I get that. I wouldn't have reacted well... " Millie admits, then continues, "... it's Austin, you know. I will always love him, just not in that way. I mean, I never expected it to happen with him, but at least he's a good man."

"But what about Will?"

Millie lowers her gaze while her fingers toy with her wedding ring. "He is less forgiving than me. He can't seem to get past the whole Austin being back thing."

"But it's not going to be like that," I tell her, quick to clear up any misconception. "Austin is the baby's father, but we're not together. So, I don't see why Will is freaking out. It's not like Austin lives with me or anything."

"He doesn't see it that way. He thinks there will be birthdays and Christmas. And he's adamant you'll get married."

"Married?" I choke, instantly feeling the heat in my cheeks rise. Suddenly, I feel guilty for hiding what happened between us weeks ago. But Millie isn't the right person to divulge all my intimate secrets to, especially when it involves her ex. "Wh... why would he think that?"

"I don't know, Ava."

"Okay, so entertaining Wills theory, hypothetically," I profess, stalling for just a moment to make sure I word my thoughts right for once. "Why would that bother him? If it meant that Austin married me, it's not like he'd do that to get close to you? Getting married is a commitment of love, right? We would have to love each other to commit for life."

"Try explaining that to a billionaire who knows how to decode a computer in like zero point two seconds, but when it comes to his wife, it's a whole other story."

My chest hitches before my shoulders fall. Just when I think it will all work out, I am yet to encounter my brother-in-law in beast mode.

"Is Will here, in Manhattan?"

Millie nods. "He took Ashton to Central Park Zoo

today."

"How long are you in the city for? I'd like to spend some time with you without everyone watching us like we're on some reality show."

From where they stand, Addy and Alexa are gawking like stalkers. The second they notice I'm looking at them, they turn away, pretending to be engrossed in a conversation.

"I've got a few hours tomorrow before we fly out in the evening," Millie informs me. "But, Ava, so that you know, I'm trying my hardest here. It feels like I'm caught in the middle, trying to juggle being supportive to you but also a husband who has gone completely irrational on me. I'm not sure how Austin feels, but all of this will take some adjustment."

I nod, then place my hands on my stomach for the baby to kick.

"The baby is reacting to all the cake I ate," I groan.

Millie's face lights up, immediately placing her hand on the spot where the baby kicks.

Suddenly, it happens again.

"Oh, my God!" Millie almost screams. "It kicked me. The baby kicked me."

I rest my head against the chair as my sister continues to talk to my belly about how awesome she is.

The truth is, Millie Edwards Romano is awesome.

The best sister I could've asked for.

But, she's married to a man who is known to be ruthless when he doesn't get what he wants.

Only time will tell just how far he'll go to protect his wife.

Or maybe, his protection is what will drive my sister and me apart again.

NINETEEN

AUSTIN

"It says to take part B and connect it to part C."

Ava draws her brows while staring at the instruction booklet in front of her. Her back leans against the spare bed with legs stretched out and feet bare. The blue dress she wears barely reaches her knees.

Unable to hide my grin, I continue to connect the pieces to the sounds of her frustrated huffs, followed by theatrical groaning. Typical Ava—she has zero patience.

"This makes no sense at all," Ava complains, placing the booklet in her lap. "How are all these pieces supposed to be a crib?"

"Patience, Miss Edwards," I remind her gently, not sweating this at all. I've done far worse in med school. "It'll come to fruition if you just follow procedure."

"You sound like a doctor."

"Lucky I am one." I smirk until she throws a piece of scrunched-up paper at me.

Ava's guest bedroom has been turned into a nursery. After her baby shower weeks ago, the gifts just sat in here because Ava had no clue what to do. So I offered to help build the crib, thinking it's the best starting point since we both have no idea how to raise a baby.

"So, have you got anything for your place? There are a lot of double-ups, and I'm sure I can go through it and give you some."

"Not yet," I tell her, pausing momentarily, then continuing, "I'm actually looking to buy a place, so it doesn't make sense to move more things."

"Oh?" Ava's mouth falls open. She's never one to keep her thoughts at bay, her bright eyes revealing everything. "I remember you mentioned that. Have you found anything yet?"

"Narrowed it down to two places. We'll see."

Ava tilts her head with a gaze that falls upon her knees. Her fingers scratch at the skin, yet it appears she's distracting herself more than relieving an itch.

"I mean, if you need money or anything, I'm happy to help. I'm not Lex Edwards, but my company has done well."

My chest caves slightly, annoyed at her presumption of me not having money nor being able to take care of the child financially. When it came to money handouts, I accepted my parents paying for my college tuition since med school is expensive. Then, when my grandfather passed away, I inherited a property and some cash. Enough to get me settled when I'm ready.

During my college years, I worked while studying then was fortunate enough to get a paid residency.

I wasn't born into billionaire wealth like the Edwards girls.

The tension in my shoulders mounts, but then I remember my dad teaching me to respect offerings, no matter who they may come from. It's about the gesture and not my ego.

"It's fine." I shrug, with a flat tone in my voice. "When my grandfather passed away, he left me a condo in San Francisco. It's on the market now. Once that sells, I'll add some from my savings and can afford a two-bedroom. That's all I need anyway."

"Uh, sure, I guess that's good then. So you don't have to worry about money?"

"I don't, but I also don't live an extravagant existence," I remark, knowing she's probably cringing inside. But, after all, we're talking about Ava Edwards. Once, she demanded her father organize a private plane because she wanted to fly to Vegas for some fashion show which gave out free designer bags. Bags, shoes—something ridiculous like that. "If I'm not at work, I'm at the gym or sleeping. I'm lucky to socialize once a month."

"But I don't understand how you'll see the baby," Ava blurts out, to then purse her lips. "I'm sorry, that shouldn't have come out so rudely."

There are so many unanswered questions. The situation we find ourselves in is less than conventional, and there have been times when it almost seems easier just to move in together, so we get the best of both worlds.

But then—we crossed to the other side.

It didn't surprise me one bit Ava ran after we fucked again. In the heat of the moment, we both said things. Words that took whatever it is between us to another level.

In a way, Ava traveling and distancing herself should have given me space to think, but all I did was busy myself with work. We were incredibly short-staffed, so the distraction was welcoming.

We agreed on one thing, neither one of us would

involve ourselves sexually with anyone else. Easier said than done. My dick has been a nightmare since that night. No amount of pleasuring myself is solving the problem, and it's not exactly like I can ravish Ava given how far along she is. Not to mention the fact she is struggling with her size and getting comfortable.

My dick just needs a god damn raincheck.

However, Ava doesn't look like she has the same predicament as me. More than ever, she has been complaining about back pain. We both have busy schedules, so when we see each other, time has passed, and Ava's stomach continues to grow.

"I don't know how it will work, okay?" I distract myself with another bolt, screwing the piece in. "Once the baby is here, we can figure it out."

We work quietly, Ava reading out instructions and me piecing it all together. Then, when the final piece is on, I reach my hand out so Ava can stand up.

"Oh, my god, it's an actual crib."

I chuckle softly. "That it is."

"For a baby to sleep in."

We both stare in awe until Ava rubs her belly. Even in her third trimester, she still looks as beautiful as ever. If you look from behind, she doesn't even look pregnant, carrying all in the front.

Ava reaches out for my hand to place it on her stomach. A small kick hits my palm, causing my lips to curve upward into a smile. A warm sensation spreads throughout my chest from connecting with our baby, who is clearly excited the crib is built.

"The baby is very active today," Ava beams, placing her hand near mine. 'It's either because you're around or the brownie and cookie combo I ate earlier."

"Not long to go now," I remind her with ease. "Have you thought about a birthing plan?"

"Birthing plan?"

"Yeah, like if you're open to pain relief, natural birth, water birth."

Shaking her head, Ava almost looks mortified. "Um, no to the water birth. Open to pain relief. I think, if it's safe?"

"It's safe, Ava, just something to think about."

"Do I have to think about it now?"

"Not right now, but you're thirty-four weeks tomorrow."

Ava acknowledges with a silent nod, then takes a seat on the rocker chair her Aunty delivered to her.

"It's happening." Ava gulps while pressing her hands on her lap. "Thank God my sisters are keeping me sane by sending me videos of random things like a flamingo dancing to some old '80's song."

I'm glad Ava and Millie finally moved past their differences. Without mentioning anything to Ava, I've seen a noticeable change in her behavior. She's back to her usual self, being dramatic over the smallest of things and gossiping about stories that are of no interest to me whatsoever.

The two of them have been inseparable for as long as I've known them. When Millie left for college, Ava was lost without her. They have a sisterly bond no one can break, so reconciling is a good thing.

"Even as a lawyer, I'm glad Millie still has the time to entertain you," I muse, glancing at the crib, proud of my efforts.

"Between her and Addy, I don't know how they get anything done. It reminds me why I muted their conversations back when I was a workaholic."

"What do you mean back when you were a workaholic?" I tease with a grin. "You still are. Lex Edwards' work ethic is part of your DNA."

"Hey," Ava raises her voice in annoyance, then crosses her arms in defiance. "I resent that. Last night I didn't even take my laptop to bed."

"Oh yeah? What did you do then?"

Ava's eyes widen, her cheeks turning bright red. She immediately drops her gaze to the floor. "Um, just scrolling my phone, you know, watching videos."

"Videos? Work videos?"

She rubs the back of her neck, still unable to make eye contact with me. "Uh, no. More adult content."

Throwing my hands to my face, laughter escapes me. She will be the *death* of me.

"You're killing me, Ava. You know that?"

Biting her lip with a mischievous grin, she places her hand on her chest. "Me? How about you stop standing there looking like a piece of delicious candy, and I can't have it because I'm diabetic."

"But you don't have diabetes?" I tease.

"You know what I mean. It's off-limits, or the consequences are dire." The sound of her phone distracts us both. "Saved by the bell."

Gritting her teeth, Ava presses her lips tight before answering the call, but I welcome the change in the conversation since my pants start to become tight with my dick falling hard again.

"Hey, Luna, what's up? I've got you on speaker, and Austin is here."

"Oh, hey, Austin!"

"Hi, Luna, long time no speak. How are you?"

"Good, frazzled, I don't know. Did you guys know Andy won this significant award?"

We both look at each other and shrug our shoulders.

"I'll take that silence as a no," Luna concurs, her breathing unusually heavy over the speaker. "I'm flying out tomorrow but want to organize an intimate dinner for tomorrow night. Just Andy, my parents, Nikki and Rocky, and you guys if you're free?"

"We'll be there," Ava confirms, then closes her eyes momentarily while scowling. "See you then."

She hangs up the call then lifts her eyes to meet mine.

"Okay, I'm sorry I just assumed you were free or would want to go."

"It's fine," I assure her. "Andy deserves to celebrate his success."

"Are you sure? I mean, it's not like a date. We're going as friends of Andy's. Well, I'm his cousin, but you know what I mean," she rushes nervously.

I rub my chin while continuing to lean against the wall. My eyes fixate on her, and notably, she can't seem to sit still, fidgeting with her jewelry.

"You seem nervous? Is there something on your mind that you want to share?"

"No..." Ava shakes her head vigorously. "I don't know what you're talking about?"

"Okay. It just seems like you're kind of awkward around me." I lower my gaze, hiding my smirk, waiting for her filter to disappear.

"Addy thinks I'm falling in love with you."

And there it is...

With a dazed stare, my posture stiffens. At the same time, a tightness inside my chest restricts my ability to breathe at a normal pace.

Fuck, I didn't see that coming.

"And Will thinks we're going to get married."

It's just one explosion after another, detonating while leaving me speechless. I practice my methods to remain calm, trying to think logically about everything Ava just blurted out.

When the shock begins to wear off, my eyes narrow as they fall upon Ava with a grimace.

"That's a lot of opinions from people who aren't in our shoes, don't you think?"

"Yes," Ava mutters, then glances sideways. "You asked for the truth. There it is."

I expected neither one of those things to come out of Ava's mouth. But now, I'm presented with a bigger problem.

Does Ava feel this way?

Sure, the thought has crossed my mind. There are feelings, though probably clouded because having a child together can evoke so many emotions. Is it love? Who the fuck knows. The last time I claimed to 'love' someone, I was severely burnt.

And I refuse to go through that again, not if I have a say in the matter.

"So, tell me, Ava. Do you believe them?"

The question is weighted, but so is having a child together. We can't keep bending the rules or fooling around like we are fuck buddies or whatever people call them now. The one who will hurt the most from our fleeting actions will be our child.

"I like being around you," Ava says faintly like she's actually careful with her words for once. "It's just so easy between us. I mean, you know, when we're not fucking each other's brains out."

Cocking my head, I'm unable to hide my smile. "I feel the same."

"I don't know what love is, but I do know this baby will be incredibly loved."

Ava stands up from the rocking chair and moves close to the dresser. She touches the stuffed bunny sitting on top, staring at it wistfully.

"It's wrong...to have feelings for you," she stammers, with her back toward me. "This was always meant to be platonic. But, I guess, the pregnancy is probably stirring things..."

"It may be the hormones," I mention in a low voice, moving toward Ava until my body is flush with hers. With her back against my chest, my fingers move on their own accord, carefully moving her hair away from her shoulder to inhale her scent better.

"Ava, what if I told you I felt the same way?"

"*Austin...*" she murmurs.

Running my nose along her shoulder, her scent instantly heightens everything in my body. Of course, everything standing before me is what I shouldn't be wanting and desiring, but fuck, she drives me insane.

My hands wrap around her stomach, desperate to bring us closer. Right now, it is just us, and I don't give a fuck who has an opinion. Ava releases a sigh as her head falls onto my chest. If she turns around, there is no knowing what I will do, a part of me begging her to stay just as is.

"There's no rule book here, Ava. We set the rules. We do what we want, not what other people think we should do."

"I'm scared, okay?" I hear it in her voice, the quiet, shaky tone. "There's just so much going on, and the last thing I want is to bring this baby into the world with confusion."

Placing a kiss on her neck, I understand exactly how she

feels. "There's no rush. But for now, I need to take a step back."

I do just that, distancing myself from her. Instantly, she turns around with a pained stare. The emerald orbs make it incredibly difficult to move a limb, but I force myself to gain control of the situation.

"If I leave now, I can't be held accountable for my actions," I say, struggling to control my urges. "I'll see you tomorrow night, okay?"

Without even waiting for an answer, I leave the room to walk down the hall to exit her apartment.

Some things are best to walk away from, no matter how much it aches in the moment.

Today is my rostered day off, and I spent all day at the gym killing myself. I've done everything to take my mind off last night.

Yet continue to feel like I'm running in circles.

The usual trainer, Geoff, who did the rounds, complimented me on my dedication and persistence. He doesn't know I'm trying to exert my frustrations because I'm starting to go fucking crazy.

Ava Edwards is all I can think about.

Everything I'm not supposed to think about in that way.

And we haven't even reached the hard part yet.

"You know, for someone who is a doctor, you scrub up well outside the hospital."

Ava is walking beside me, wearing a tight burgundy dress that sits a bit short for my liking. It's fitted nicely, accentuating her curves, including her protruding stomach. Her hair is tied back into a ponytail, exposing her neck.

What the hell is it about her neck which draws you in and makes you want to blow in your god damn pants?

I bite down, ignoring my weakness.

"Was that meant to be a pun? But you got too excited, and it came off wrong?"

Ava knocks into my side. "I need to get better at that, huh?"

Once again, she breaks the tension between us. It will be a long night, but I need to relax and forget about what happened last night.

We enter the restaurant to find Julian, Adriana, and Nikki. We say hello to learn Rocky has some stomach flu.

"He says he's not lactose intolerant, but then he spends all night on the toilet sounding like he's having an exorcism," Nikki complains.

Adriana cringes. "I'm not sure whether to feel sorry for him or be disgusted."

"Don't feel sorry for him," Nikki drags, then turns to face me. "It's good to see you again, Austin. It's been how long?"

"Years," I remind her with a smile, not wanting a reminder of exactly when.

"And you're a doctor now?" Adriana smiles fondly, linking her arm into mine as we walk to the table. "If you've done one thing right by Lex, it's that."

"Second-year resident, still not entirely there yet."

When we reach the table, Julian shakes my hand. I've known him since I first started dating Millie, and much like Lex, the man never ages.

The last time we spoke, he was trying to calm me down after it was confirmed Millie and Romano were fucking behind my back.

. . .

"Buddy, you need to calm down," Julian holds me back, clutching my shirt with force.

Standing across the patio is Romano with a satisfied smirk on his god damn face. Lex is beside him, angry as hell but trying to push him further away to create distance between us.

She's fucked him. Who the hell knows how many times or how long this has been going on.

It's over.

"Let's go. I'll take you back to the city."

I turn around, refusing to stay here a second longer and be humiliated by a woman who agreed to marry me. A woman who promised me it would be just us for the rest of our fucking lives.

Inside the car, the radio plays soft music. I stare out the window, attempting to numb the pain.

"I've been where you've been," Julian mentions, breaking the silence between us. "It'll sting for a long while before you begin to heal. Don't let this ruin everything you have going for you. That, out of everything, was the biggest mistake I made."

I wasn't like him. I refused to let Amelia Edwards destroy me. She can have her happily ever after with her prince charming.

I don't need her or her family.

As far as I'm concerned, they're dead to me.

The memory disappears the moment Andy walks through the door. He stops mid-step with a dazed look, his eyes widening at the sight of everyone.

"Surprise!" Luna shouts, running toward where he stands and throwing her arms around him.

After a brief hug, Andy appears surprised, but something else seems to be on his mind. He's dressed rather casually in a pair of jeans and black tee, never one to dress formally. His focus shifts onto Ava and me with a forced smile. "Oh, look, it's everyone."

"Well, of course, it's everyone in Manhattan," Luna sneers, rolling her eyes at her brother. "We have to celebrate your achievement. You didn't think you could go under the radar again, did you?"

The moment he opens his mouth, the door opens, and my eyes lock onto the eyes of the woman who once owned me.

Fuck.

Now I know why Andy appeared surprised to see us. I drop my gaze, then press my lips, not believing my luck.

Beside me, Ava lets out a small huff followed by, "Great, the jealous brother-in-law is here."

In hindsight, I never should have agreed to this. I don't have the patience to deal with the conniving billionaire right now. But this isn't about him. It's Andy's night. With that thought in my head, I glance up to see a furious man standing beside his wife.

"Oh, crap," Luna mouths.

Adriana pats her on the shoulder. "It'll be fine. We're all adults."

"Adriana?" Nikki sighs heavily. "Have you met my son?"

"You know what?" Ava begins, straightening her shoulders, "This is about Andy. I'm sure we can all be in the same room for an hour."

The three of them walk around to say hello to everyone until Millie stands in front of me. She hasn't changed much. Her hair is shorter or lighter. Aside from that, nothing else has changed except this weird feeling when I'm around her.

Almost like she's a stranger.

Millie keeps her distance, and to respect her wishes, I don't go in for a friendly hug, almost feeling the heat coming off her husband.

"It's nice to see you, Austin," she greets in a formal tone. "I didn't realize you would be here tonight."

"I called Ava last night and spoke to Austin as well," Luna jumps in, eyeing the both of us. "I had no idea you and Will were coming into the city."

Millie keeps her smile fixed. "Andy called us, so Mom and Dad stayed with Ashton."

Ava doesn't go to hug her sister. Instead, they speak with their eyes—something they've always done which used to annoy me.

"Why don't we all sit down," Luna suggests, then purposely directs people to sit in certain spots.

Of course, Romano is across from me, enough that he can't seem to stop glaring. I don't know what the fuck his problem is, but I turn away, trying to keep my anger at bay.

Once we're all seated, Luna orders wine to celebrate. Andy, who is humble as ever, briefly talks about the award. His parents watch on proudly, with Julian being his number one supporter. I've always admired their bond, and it's easy to see where Andy gets his drive and ambition from.

"So proud of you, Andy," Millie cheers, raising her glass.

"All those photos I took of you and Ava during your teen years have paid off. I remember Ava wanted me to convince the school to swap her yearbook photo."

"The photo they took of me looked hideous." Ava scowls with an exaggerated sigh.

"Of course, they didn't allow me to swap it."

Everyone but Romano laughs. He toys with the edge of his glass, then drinks it in one sitting. A tightness forms in his eyes until he tilts his chin, keeping his gaze downward.

"Didn't get what you want for once?" Romano utters from across the table, placing his arm around Millie like he's trying to fucking prove a point. "That's surprising."

Ava crosses her arms beside me. "What's that supposed to mean?"

"Well, you're always one to get what you want, right? Even if it means you have to ruin people around you."

"Will, don't," Millie mumbles beside him.

Turning to look at Ava, I grab her hand beneath the table and squeeze it tight. The last thing she needs right now is a raised blood pressure from stress. Then, leaning in, I whisper, "Don't let him get to you. You know what he is like."

The moment I pull away, Will shakes his head with a smug expression. "Does your boyfriend make it all better? It's all very convenient, right? The two of you making love, having a baby, playing happy families."

"Will," Nikki snaps, crossing her arms just like Ava. "Get a grip on yourself."

Ava stands up, throwing her napkin on the table.

"You are a god damn jerk, Will Romano. The world doesn't revolve around you." Ava's face turns bright red, and I stand up with her, no longer wanting to be subjected to his childish behavior. "I'm sorry, Andy. Congratulations on your award. We can celebrate another time."

She storms off as I drop my head, keeping my hands on the back of the chair. With anger slowly seeping into every crevice, my gaze shifts until I'm staring into the eyes of the man I once loathed more than anything.

The same man who disregarded my intentions to marry Millie, then went in for what *he* selfishly wanted.

"It takes a man to admit his mistakes," I begin in a controlled voice, trying to suppress my anger. "I'm not perfect, and neither is Ava. And from memory, you once ruined my life to get what you wanted. So, before you judge Ava or me, perhaps you should stop throwing stones in your glass house."

I quickly nod goodbye to everyone, then exit the restaurant to an empty sidewalk.

With my fists clenched tight, I scan the area around me. Ava is nowhere to be found.

Suddenly, my eyes fall upon the concrete sidewalk to see the bracelet she wore on the ground. I pick it up, remembering on the walk over here how she said she loved it so much that if she ever lost it, she'd be so upset, which is why she never wore it.

Placing it safely in my pocket, I then extend my hand to hail a cab.

Romano may have ruined the night, but my concern is Ava.

"Addy thinks I'm falling in love with you."

Her words repeat inside my head.

And like a wind knocking the air out of me, I can't deny it any longer.

I think I'm falling in love with her too.

TWENTY

AVA

The anger tearing through me is like a hurricane making landfall, destroying everything in its path.

My muscles continue to quiver, and the speed of my pulse rises as I stand here on the sidewalk outside the restaurant.

A cab is not too far in the distance, so I stretch my arm, and it pulls over to the curb.

Desperate to escape, I hop inside and quickly give the driver my address without a second thought.

The anger begins to shift as I stare out the window, riddled with humiliation. How dare he say those things to me in front of my family. What gave him the right to voice his opinion thinking he has the slightest clue what I've gone through.

He couldn't be further from the truth.

Will Romano is a selfish man. The irony is *he* always gets what he wants.

It only takes ten minutes to get home, and during that time, my phone rings non-stop.

When I exit the cab, I move quickly, eager to be alone inside my apartment and not deal with the human race.

As my steps quicken, a pain strikes my lower body. I flinch, clutching my stomach while being forced to stop momentarily. The sensation is different from the baby's usual kicks, sharper and spreading across my entire abdomen.

I take controlled breaths in and out until the pain turns into an ache which eventually subsides. When it's completely gone, I am able to move again freely.

In the sanctuary of my home, I breathe a sigh of relief, purposely ignoring my phone. The continuous ring is driving me mad. My hands reach for the phone inside the beaded clutch to turn it off. Without a second thought, I throw it on the sofa, not wanting to talk to anyone.

All I can think about is Will's words and the conviction in his eyes while he sat there like an arrogant prick. The more I think about it, the more my blood boils. Will Romano needs to be taken down a notch, and I have no issue telling Millie to control her self-absorbed husband.

As for right now, the only thing to clear my mind is a shower. So I make my way to the bathroom, removing my clothes and shoes, then turn on the faucet.

The water is hot, easing my muscles but not my mind. Thankfully, the pain in my stomach has stopped. It must have been hunger pains since I'm unable to recall when I ate last.

After what feels like only a short time, my skin begins to wrinkle, prompting me to get out. I throw my robe on with nothing underneath, quickly brushing my hair to the side without worrying about any face creams since exhaustion begins to hit hard.

Upon my walk back to the kitchen, a noise distracts me.

Out of the corner of my eye, I see Austin is pacing the living room with his arms crossed beneath his chest. The skin bunches around his eyes along with a clenched jaw, unlike his usually calm expression.

"How did you get in here?" I ask, considering he doesn't have a key or my code.

"Your doorman, Harry. I said you weren't answering your calls, which you were not," he answers coldly, then shakes his head with a frustrated stare. "God, Ava. Do you know how worried I was about you? You run off, don't answer your phone. Anything could have happened to you!"

I lower my gaze, tightening the knot of my robe. "I'm here, alive, as you can see."

"It's not just about you anymore," Austin shouts, running his hands through his hair with a tortured gaze. "Do you understand that?"

"I understand that!" I yell back in frustration. "I have the baby to think about. I'm not as selfish as Will paints me out to be. Everyone thinks I'm some heartless person who only thinks about herself."

Austin drops his head, bringing his hand to his mouth. "You're not selfish, Ava. Far from it. But it's not just the baby..."

It takes a moment for it to register, and it becomes apparent when his gaze locks onto mine. The warmth of his honey-colored eyes spreads all over me like a breeze on a perfect summer's day.

And then, I remember our conversation last night, when he admitted his feelings for me have shifted, and I'm not alone in this. This thing happening between us isn't just in my imagination.

I no longer care what Will thinks, or anyone else for that

matter. Why should I continue to fight against all odds when the most kind-hearted, beautiful, and brilliant man is standing in front of me?

The father of my child.

And I can't deny my heart of what it so desperately wants.

"Stay with me," I breathe, unable to break his longing stare. "Stay with me tonight."

"Ava, I don't think you know what you're asking me to do."

"I need to hear it, Austin, from your lips. Tell me I'm not crazy. Tell me it isn't just this pregnancy," I beg of him.

His feet move slowly, my eyes falling upon every step until he's inches away. Then, finally, Austin raises his hand, placing it on my cheek as I lean in. My eyes close of their own accord, the comfort of his touch so right I never want to feel anything else.

"This is more than tonight."

Austin's lips fall upon my forehead. Slowly, he pulls away but keeps me in his arms. This magnetic force between us is so strong, like gravity pulling us together to sync the beat of our hearts.

And between us, a tiny heartbeat connects us in the most profound way possible.

The graze of his finger touches my chin, and gently, he lifts it, so our eyes meet.

"I'm falling in love with you," he whispers so delicately.

Tilting my head, he laces his hand around my neck and brings me closer. Our soft breaths mix until our lips graze, forcing me to suck in my breath to control my heated urges.

Austin's lips are warm, teasing me with a gentle roll of the tongue. Soft moans escape me while we both lose ourselves in the moment. A kiss, while simple to some, is so much more when it's with the person who owns your heart.

Suddenly, the door buzzes, both of us are startled by the loud sound.

I run my finger down Austin's cheek before walking toward the intercom.

"Yes, Harry?"

"Miss Edwards, it's your sister Amelia."

My eyes close momentarily, to then open with a heavy sigh. "Let her up."

Turning back around, I see Austin watching me with a smile which begins to waver. He runs his hands through his hair, and just like me, exhales a deep breath.

The knock on the door is soft, not at all like Millie's usually demanding bang.

My fingers punch the code, followed by turning the handle. As soon as the door opens, my gaze falls upon Millie's puffy face. Her usually vibrant eyes are surrounded by red, dulling down the emerald green we have in common.

Millie sniffs, crossing her arms at the same time she glances upward to the ceiling.

"I'm sorry, I had nowhere else to go."

I pull her into the apartment for her eyes to widen upon noticing Austin.

"Oh." She shakes her head in confusion. "I didn't think you'd be here. I'm sorry if I'm interrupting something."

"No," I tell her softly. "It's okay. We were just talking."

With a quick side glance, I plead with my eyes for Austin to understand why I just hid the truth.

"I should probably leave you guys…"

"Millie, no. You're upset. What happened?"

Austin clears his throat. "Listen, I'll leave you two to talk. Besides, I have an early shift tomorrow."

We keep our distance, despite our earlier admission of our feelings for one another.

"Millie?" Austin calls softly while standing at the door. "He's angry. I remember once being in the same position. The difference is, he will calm down and apologize because he can't bear the thought of losing you."

Tears shimmer in Millie's eyes. "I'm sorry for what happened at the Hamptons. It was wrong of me to treat you that way."

"Life has a way of working out. But for now, maybe a little bit of breathing space will clear your mind."

And with his final words, he glances up at me with a knowing look, then closes the door behind him.

"When did Austin become the rational one?" Millie says the moment he leaves.

I chuckle softly. "Austin has always been the rational one. Will, on the other hand—"

"Is a giant dickhead," Millie finishes off.

"No argument from me right now, but what happened? I mean, after I left."

Millie moves toward the sofa, throwing herself on it with a frustrated huff.

"It's just been so tense between us," she admits, hugging the navy velvet cushion against her chest. "Ashton is a handful, which Mom says is normal for a two-year-old, but it feels like I'm the only one worrying. Of course, Ashton always wants to be by my side. So I'm constantly asking Will to help, but his work is more important than mine."

Millie takes a deep breath, then continues, "Mom said when she and Dad had me, they went through the exact same thing. It's just learning how to sustain a marriage, career, and family."

"They made it work, that's for sure."

"Yeah, I know. Although last week Mom absolutely blasted Dad for having to leave town."

"Really?" I raise my brows. "I didn't think they got caught up in arguments like that anymore."

"Aunt Adriana told me it was because some young woman has been trying to hit on Dad at these conventions. Dad laughed it off as a joke and teased Mom about being jealous. Then Mom lost her shit."

I struggle to hold back my smile. "It's kind of relieving to know we're not the only dramatic ones. But back to you and Will."

"He's been short-fused. So, naturally, I'm like, if you want to act like that, I'm not having sex with you. I deserve respect, and frankly, his asshole behavior won't slide with me."

I purse my lips, knowing that's probably what has contributed to Will's angered behavior.

"Just like Austin said, Will is hurting and will come around to realize he's hurting you."

Millie bites her bottom lip while lowering her gaze. "He said things tonight which really hurt. First, he accused me of supporting you because he thinks I want to get back together with Austin."

Falling silent, I'm unsure what to say, mainly because my feelings involving Austin still feel new. Given their past, it doesn't seem appropriate to comment.

"You know what?" I tell her, then grab my phone to scroll through my apps. "I'm ordering us food. Pizza, Chinese, and those amazing donuts from that place near my office."

The corners of Millie's lips curve upward. "You sure know how to cheer me up."

We order food, and while waiting, turn on a streaming service to binge-watch until the food arrives. It's not unusual for us to devour an array of food just to ourselves, and it's the small things like this that I miss about not living close to Millie.

Our food coma knocks us hard, so we head to bed to lay in the dark and just talk.

"I wonder what Will is doing now," I say out loud.

"He texted me. It's a bunch of misspelled words. But apparently, he's at Andy's, drunk on God knows what."

"Andy will take care of him," I assure her, at the same time trying to roll over to my side. My back has been aching all night, more so than usual. "Even though he deserves the nasty hangover for being a jerk."

"Ava?" Millie whispers in the dark. "Is there something going on between you and Austin?"

Even in the night, with darkness shadowing the room, my eyes widen, and everything feels bright. I shuffle uncomfortably again, trying to think of something to say which isn't the truth.

"We're close," is all I manage.

"Ava, it's me. I know I have a past with Austin, but he was never supposed to be my future. So as much as my asshole husband is upsetting me right now, there will never be anyone but him."

"I know."

"It's okay, you know. The two of you are expecting a baby together. So why not make yourselves a proper family if you also feel that way about each other?"

Here is my sister giving me the green light. The one person I thought would never forgive me for my mistakes.

But as I continue to lay here beside her, my chest begins to expand at the thought of making a family a possibility.

My mind imagines Austin in bed with me each night, making sweet love to me like I'm the only woman he'll ever need. Then, I see a ring, him getting on one knee. But like a splash of cold water, all of these daydreams remind me of the life Austin and Millie once shared together.

"I'm tired, Millie. It's been a long night."

"Okay," Millie agrees faintly. "Falling in love with Austin isn't the hardest part, Ava, but losing him to someone else will be."

Millie left early the following day to have a meeting at Nikki's office over some legal matter.

Alone, with my thoughts, there's only one thing plaguing my mind.

I leave my apartment dressed in a maxi dress because the humidity is at an all-time high today. My hair bothers me, so in the cab, I tie it up into a loose bun, not caring how unkempt I look.

I am a woman on a mission, ready to step into the boxing ring.

"I'm here to see Will Romano."

The receptionist is an older lady, maybe late forties. Will was smart enough to ditch the bimbos, or perhaps that's Millie's doing. Though truthfully, the woman could go easy on the lip injectors. Unless she's a cocksucker. *Oh, my God, is that why she was hired?*

"Do you have an appointment?" she asks rudely.

"No, trust me. He will see me."

"I'm sorry. Mr. Romano is only seeing appointments."

"Look, lady," I hiss while leaning on the desk for support. "I'm his sister-in-law, and I'm going to drop a baby soon. Do you really think I care about your stupid appointments rule?"

The woman picks up her phone. "I can ask him if he'll see you."

"You know what?" I raise my palm to stop her. "I will see myself in."

Walking to his office, I don't even knock. When I enter, he is on the phone and appears annoyed to see me. Will is usually very well-groomed, but today, he's sporting an unshaven face, loose tie, and his hair looks wild like he's been running his hands through it repeatedly.

"Walker, let me call you back."

He presses his phone and sits back in his chair like the arrogant asshole he is.

"Don't look at me like that," I warn him.

"Like what, Ava? You barge into my office unannounced. Please tell me how I should look at you?"

"You're an asshole," I tell him, my heart rate spiking. "How dare you humiliate me in front of my family! If my father were there, he'd have put you in your goddamn place."

I take a breath, but a pain rips through my abdomen, causing my chest to hitch.

"I deserve an apology, and so does Austin," I fume, then to remember Millie. "And you know who else deserves one? Your wife. My sister is upset, and it's all your fault."

Will crosses his arms with laughter escaping him. "You expect me to give him an apology?"

The pain rips through me again, causing my hands to clutch my stomach. I close my eyes, willing whatever this is to stop.

"Ava?" Will calls. "Ava?"

My breaths come hard and fast, unable to even string a sentence together.

Will quickly moves off his chair with his phone in hand. I continue to breathe heavily as the phone dials.

"Amelia," Will rushes, panicked. "Ava is in my office, and she's in pain."

"What do you mean she's in your office? And what pain?"

I shake my head, biting down, crippled by the intensity of the cramp-like feeling.

"Millie," I say out of breath, "I..."

The second the pain rips through me again, a gush of warm liquid runs between my legs, causing me to gasp.

"Um, what the hell was that?" Will shouts.

"Will, what? What's wrong?"

"All this water just came out of her."

"Oh, my God! Her water just broke. Shit, hold on, let me conference in Mom."

"Amelia! Don't fucking hang up the phone."

The line goes silent for Will's growl to become louder inside his quiet office.

"I can't get a hold of Mom, it's Dad," Millie rushes, "Ava's water just broke!"

"Where is she?" Dad quickly questions.

"She's in my office," Will informs him, his face turning white. "She started wincing in pain, and her water just broke."

"Ava, sweetheart?"

"Dad." I begin to panic with a hard swallow. "I'm only thirty-four weeks."

"Will, get her to the hospital now. Ava, where is Austin?"

"Work," I choke.

"Amelia, call him and let him know what's happening."

"I...I can't do this," I stammer, terrified of what is happening. "It's too early."

"Sweetheart, just breathe, you're in labor, and you need to get to the hospital."

Dad gives Will instructions then lets him know he and Mom will fly out immediately and leave Ashton with Adriana.

Will grabs my hand to take me downstairs, ignoring the panic from his office staff when they see what's happening.

We hop in a cab to take us to the hospital. Will's instructions to the driver are to haul ass. For what should be a short cab ride, it feels like an eternity to get there.

As we walk through the ER doors, every step becomes more difficult. Will quickly abandons me to talk to the nurse behind the desk.

"Austin," I barely breathe out. "Ask for Dr. Carter."

I don't know how long it all happens. Time is lost on me as the contractions come hard and fast, only minutes between each other. Finally, I'm placed into a wheelchair before Austin comes running out of the double doors, wearing his navy-blue scrubs.

"Ava?" Austin's eyes are wide as he bends down to my level.

"Her water broke." Will pants.

Austin glances up at him, confused. "Her water broke? What happened?"

"She came to my office, we were arguing, and then she started having pains. So I called Amelia when it broke. Amelia then called Lex, and now we're here."

Austin shifts his attention back to me, his expression softening.

"It's going to be okay. I'm going to take you up to the labor and delivery ward so you can be examined."

I grab his arm, clutching tight. *"I can't lose this baby."*

He touches my cheek with a reassuring smile. "I promise you won't, but we need to take you now."

My hands clutch my stomach while nodding. Austin wheels me through the hospital as Will follows. He is on the phone, and I assume he's talking to Dad or Millie.

"Okay, we're here."

"Amelia is on her way. Your parents are on their way to the airport," Will informs me, trying to control his panic, but it is clear he's worried. "It's going to be okay."

I press my lips together, unable to respond besides the nod of my head.

Will clutches my hand, squeezing it tight. "I'm sorry for what I said. It was uncalled for."

"It was," I concur, squeezing his hand back but manage to smile faintly. "You're still an asshole, though."

"I am." Will grins, leaning in to kiss my forehead before glancing at Austin. "Take care of my sister, please."

Austin tilts his head, acknowledging Will. "I promise to. She's stuck with me forever now."

TWENTY-ONE

AVA

"Ava, one more push."

My hand squeezes tight as I buckle forward to push for the third time. The pressure is too much to bear, my entire body aching with this godawful pain that tears throughout me. I begged for pain relief the moment the contractions intensified, but it was too late, according to the nurse. With a team of medical staff around me, this baby is coming now.

A burning sensation causes me to moan until Austin's face spreads into a wide grin. "The baby is here, Ava. It's a girl."

There is no cry, no sound besides people talking in medical jargon. My heavy panting refuses to subside, but I manage to tilt my head just enough to see the baby when the doctor raises her for just a split moment.

She's so tiny and fragile-looking, the smallest baby I've ever seen.

Inside the doctor's arms, she's taken away to the other side of the room, where an incubator is on standby.

The absence of the long-awaited cry stresses me out.

My body shakes with tremors even in my state of exhaustion.

"Why isn't the baby crying?" I panic, out of breath.

And then, a soft wail, barely audible inside a room full of people, is music to my ears.

Tears cascade down my cheeks, the salty taste mixing with my dry lips. With clouded eyes, I turn to gaze at Austin.

"I'm so proud of you," Austin mouths, having never left my side throughout the whole birth. Even though he's used to being a professional, not once did he abandon me. "I know that wasn't easy."

"A girl?" I ask with a croaky voice. "Can I hold her?"

Austin rubs my hand, still remaining calm. "She needs to go to the NICU. At thirty-four weeks, her lungs are still underdeveloped, so she will most likely need a ventilator."

I nod through my tears, my emotions mixed with worry and relief she is here.

"Hey," Austin calls softly. "It's going to be okay. You did amazing."

"But she's so little. I should've done better to keep her safe inside me."

With a deep sigh and soft expression, Austin strokes my hair. His simple touch calms my racing heartbeat, allowing me to control my erratic breathing.

"There's nothing you could have done, Ava. She was meant to come early."

"Dr. Carter?" A nurse calls from across the room. "We're taking her to the NICU now."

"Stay with her, please," I beg of him, not wanting our baby to be alone. "I'll feel better knowing you're with her."

"Are you sure?"

"Go," I insist, managing a smile. "I'll be fine, and Millie will be here soon anyway."

"She's outside. Do you want me to tell her to come in?"

I nod, then Austin kisses my hand, pulling away with a yearning look. The loss of contact aches, but it isn't just about me anymore. Our baby needs him.

The nurses are still between my legs doing something I prefer not to ask exactly what. My head rests against the pillow when Millie peeks her head through the doorway. The moment my eyes fall upon her, I begin to cry again.

She rushes to my side. "Ava? What's wrong?"

"I don't know." I gulp through my tears. "I'm scared. She's so little, and that was the most terrifying thing I've ever been through."

Millie grabs my hand, squeezing it tight. "Austin spoke to us for a moment. She's going to the NICU, and you know what, she is going to be just fine. I saw her briefly when they wheeled her past."

"How do you know she's going to be okay?"

A smile graces Millie's face. "She has the Edwards blood. Can you believe it, Ava? A girl."

"A girl," I murmur, still in disbelief.

"I can't believe how fast she came. You were only in here for an hour. Austin mentioned how they tried to stop the contractions, but it was too late."

Half-listening, I'm too tired to comprehend anything until Will comes to mind.

"Wait, where's Will?"

"In the corridor, freaking out, of course."

My reaction is to laugh, but exhaustion weakens my entire body. "Tell him I said thank you. If I were alone, I don't think I'd have gotten myself to the hospital fast enough."

"I will pass the message on," she assures me, softening her tone. "You need to get some rest."

"I know." I yawn before my eyes fall heavily, and sleep is imminent.

~

My eyes flutter, the fluorescent light blinding me and making it difficult to open them wide. On my second attempt, the surroundings come into focus. I'm in a hospital room, though it looks slightly different from the one I was previously in.

Millie is beside me, watching with a watery gaze. Behind her, Will is also inside the room.

"What happened?" I croak, barely able to talk from a scratchy throat.

Millie grabs the cup with a straw on the table next to me, then encourages me to have a drink of water. I move my body slowly, so I'm slightly upright, but everything is sore.

After managing a few sips, I start to feel a bit better.

"They moved you out of the delivery suite," Millie informs me, placing the cup down. "Now, don't be alarmed. You were bleeding more than usual, which is why you were so tired. They managed to stop the bleeding but want to keep an eye on you."

"But the baby?"

Will moves closer to me, resting his hand on mine. "She's beautiful, Ava. I remember when Ashton was born, he was even smaller."

Millie nods in agreement. "It's true. He was born at twenty-nine weeks, but look at him now, he's healthy and even enjoys eating mud if you don't watch him."

I smile gently, unable to muster up a simple laugh. "Do you know when I can see her?"

"Austin said as soon as you get your energy levels up," Will mentions, yet worry still etches his face. "So you need to drink and eat something."

There's a knock on the door, and a hospital worker pops her head in with a tray of lunch. With Will and Millie's help, I manage to sit up to eat what I'll call a less than desirable meal.

But beggars can't be choosers. I end up finishing the mush and whatever brown thing they passed off as meat.

Somewhere during my rice pudding, there's another knock on the door.

"Come in," Millie says.

When the door opens, I see my parents' faces. Mom looks relieved to see me, pressing her hand against her chest, then places her purse down to hug me. She pulls away as Dad hovers behind her. He draws his brows together, repeatedly rubbing his face. I instantly notice how disheveled he looks, not like the usually well-groomed Lex Edwards the world is used to seeing. Of course, he's dressed in a navy suit, but his tie has been removed, and the shirt beneath looks creased.

"Hey, Dad."

Mom touches his arm to comfort him. Then he moves closer to me as I wrap my arms around him. Inside his embrace, I bask in the familiarity, thanking my lucky stars they're both here. Finally, we both pull away, but he lingers close by, sweeping the hair away from my forehead.

"You had us worried, sweetheart."

"I know." I sigh, then faintly smile. "I had me worried too."

The door opens again, but this time, Austin walks

through. The moment my eyes lay on him, I breathe a sigh of relief he is still around. As much as I love my family, seeing him brings a sense of calm.

He moves to my other side for Mom to ask about the condition of the baby.

"She's doing well and weighing heavier than expected for her age."

"And her heart?" Dad questions.

"Beating perfectly," Austin assures him. "Our focus is her lungs. She's on the ventilator right now. We're closely monitoring how she progresses before we can remove it."

"When can I see her?"

Austin's mouth curves upward, and his reassuring smile is enough for me to relax for just a moment.

"Right now, if you're up for it. She's due for a feed."

"Feed?" I ask, unsure what I'm supposed to do. "As in breastfeed?"

"There's a lactation nurse on hand. She can help teach you how to position the baby to latch on."

In the corner of the room sits a wheelchair. Will brings it over, and Austin and Dad help me transfer from the bed to the wheelchair. My legs are like jelly, unable to stand on their own. A simple task like moving is so much harder than I think.

Austin wheels me down the corridor to the NICU as my family follows. We reach the door, which instructs us to stop and protect ourselves before entering. Mom helps me with a gown, sanitizes my hands, and fits me with a mask.

"One person can come in with you," Austin informs me.

I turn to look at my parents. Dad nods with a smile. "Take your mother in. She can help you with the baby."

"Are you sure?" Mom asks, knowing how tight my bond is with Dad.

"Of course, Charlotte."

Mom follows the protocol as well, dressing in a gown and sanitizing her hands. Then, when her mask is on, Austin wheels me to the incubator in the middle of the room as she follows.

With each step he takes, our baby comes to full view.

I stare in awe at this tiny baby lying inside the heated incubator. Inside my head, I count the fingers and toes—ten and ten—just perfect.

It's hard to believe that she was inside of me only a few short hours ago, and now she's here living and breathing.

Austin places his hand on the incubator. "You ready to hold her?"

Nodding, I then watch as Austin carefully removes her. He does so with such delicacy, and when she's in his arms, I take a moment to admire our little girl being held by her daddy.

My arms shift into position while Austin slowly places her in my arms. The second she's in my embrace, my heart gushes with a warm sensation and this burst of over-whelming love I've never experienced in my life.

"She's so little," I whisper, touching her fingers.

Austin crouches down, so he's at my level. We both stare into her face, mesmerized by this tiny human who is ours. Never in my wildest dreams could I ever imagine what it would feel like to hold my baby for the first time. I want to capture this moment for the rest of my life, catalog it in my memories. And to think, my mother did this four times.

"Congratulations to you both," Mom says with a proud smile. "Have you thought about a name?"

I have my own ideas, but nothing stands out when I look at her. Nothing is worthy of this beautiful little girl in my arms.

"I have a name," Austin murmurs. "It's not conventional."

"What is it?" I breathe in anticipation.

"Emerald," Austin begins with a wistful stare. "It was actually my great-grandmother's name. Though people actually called her Emmy for short."

My eyes fall upon our daughter's face.

Emerald—I can't think of a more perfect name.

"It's beautiful, Austin."

"Plus, you know she'll have emerald eyes, right?"

A grin spreads across my face. "How do you know? She hasn't opened her eyes yet?"

"Because, Ava, the Edwards' gene is strong."

I wish she would open her eyes, but as she continues to sleep peacefully in my arms, I can't help but think just how perfect this moment is.

"Emerald Charlotte Carter," I say out loud.

"Oh, honey," Mom almost chokes, "you don't have to."

I look up at Austin, his gaze so loving and pure. "Needs one more adjustment..."

"Oh?" Me and Mom mouth at the same time.

"Emerald Charlotte Edwards-Carter," Austin tells us. "The full circle."

TWENTY-TWO

AUSTIN

It's not unusual for laboring women to arrive at the ER almost every day. During my time working at this hospital, I've assisted in multiple deliveries that never made it to the delivery suite.

I just never expected Ava to be the one to walk through those doors and with Romano out of all people.

And at only thirty-four weeks gestation.

There was no time to even get angry at Will for arguing with Ava. It was my job to remain calm throughout the whole ordeal.

No matter what the team tried, nothing was going to stop this baby from coming. Ava had dilated, ready to push.

And that she did, at exactly 10:47 a.m.

The hardest part of being inside the room was controlling this overwhelming feeling of unconditional love for our baby while battling the statistics I know come with premature babies. Thankfully, she checked out healthy in all areas we were concerned about.

Ava finally gets to feed Emmy, and I'm glad we both agreed to the name. In fact, Ava thought it fit her perfectly.

Emerald Charlotte Edwards-Carter.

My daughter.

It still feels surreal.

The lactation nurse assists Ava with nursing as I watch on, trying to retain the information but mesmerized by our baby enjoying her first feed. Ava's milk is yet to come in though it doesn't stop her from feeding.

"How does it feel?"

Ava purses her lips. "Weird. How long does a woman breastfeed for?"

"It's completely up to the individual," I inform her.

Charlie shuffles beside us, stroking Emmy's hair gently. "You and Amelia were about six months. With Addison, I suffered from mastitis, so she pretty much went straight to formula. As for Alexa, she was about a year."

Ava laughs faintly. "Addison is the smart one. Maybe the experts are wrong? Breastfeeding doesn't equal intelligence. I mean, look at Alexa."

Charlie presses her lips flat, trying to hide her smirk. "Alexa is gifted in other areas."

"Texting friends doesn't count, Mom," Ava quips.

Ava mentioned Alexa going through her wild phase, leaving the sordid details out of our conversation. At the time, I laughed, thinking Lex had it tough. But then it dawns on me that I have a daughter now, and I will probably be in Lex's position one day.

Suddenly, it's no longer a laughing matter.

The moment I held my daughter, I knew I'd never be the same. She instilled this confidence in me to become a better person. To be a role model and give her the best life possible.

And going through this experience made me look at Ava differently.

To watch a woman go through the birth of a child, and that child being your own, is a life-changing moment.

Ava's endurance, determination, and knowing just how much pain she was in delivering our beautiful daughter, she deserves only the best, but with everything going on, our moments in private are far and few between.

As the days wear on, Lex and Charlie are with Ava almost all day, every day. Will and Millie left the day after Emmy was born as they didn't want to leave their son alone for too long.

We somewhat called a truce, though not verbally agreeing to anything. I have no issues with their relationship. I just don't want Ava subjected to any more negativity nor criticized for her involvement with me.

There's a stream of visitors, including my parents, who flew over. As much as I want to spend more time with them, I am already juggling work and trying to support Ava.

On the day of Emmy's birth, my supervising doctor was more than accommodating, allowing me to spend the day up in the maternity ward. However, the next day, it was back to usual.

Whenever I have a break, plus before and after my shift, I sneak upstairs to check on Emmy and her progress, then pop my head in to see how Ava is going.

Despite my dissapproval, I barely manage to get her alone, especially when Eric insists on setting up his office in Ava's room.

"I'm keeping her company." Eric tries to justify with an intimidating stare.

"Just make sure she gets some rest."

"Of course, Dr. Carter. So..." Eric claps his hands with a cheerful smile. "Show me the room where all the doctors are getting a quick bam bam, thank you, ma'am."

"Eric," Ava scolds, tilting her head. "Is it that room marked private near the elevator? I swear I heard something."

I shake my head at the two of them. "Believe it or not, we're all professionals."

Both Eric and Ava roll their eyes at the same time they release an exaggerated groan.

"You're telling me that out of all the hot doctors roaming around this hospital, no one is even getting any fellatus?"

Ava bursts out laughing. "Just because you say it in Latin doesn't make it any less crass, Eric."

Eric beams with an upturned gaze. "I can imagine it now, two hot doctors, cloaks ripped off, stethoscope falls to the ground..."

"Oh, my God, stop," Ava chastises, throwing her hands to cover her face. "It's disturbing, and I'm pretty certain I'll never have sex again because stitches mean something tore, and I really don't want to know what exactly."

"Well, honey," Eric begins, fixing his cufflinks at the same time. "You can start off with a small wiener. You know, get that pencil in you before you transition to the king-sized sharpie."

"Eric, your analogy is next level. Actually, I don't even have words for you right now."

Quickly checking Ava's chart, I hide my smirk over this ridiculous conversation.

"Your tear will heal," I advise her in a serious tone, not wanting her to think I'm desperate to fuck her. "You'll be able to have sex again when it's safe to do so after six weeks."

Eric raises his finger to his lips. "But with who, exactly? So what are you saying? Technically, Miss Edwards is able to perform the act of fellatus on, let's say, a man who is in desperate need. Perhaps, hasn't had any activity for months..."

I check my watch as Ava drops her head, trying to cover her grin.

"Would you look at the time? I need to head back now." I lean in, quickly kissing Ava on the forehead. "Make sure Eric behaves, please. I don't want security scouring the halls wondering why the storage closet is locked again."

Eric's mouth falls open, his eyes widening. "Storage closet! I knew there was a place."

As I close the door behind me and begin my walk back to the ER, my phone buzzes inside my pocket. I pull it out to read a text from Ava.

Ava: *Ignore Eric. He is not getting laid since Tristan is back in LA for the week.*

Me: *His obsession with the word 'fellatus' is oddly disturbing*

Ava: *A simple blow job should suffice.*

Bowing my head inside the elevator, I forget what a blow job feels like since it's been forever. Not to mention Ava and I have never officially engaged that way.

Me: *It should. It would.*

Ava: *Well played, Dr. Carter. I walked into that. See you after your shift.*

∾

My parents left for a quick weekend away in Montauk before heading back to LA. I'm somewhat relieved they left since juggling the baby and Ava's family—is beginning to take its toll. Everyone has an opinion on everything, and I'm not used to being surrounded by so much family.

Inside the breakout room, I stretch my arms, then crack my neck, desperate to alleviate the stress. My hands reach out for the coffee machine, but I retreat since I've already drunk multiple cups.

Today tested me with a patient admitted with multiple bullet wounds. We tried our best to revive the man who remained under police guard, but in the end, his injuries were too horrific.

His teenage children wept in the corridor, the trauma too much to handle as they apparently witnessed the whole aftermath.

Closing my eyes, I intake a breath, and when I open them again, Ava's face comes to mind. For the last week, it's been weighing on my mind where we go from here. Ava's treating doctor advised she can be discharged on Monday with Emmy. Everything is progressing nicely, and as long as Emmy continues her routine check-ups, she doesn't see the need for either one of them to stay any longer.

The news is great, and although I'm yet to tell Ava, there is the matter of where we stand.

I don't want Ava to be alone, knowing she needs support. But where does that leave us?

Aside from the constant visitors, Ava spends any free moment she has in the NICU. When she returns to her room, she always falls asleep.

I just need her to be alone, to confess how I feel, and ask her if she would consider living together. The thought of being apart from Emmy leaves me unsettled. I don't want to miss her milestones because it isn't my day to take care of her.

But things are complicated.

If I bring this up, and Ava agrees, there's no turning back.

This isn't a break-up-get-back-together situation. We have a child to consider, and we can't play Russian roulette with our relationship.

Also, Ava's emotions have been somewhat heightened of late. So it really could go either way.

"Hey, stranger," a voice says behind me.

I swiftly turn around to see Lane. It's been a few weeks since I saw her last. Our shifts never rostered at the same time.

"Hey yourself."

"Rumor has it you had a baby?"

I nod with a proud smile, leaning back against the locker. "Yes, she came early."

"Congratulations," Lane offers, then grins. "You know, a bunch of the new nurses are deeply disappointed you're in a relationship."

"The girls in the geriatric ward?"

Lane laughs, crossing her arms, still dressed in her scrubs. "Yeah, there was some pool on who could get into bed with you first."

I drop my head to chuckle, then rub my face. "How do you know all this?"

"Hmm, the gossip train moves fast. They somehow found out we were together and, um, wanted specifics on, your um... anatomy."

My lips press together, unsure of what to say. "I'm not sure how to respond to that, but Ava and I are just co-parenting right now."

Lane watches me attentively, her lips twisting with sympathy.

"Austin, when are you just going to tell her you love her? You have a family now, and this isn't some fling."

"It's not that simple, Lane," I tell her, honestly. "We have this history, and Ava isn't like anyone else. I don't want to push her, not when she has a history of fleeing when she loses interest."

"You think Ava will lose interest in you?"

"You don't know her like I do," I mumble.

"I don't, but I do know that it's not possible to lose interest in Austin Carter. You're a great guy, and you will be an amazing father," Lane admits, keeping her gaze fixed with a warm smile. "Now, any chance I can meet your daughter?"

"Sure, I was just about to go there myself."

We leave the breakout room and chat on our way up to the NICU. Our conversations usually revolve around work. That is when we do run into each other and have time to chat.

Upon arriving at the NICU, we follow protocol then enter, where I lead her to the incubator.

"Oh, Austin," Lane murmurs, her eyes lighting up. "She's beautiful."

"Can't argue with that. She's progressing nicely, and if all goes well, she should be able to go home on Monday."

"You must be so relieved."

"I am. It's been a stressful week. I would have liked to take time off, but we're too busy, and my leave is scheduled for when the baby was supposed to be due."

Lane has a look at the chart, reading some of the information which we discuss in more detail.

A noise interrupts our conversation, prompting me to

turn around. Ava is standing a few feet away, dressed in her blue silk pajamas. She must have just showered as her hair is still wet yet brushed neatly to the side.

Ava stares at Lane and me with a pinched expression, crossing her arms beneath her chest.

"Sorry, I didn't mean to interrupt the two of you."

"Of course you didn't. We were just discussing her breathing levels." I tilt my head, questioning Ava's mood. "You remember Lane, don't you?"

Ava forces a smile. "How could I forget?"

I check my watch, noting the time. "Are you here to feed?"

She turns away with a slight nod and sits in the recliner while the nurse removes Emmy from the incubator, then places her in Ava's arms. Lane quickly says goodbye to head over to the cardiac ward to check on a patient.

Ava shuffles, trying to get comfortable while unbuttoning her top. Her milk came in a few days ago, and since then, Ava's breasts grew to double the size. They are impossible to ignore, and if anything, look extremely uncomfortable.

In her arms, Emmy appears to be fussy and not latching on.

"C'mon, baby girl," Ava cries in frustration. "Why don't you want to feed?"

Leaning down, I stroke Emmy's cheek to relax her. She begins to suck as Ava breathes a sigh of relief, closing her eyes momentarily.

"Oh, thank God."

"Better?" I ask, trying to soothe her.

Ava is exhausted, which doesn't surprise me. Her body has undergone so many changes over the last week, and it's usual for a woman's hormones to be unbalanced after giving birth.

"Does Lane always work the same shift as you?"

I purse my lips and shake my head. "No, sometimes we cross paths, but not daily."

She shifts her gaze back onto Emmy, avoiding my eyes. I sense her jealousy, though it's ludicrous given I broke it off with Lane months ago. This is the last thing she should be worrying about.

"You know, Ava. We haven't had much time to talk in private, but when I said I was falling in love with you a week ago, I meant it."

Ava releases a breath, then slowly, she glances up until our eyes finally meet.

"I just... " she trails off, then continues, "... when I see her with you, something stirs within me. I can't explain it."

I lower my body, bending my knees until our faces are at the same level. My fingers reach out for her cheek, gently stroking it. Ava sighs softly as I lean in to place a kiss on her lips.

Albeit brief, her kiss is pure and everything I need.

"We'll work this out, okay? But right now, we need to take our baby home and learn how to raise a child together."

Ava nods, a slow smile escaping her. "Mom said my apartment is ready. Your mom helped her wash all the baby clothes and set up the diaper table."

"That sounds like Mom," I tell her while grinning. "So, Monday is the big day. I'll try to swap my shift so we can leave together. How does that sound?"

Ava touches my face, never breaking her gaze. "It sounds perfect, Austin."

I stay for a few minutes before my pager goes off. The

emergency beeping means they need me downstairs immediately.

"I have to go," I quickly advise, despite my desperate need to go home and sleep. "Sorry, they've got multiple trauma cases arriving."

"Go," she says, then leans over to kiss me one more time. "Do what you need to do. Emmy and I will be just fine."

Standing up to leave, I stop, then lean down to kiss her one more time.

"Keep thinking the things you're thinking," I whisper with a simper.

Ava grins knowingly. "I will, Dr. Carter. Promise I won't stop."

TWENTY-THREE

AVA

Everything I have ever learned about being a mother up to this point is a lie.

The movies, the articles, and even these stupid books which people *insisted* I read.

No one tells you what happens after you give birth. First, there are the stitches down below and the mere thought of a needle being used to sew up a vagina. There's the struggle to use the toilet, worried you'll tear something. Then, to the airplane-sized pads you're forced to wear because of the continuous bleeding.

As someone who has only experienced light menstrual bleeding, this is a shock in itself.

The body aches, and my limbs are sore. And let's not forget my breasts—they're enormous. My nipples look like they belong on a cover of *National Geographic*. All I'm missing is a grass skirt and a jungle background.

Another thing people forget to disclose is when your milk comes in, it is excruciating, and there is no other way to explain it. One minute, I'm barely able to squeeze the colostrum from them. To the next, they're pouring out like an overflowing river of milk.

It means my diet had to change because everything I eat or drink is passed onto Emmy.

But aside from my body feeling like a punching bag, Emmy has decided that sleeping at night is for the weak.

Why sleep when you can cry instead?

The nights are the hardest, feeding in solitude while trying not to fall asleep at the same time. She doesn't wake up just once a night but more like four to five times. The longest stretch of sleep is from four in the morning to about seven. Three glorious straight hours of sleep before the sun rises and we're up again.

I lose track of days, almost every day feeling like Groundhog Day.

Mom staying with me has helped so much. With her experience and knowledge, she suggests we work on getting Emmy to sleep for longer stretches by recommending we bathe her at night and then finish with two feeds. Mom said that the first feed after a bath is usually short because the baby is too tired. The downfall, the baby will wake up really hungry in a few hours.

So that's what we do, bathe Emmy around seven in the evening followed by a quick feed so she sleeps to about eleven. When she wakes around that time, she drinks much more, which changes the way she sleeps. We've started noticing she goes straight through until about four in the morning, giving me some relief.

"No wonder you had four kids," I utter to Mom as we sit on the sofa while I feed Emmy. "You're a pro at this. Just getting those few extra hours of sleep feels like heaven."

"It'll get easier when you have more kids."

"More kids?" I raise my brows, then tuck in my upper lip. "I think I'm done."

Mom chuckles softly. "That's what every woman says. Just wait. One day you'll surprise yourself when you yearn to hold a baby in your arms, and you miss the newborn smell."

Leaning in, I inhale Emmy's scent. Something about it is so pure, a mix of baby products and something else I can't quite figure out.

"I guess you have to be married to make that happen for the second time."

Mom wraps her hand around the warm cup, blowing the steam away to take a sip of her coffee. *God, what I'd give for coffee right now.*

"Austin is a good man and a great father," she begins with, then stalls, waiting for my reaction. "You know I've always been fond of him, and your father respects Austin."

"But?"

"No buts, honey. I just want you to know that whichever way you decide to take your relationship with Austin, we're here to support you."

My gaze falls upon Emmy, the sweet little angel in my arms. She's grown a lot and making these cute sounds which sometimes can sound like she's sighing.

"He's a good guy, great, in fact. It's just not that easy, Mom. There are so many things going on, not to mention Millie's history with him. I just think our emotions can sometimes be clouded amongst the chaos."

Mom nods quietly, her eyes brightening as she appears to be reflecting.

"My entire life has been chaos since the moment I fell in love with your father. Nothing we did was conventional. We didn't date, as you know, he was my best friend's older brother and married at the time. Then, eight years later, when our paths crossed, I was engaged to Julian. Our timing was never right, but perhaps in hindsight, it's what tested our strength and willingness to fight for one another."

"But did you doubt yourself? Wondering if you were worthy of the man you fell in love with?"

A fond smile spreads across Mom's face. "I mean, all the time. The great Lex Edwards? C'mon, every woman wants him. So, why me? What made me so special?"

"I'm sure, if you ask Dad... " I say with a smile, then continue, "... he'd say, the great Charlotte Mason? Why would she want a controlling and jealous billionaire like me?"

We both laugh, releasing a sigh at the same time.

"God, he loves you, Mom. I've never ever seen him even bat an eye or look at another woman. He worships the ground you walk on. When you've grown up watching how a man should treat a woman, it sets your own expectations really high."

"Your father and I aren't perfect. We've grown together. But, Ava, you must understand that fairy tales are just that. Love can be hard work. Sometimes, when we love so hard, we make wrong decisions. My point is, don't be afraid to give your heart away, but also don't expect that if you do, it's a guaranteed happily ever after. You've got to fight hard, and that's what will strengthen the bond between you and the man you love. Just like when you see him fighting just as hard for you."

Mom gives me a lot to think about, and perhaps what she says is true. I've grown up reading fairy tales, thinking that once you fall in love, it's a guaranteed happily ever after. The hard work is done, right?

But those closest to me are prime examples of how

falling in love isn't easy. Will and Millie's story sticks out the most, mainly because it doesn't feel like so long ago. Things would have been a lot different if they didn't break up and Will didn't move to London. Though, just like Mom said, they fought hard to be together, and it was all about timing, especially for them.

During Mom's stay, I welcome our chats over tea and coffee. However, with Austin working nights and some-times double shifts, he usually only has an hour to spend with Emmy before going home to crash. I begin to see just how exhausted he is, and so with that, I don't put any pres-sure on him to talk about us so he can focus on bonding with Emmy.

Yet like all good things, Mom needs to go home. So with her bags packed, she extends her arms to bring me in for a hug.

"I'm going to miss you, Mom. This whole parent gig is full-on."

"You're telling me, kid," she answers with a grin. "Twenty-five years later, and I'm still fussing over you."

"Twenty-six next week."

"Of course. My baby girl just keeps on growing."

I laugh. "You're just as bad as Dad. But honestly, Mom, thank you for everything."

"Anytime, honey. Think about coming to visit or stay a bit with us, okay?"

I nod with a smile. "I will, Mom."

~

"Happy birthday!"

Eric and Nikki are at my door, not even waiting for a

'come in' and just barging into my apartment with their hands full of gifts.

Nikki is wearing a beautiful olive Dior dress. I recognize it from the summer collection. She's never one to dress casually, always looking like a runway model and half her actual age. People often think she is Will's sister. That's how youthful she looks.

As for Eric, he's dressed in his well-pressed Burberry suit, and his hair strategically styled to the side with not a single strand out of place.

"Thank you, guys. You didn't have to."

"Are you kidding me? This is just a small portion of the gifts which have arrived today. Your office is covered in presents, and sweetie, your designer bag heart is going to literally *come* when you see what you've been given."

"Um, sure." I laugh, glad to have Eric here to lighten my mood. "I spy a pink bag in your hands?"

Nikki and Eric look at each other with a mischievous grin, then sing in unison Happy Birthday. They pass the bag over, insisting I see what's inside.

Removing the white tissue paper first, I then reach in and pull out a black lace one-piece which is entirely transparent. The bikini line is high, and when I tilt my head, I notice the split in the crotch, which I can only assume was designed on purpose.

"Okay, wow. Nice, for someone getting laid," I tell them, forcing a smile.

"There's more," Eric coerces. "C'mon, you'll love it."

I then pull out a clitoral vibrator-looking thing, nipple clamps, anal plug, and strawberry flavored lube.

"You guys shouldn't have." I try my best to hide my sarcasm because let's face it, I'm not fucking Austin nor anyone else right now, despite my hormones raging like a bull with a red flag being waved.

"Oh, it's all our pleasure," Nikki sneers with a lick of her lips. "And yours soon, now that Mommy has left the building and gone back to LA."

I shake my head, placing the gifts back into the bag. "It's not like that. We're co-parenting."

"Maybe it's time to co-parent his ding-a-ling?" Eric remarks, followed by his lips pressing together while deliberately cocking his head.

"I take it back. That tops the list of disturbing things you've said. Emmy is our priority, end of the story."

I don't want to admit to either one of them that I've been thinking a lot about Austin and his so-called ding-a-ling. *Damn Eric!* Rephrase, beautiful cock, from what I remember. It's gotten to the point of being so highly aroused, I'm unable to take a decent shower without extending the shower head between my legs for some relief.

But it's only been four weeks since I gave birth, and I'm terrified of sex hurting or even an orgasm hurting me.

"Where's my little girl?" Nikki moves toward the bassinet, which I wheeled into the living room. Slowly, she removes her from it and cradles Emmy in her arms. "I miss the baby smell. Ashton feels so big now, and when I hug him, he wriggles out because Rocky is his favorite."

"Funny that," I mention with a slight chuckle. "Ashton won't let go of Dad either. Must be a boy thing."

"Honey, if Lex could hold me, I'd be running to him too," Eric tells us.

I scrunch my nose. "Too far, Eric. Too far."

"How is Austin coping with being a new dad?" Nikki asks, followed by a coo as Emmy slowly opens her eyes.

"Okay, I guess. He's been working nights. So after he

showers and changes, he comes over for two hours, and then ends up crashing, to then get up and go to work."

Eric and Nikki both look at each other, like a secret lies between them. But, I swear, the two of them together do my head in at times.

"What?"

"Why doesn't he just move in?" Eric asks

"He said it... " Nikki blurts out, "... not me."

"Because we haven't spoken about anything."

Eric sighs heavily with exaggeration. "Why not?"

"Why not? Because we just had a baby."

"That was four weeks ago."

"Yeah, and having a baby isn't easy," I inform him, annoyed he thinks I'm sitting around here doing nothing. "It's exhausting."

"Eric, give her a break," Nikki chastises. "Besides, once the hormones get a hold of you, good luck."

"What hormones?" I ask, pretending I have no clue what she's talking about.

Nikki laughs. "The ones which make you think about dick twenty-four-seven."

"She said it..." Eric blurts out this time, "... not me."

I intake a deep breath, not wanting to delve into this topic since every time I bring it up in my head, I end up at a dead end. Still horny, of course.

"I have an idea," Nikki begins, then continues, "it's your birthday. How about Eric and I stay here for a few hours to take care of Emmy? Why don't you put something nice on and go to the office to open all your fabulous gifts? You've got extra milk stored in the fridge?"

"Yes, I pumped only an hour ago. I have about a weeks' worth of milk stored in the fridge."

"Great," Nikki announces with an overbearing grin. "I'm sure a small break won't hurt you."

"I could," I admit, then smile slowly. "But I'll only be gone for a few short hours. I don't know how I feel about leaving her."

"Absence makes the heart grow fonder," Eric sings with an over-joyed expression. "Let's go find you a fabulous birthday outfit."

Eric's mission in life is to make everyone look fabulous. So he picks out a sweetheart neck Dolce & Gabbana dress hanging in my closet, which surprisingly fits. Aside from one massive problem, and when I say massive, I mean my breasts.

They are really popping out.

"Oh, honey, that rack of yours. I'd come in my pants if I were a straight man."

"Ew," I say with a scowl. "Great for motorboating if I had someone to drive the boat."

Eric bursts out into laughter. "Oh, child, I've taught you well."

As difficult as it is to say goodbye, I leave my apartment, though I contemplate going back inside the elevator and upstairs when the overwhelm hits, and it feels wrong to leave Emmy.

However, when I exit the building, into the beautiful fresh air and sound of the city, a sigh of relief washes over me.

Freedom.

I take a cab to my office, and upon entering the building again, it feels like a breath of fresh air. My heels click against the marble floor, a simple sound that instills confidence in me—something I've battled with my entire pregnancy.

When I reach my floor, my team is standing in the foyer to then yell, "Happy Birthday!"

There are plenty of hugs and presents given. A table sits in the middle with food plus a giant birthday cake. Champagne is handed out, and I quickly google if I'm allowed to drink. One glass is supposed to be okay if I wait two hours to feed. I also read up on pumping and dumping, though the information is conflicted. I decide maybe half a glass is safer, plus a pump and dump just to be sure.

Eric isn't wrong in his description of the gifts. Every company I've ever worked with has sent me a gift—plenty of designer names. I quickly ask my marketing team to organize photos and thank you cards to make sure we credit and give thanks where due.

After spending two hours in the office, socializing and incorporating some work, I decide to head home.

As I sit in the cab, reliving what a wonderful day it's been, my mind wanders to Austin.

"Sir, change of address, please."

I give the driver Austin's address, which thankfully is only a slight detour.

Inside Austin's building, I knock on the door for Jonah to open up.

"Hey, Ava," Jonah greets, to then scan the area around me. "Where's Emmy?"

"With my aunt and friend. Is Austin around?"

"Yeah, sure. Come in."

I follow Jonah inside, only for him to throw a bag over his shoulder. "He's in the shower. He should be out soon. I'll catch you later. I've got a photoshoot with Andy, which I'm late for."

With a smile, I forgot Jonah worked along with Andy. Apparently, Jonah was studying medicine which is how he met Austin, but he changed his mind to pursue a creative career.

He closes the door behind him, leaving me alone in the apartment.

Pacing the living room with my phone in hand, I don't want to sit down nor interrupt Austin. My phone has been buzzing all day with calls and messages, so I take the opportunity to respond to everyone. Millie is the worst offender, uploading all these baby photos of me onto her social media, and in almost every photo, I'm crying beside her while she has a devilish grin on her face.

> **Me:** *You're going to pay for those pictures. Wait until it's your birthday. I'm going to whip out that video of you when you were two and you pooped in the bathtub.*

> **Millie:** *You wouldn't dare!*

> **Me:** *Game on, sis.*

With a grin spreading across my face, a noise forces me to glance up. Austin is standing a few feet away with only a towel wrapped around his waist. His chest is completely dry, standing out so gloriously with his defined six-pack and that V part.

Stop looking, now.

My eyes quickly divert to his face, where I can see him staring at my chest with a tortured expression.

"If it isn't the birthday girl," he says with the corner of his mouth curled up into a smirk. "I was just about to head over to see you."

"Nikki and Eric insisted on taking care of Emmy for a

few hours, so I could go to the office. They didn't tell me the team had organized a mini party. There was champagne."

"Hmm," he mouths, moving closer, which causes my breath to hitch. "It would explain why your cheeks are flushed."

"It was only half a glass. I googled what was safe, just in case you get all doctor on me. Besides, I pumped enough for Emmy to drink tonight, so yeah..." I rush, my temperature suddenly rising. "Do you mind if I have some water? It's awfully hot in here."

I don't even wait for an answer, moving to the kitchen, where I grab a bottle of water from the refrigerator. Somehow, I manage to twist the lid off and gulp down a fair amount. When I turn around to close the door, Austin is only inches away.

"So tell me, what does the birthday girl want?"

He smells so fresh like soap and aftershave. Between my legs, a persistent throb makes it challenging to get my words out. What did I want? *For him to fuck me like I'm the last woman on earth.*

"Honestly, Austin. You don't need to get me anything. I have everything I want."

Austin leans closer, tilting his head so his lips are close to my ear. "I would hate to think you have everything you want. Otherwise, that would mean another man has touched you."

My chest tightens with Austin's deep, prolonged stare into my eyes. I trail my finger down his chest, unable to stop myself from reaching out to touch him.

"I promise you no one else has touched me," I murmur, biting down on my lip to control my urges. "But I lied. I don't have everything I want."

Austin's gaze falls upon my lips. "What does the birthday girl want?"

I'm done with waiting and done with playing it safe. What do I have to lose, anyway? Without a second thought, I grab his hand to guide him between my legs. When his fingers graze against my clit, I intake a sharp breath.

His fingers sit above my panties, rubbing at a slow and agonizing pace. I throw my arms around his neck for my lips to crash against his. Austin's tongue is smooth, causing me to moan in amidst of our heated kiss. His breathing is heavy when he pulls back, but he never stops the motion between my legs.

"I think... " he begins with, keeping his voice low, "... that the birthday girl is in desperate need to come."

Nodding, I'm unable to even scream the words 'fuck yes.'

"But I want to hear it," Austin demands while grazing my lobe with his teeth. "I want you to look me in the eye and tell me exactly what you want me to do."

He pulls back, so we're face to face, and with my breathing growing fast and more audible, my eyes focus on his.

"I want you between my legs. I need to feel your fingers rub against my clit and bring me to an orgasm. I want you, Austin, that's all I've been thinking about, and it's driving me insane."

With a smirk playing on his lips, he moves his fingers into my panties, causing me to moan at his touch.

"Good girl. If you ask, you shall receive."

His fingers move on their own accord as my whole body reacts with pleasure. Then, with his head buried in my neck, he kisses beneath my ear. "I've been only thinking about you, Ava. I remember how amazing it felt to be inside you. Thinking about all the things I want to do to your body. You drive me fucking crazy all the time."

"Austin." I gulp, throwing my head back against the refrigerator. "I'm close..."

"Come for me... now," he commands with grit in his voice.

Closing my eyes tight, I feel the sensations tear throughout my entire body, and the euphoria spreads to every inch, causing me to ache in delight. My moans become louder until my breath gets stuck to become a heightened groan. My breathing is uneven, and my throat raspy and dry.

I open my eyes to see this beautiful man with a very satisfied smile on his face. But then, my eyes fall upon his perfectly sculpted chest, and the ache between my legs begins to throb again.

"It is my birthday, and you said I could have anything I want."

"Hmm," he murmurs, brushing his thumb against my lip. "I did say that."

My fingers run down his chest until they reach the top of his towel. Then, swiftly, I tug to remove it as his cock springs free.

With my hands placed on his hips, I lick my lips then whisper, "I want you in my mouth. If the birthday girl asks, she shall receive."

Austin expels a grunt, smashing his lips onto mine. "Get down and suck my cock, birthday girl. I've been waiting a long time for this."

TWENTY-FOUR

AUSTIN

My hand wraps around Ava's hair, pulling the ponytail as she kneels on the kitchen floor to suck my cock.

The muscles in my body tense while I try to control myself from blowing straight away, desperate to devour every moment her mouth takes me in, to the sheer desire in her eyes as she watches me from below.

I've fantasized of precisely this moment, more than I care to admit, even in the shower before I knew she was in my apartment. But dreams are sometimes so far off reality, and in this case—reality is so much better.

Her mouth opens wide, with the corners building up in saliva. I get off on the sound it makes, groaning each time her tongue circles the tip of my cock.

Pulling her hair back, I guide myself inside her until she wraps her hand around my shaft and leans back against the refrigerator, eyes wide with a wicked smirk playing on her lips.

"What do you have for me, birthday girl?" I tease,

waiting in anticipation as my cock stands hard in front of her.

At a slow and agonizing pace, she strokes my cock, and just when I think I will come this way, she opens her mouth wide to take me in.

All in.

The tip of my cock hits the back of her throat, causing my body to jerk in pleasure.

"Fuck," I moan.

Ava doesn't stop, taking me in deeper until my body stiffens, and I warn her gently I'm going to come so she can take me out.

But she doesn't.

She continues to take me deep in her throat as the sensation tears through me, and I spill into her mouth, my eyes closing as a grunt follows.

My heart is beating at a rapid rate, and I'm barely able to focus, seeing stars and slightly dizzy. With my hand resting against the door, I try to control my breathing as Ava slides back up.

"Are you okay?" She grins, licking her lips like the naughty girl she is. "You look somewhat disorientated."

Lacing my hand around her neck, I bring her in for a deep kiss. The taste of her tongue is sweet, and I get off on knowing she's swallowed without me even demanding it.

"You're perfect."

She places her hands on my chest with a small laugh. "What makes me perfect? The deep-throating or the fact that I swallowed without you asking?"

I'm unable to hide the smile on my face, staring into her eyes with a need to strip her naked and do whatever possible to her body.

"Both, all of it. You, your sexy body. You're driving me crazy, Ava Edwards."

Her eyes fall upon my cock, noticing it's hard again.

"As much as I'd love to take you in my mouth again, unfortunately, I have to go home because mama's breasts are on the verge of exploding," she informs me while tracing her fingers down my abs. "But, if you're willing to come home with me, I'm sure we can find something to do later. You did say the birthday girl gets what she wants, right?"

I press my mouth on hers and pull back with a grin. "The birthday girl is awfully demanding today, but I'm not complaining. Give me a few minutes to get changed, and I'll come with you."

"That's the plan." She winks.

～

"Well, well, well." Eric welcomes us with a knowing smile. "If it isn't, Daddy and Mommy, all happy-looking. Rejuvenated, if anything. Like something came over them."

Nikki lowers her head with a smirk. "Thirty years I've known you, Eric, and you still manage to surprise me."

"How was the afternoon?" Eric questions, examining the both of us a little too closely.

"Good. I went to the office, ate cake, and opened gifts," Ava casually mentions. "I even drank some champagne. Albeit, small but still nice."

"Uh-huh," Eric drags, his stare penetrating. "And then you ran into Austin?"

"Actually, she came to visit me, and I was just hopping out of the shower, you know, wearing a towel because that's what you do when you get out of the shower."

Ava's eyes widen as Eric throws his hand to his neck,

then purposely swallows hard.

"Well, I see it's getting quite warm in here, Dr. Carter. A towel, you said?" Eric begins to fan himself, and I'm enjoying messing with him. "I need to take a seat."

"I'm glad you had a nice afternoon," Nikki says, ignoring Eric's dramatic panting on the sofa. "Emmy is well fed and resting. As for us, we need to leave because we have an important dinner downtown."

Eric raises his brows in concern. "We do?"

Nikki forces a smile, and I sense her desire to leave us alone, which I welcome. "Yes, Mr. Kennedy. The meeting with Jane."

"Jane, who?"

"Oh, for the love of God, Eric." Nikki throws her hands up in the air. "Let these two get some alone time because you can cut the sexual tension with a god damn chain saw."

Eric and Nikki grab their things, wishing Ava happy birthday until Nikki leans into Ava, "Back door, honey. If the front is closed for repairs, take him all in the back."

Ava drops her gaze with a grin, lifting it moments later to meet my relaxed stare.

The moment they leave, I wrap my arms around Ava.

"So, Nikki's advice seems about right."

She smacks my arm playfully. "I need to pump. I'll be back soon."

Ava disappears to the bedroom while I move toward the bassinet and scoop Emmy into my arms. I place a kiss on her forehead, lingering to inhale her baby scent. I saw her two days ago, but even then, Emmy looks like she's grown.

Rocking her gently, I walk around the room, and slowly make my way toward Ava's bedroom. The door is open, and Ava is on the bed trying to type on her phone with two breast pumps pumping milk out of her.

"Don't judge. I'm trying to multi-task."

She places her phone down and removes the two pumps as I place Emmy in her cradle near the bed. Ava set up the apartment so whichever room she is in, Emmy has a place to rest.

I cross my arms with a simper, watching Ava's tits entirely out.

"You know, they're just breasts, Austin. You see them every day at work," she teases.

"I do, but they're your breasts," I say, etching closer to her. "And they're big and perfect..."

I crawl on top of her, moving my hands toward them, desperate to feel them.

"Austin... " Ava breathes, "... stay the night, please. I want you all night long."

My fingers graze her nipple, causing a small amount of milk to drip. Fuck, why did that turn me on?

"Ava, we can't fuck, not yet. I need you to heal properly because once we do, there's no stopping."

She brings my face to hers, crushing her lips onto mine.

"Fine, so you'll fuck me in the ass, then?"

I drop my head, laughing softly. "You're going to kill me. You know that, right?"

Ava slides her hand down my chest, past my abs, then into my jeans, where she grabs my cock.

"I'm tired of lying to myself. I want you to fuck me in whatever way is safe. There, I said it."

We strip off our clothes, turning the lamp on beside the bed while Emmy rests. We don't have long before she wakes up, and while it feels odd to be intimate inside the room with a baby, neither of us stops because of it.

Ava is insatiable, begging me to make her come in every

way possible. I can't get enough, devouring every inch of her but also trying to be mindful not to hurt her.

I'm in love with her boldness, her heated demands, and confidence in her body. When I slide inside her ass, I beg myself not to come straight away.

But she's fucking tight, and nothing screams dirty like a woman begging you to come in her ass.

"Ava," I breathe, trying to slow down my movements to savor this moment. "I want us to come together."

I move her carefully, so she's straddling me reverse cowgirl. Then, with her hair cascading down her back, she leans into me, spreading her legs to play with her pussy.

The angle she's in leans my cock into her ass deeper. I allow Ava to grind at her own pace, not wanting to hurt her. Finally, she warns me with her moans and the pitch of her breath. With a grunt escaping me, the same time I feel her contract around my cock, it causes me to explode inside her.

Once again, I'm barely able to see, my vision a burst of light as my entire body tingles in delight.

We both catch our breaths while I ease myself out of her.

"I'm..." she begins with, to stall, barely able to breathe, "I'm covered in milk."

The bed is a mess, her breasts lactating everywhere.

"Go shower," I tell her. "Just tell me where the sheets are, and I'll clean it up."

Ava informs me to look inside the closet in the laundry room. While she showers, I strip the bed, throw the sheets in the wash, and then make the bed. Emmy stirs, just in time for Ava to come out and feed.

I hop into the shower as well, then keep my boxers on as we lay in bed together while she feeds.

"She's looking more like you," Ava says softly. "Your

hair."

"I think she's going to be all you."

Ava shakes her head with a knowing smile. "She's going to be a daddy's girl, just like me."

As if the Universe is watching us, waiting for the perfect moment to strike, my phone goes off with a text from Lex.

Lex Edwards: *I spoke to John at Cedars-Sinai. He wants to meet with you if you can fly over. I'm arriving tomorrow morning if you want to visit me in my office to chat.*

I quickly read the text, then put my phone away. Lex pulled me aside during his visit, mentioning his contacts at Cedars-Sinai in Beverly Hills. They have a level one trauma center, but the competition to get in is fierce. Transferring mid-residency isn't easy unless, of course, Lex Edwards lends you a hand.

"Is everything okay?" Ava yawns beside me.

I nod, my smile fixed as I watch her feed our daughter. "Just perfect."

Ava and Emmy were fast asleep when I left early this morning. I rushed home to change and grab my things, then made my way into work.

Thankfully, things are quieter today, giving me some time to catch up on paperwork and get my head together. Yesterday with Ava was amazing, but neither one of us talked about the future, too caught up in devouring each other's bodies like animals in the wild.

A few patients are admitted with minor injuries and one older man who suffered from a stroke. Even with a few colleagues off sick, we still manage to stay on top of things.

"You have a minute?" Lane is beside me at the desk, her face less than pleased.

"Sure, is everything okay?"

"Yeah, I mean for me. I just want to make sure you're okay?"

"I'm fine. Why do you ask?"

"I don't want to show you here. The nurses are all watching."

Lane motions for me to follow her into the storage closet because it's true, the nurses are known for gossiping, which drives me insane because we all have better things to do.

She pulls her phone out of her pocket, clicks on something then turns the screen around to show me.

"What am I looking at?"

"Read it."

It's an article on an entertainment website with a picture of me, Ava, and Emmy in her carrier. Given Ava's social media following, I'm not surprised to see this nor care who knows I'm Emmy's father.

"So, what's new? The media are always taking photos of Ava."

Lane purses her lips. "Read below."

There is a photo of Millie and me. This would've been taken years ago. In the photo, she's in my arms, and we're kissing, both of us smiling. The article continues on, dating both those photos to last week.

"The affair between Austin Carter and his ex-Amelia Edwards-Romano has torn the family apart. Billionaire, Will

Romano, is said to be livid at the breakdown of his marriage, and close friends of the family have said Amelia has never stopped loving Austin, devastated to learn her sister fell pregnant with his child."

My blood boils as my teeth grit from the anger festering inside of me. I pass the phone back to Lane.

"So what? It's one fucking article."

Lane drops her head. "It's not one, Austin. It's all over social media. I'm sorry."

I kick the bucket in front of me, rage pouring through me at this absolute nonsense. Why the fuck can't people leave us alone? The moment Ava and I are in a good place, people need to destroy it with their greed and jealousy.

"I need to call Ava."

I open the door, but Lane calls my name. "I know they're just rumors, but maybe you should reconsider this. You know, take a break from Ava."

My head tilts, confusion setting in. "Excuse me? You don't just take a break from someone you're in love with. It doesn't work that way, Lane."

Her odd stare is unfamiliar, not like the usual loving and friendly Lane I've grown accustomed to.

"I forgot, Ava Edwards is the rich girl who gets whatever she wants, including someone else's boyfriend," Lane insults, her tone laced with malice.

As I glance at the woman who I once admired, all I can see now is the scales of her slithering skin, and the hiss of her snake-like tongue. Ava was right in questioning my association with her.

"I'd hate to think, Lane, you had anything to do with

this," I tell her coldly. "Jealousy is an ugly disease, and it doesn't look good on you."

Walking out of the room, I lift my gaze to see Ava standing a few feet away. She is dressed in sweats, her hair in a messy bun. Her worried eyes twist in sympathy, and then they shift the moment Lane walks out of the closet as well.

"Ava," I call.

The fire in her eyes burns with a molten rage. I move closer, but she raises her hand.

"Don't you dare," she warns me.

"It's not what you think. None of this is what you think."

"I think you just walked out of the storage closet with your ex. I think it's too hard for you to admit the truth when you're around me because maybe there is a truth to this article, that maybe your feelings for my sister never disappeared."

"You're ridiculous, Ava," I accuse, running my hand through my hair with frustration.

"Maybe I am. That's what happens when you're in love. You don't think straight, and when you see with your own eyes what you've been assuming all along...it only reiterates how stupid I am to think I'm all you'll ever need."

I open my mouth to say something, but she swiftly turns around and runs out down the corridor. My feet don't move, frozen in this one spot.

I should have told her I love her, and she's all I need.

But I'm just as angry, wondering why I'm the god damn villain here when I've done nothing wrong besides love Ava and not push her. I know she's always been quick to run away when the going gets tough, and forgive me for doing the right thing by her.

I desperately want to leave with only an hour left in my shift, but a pregnant woman is admitted at thirty-four weeks, just like Ava, almost fully dilated.

Uncanny timing, of course.

Just another reminder of the Universe playing its fucked-up game.

When my shift is over, my first reaction is to go talk to Ava. But I stop outside on the pavement, knowing Ava is angry and will not calm down enough to talk to me. She's hot-headed, stubborn, and I need a better way to approach this.

So, I take a cab to see the one person I know can help.

I don't expect to see Lex and Romano in the same office.

Just my luck.

Judging by Lex's sympathetic gaze and Romano's arctic glare, it's obvious to see the fake news has been brought to their attention.

"Austin, please take a seat."

I shake my head in silence, pacing Lex's office with my hand running through my hair. My chest caves in, the overwhelm too much to handle and fogging my mind at this very moment.

"I don't know what I'm supposed to do," I say while pacing, the frustration increasing my tone. "Ava is angry. She thinks I'm still in love with Millie. No matter what I say or do, it's not fucking good enough. I'm at my wit's end here. I can't keep fighting this uphill battle."

"Austin." Lex remains calm, sitting behind the desk with his posture straight. "Life has been anything but easy, especially since you've both just welcomed a baby. To add to that, you're tired, and I can only recall how exhausting it can be to work those long hours in the hospital. Ava is stubborn, and she protects herself by putting up barriers. She needs to calm down, which I will agree on. I am just about to go see her since she won't answer my calls."

"Stubborn would be an understatement," I mutter.

Lex glances at Will, his expression softening as he releases a sigh.

"This is the unfortunate nature of the beast. The Edwards family has always been subjected to media scrutiny. Charlotte and I have thick skin. We've learned over the years to pick our battles."

"It's all bullshit!" I raise my voice, desperate to kill whoever caused this nightmare. "And it's tearing my family apart."

Romano is oddly quiet, bowing his head without a word.

"Do you love my daughter?" Lex questions.

"Of course, I love her, Lex. She's the mother of my child, but what difference does it make when everyone else's opinions mean more to her than my truth?"

"Then marry her," Romano mumbles, barely audible inside the room. "Marry her, and everyone gets their own happily ever after."

My facial muscles turn slack, a flat gaze aimed at Romano, surprised to hear such words come from his mouth. From the beginning, he made it clear my relationship with Ava was orchestrated to ruin his life. Although things settled when Ava gave birth, I wasn't expecting him to encourage me to join the family completely.

Lex appears to be just as stunned, blinking slowly with his brows furrowing.

"Do you love Ava because she's the mother of your

child?"

"I can't breathe without her, Lex."

He nods, then places his hands on his desk.

"Then it's settled. Just as Will suggested, marry Ava. If you both love each other, then stop ruining it for each other. You're just delaying the inevitable."

I watch on with confusion. "Did I just hear right? So you've given me your blessing to propose marriage to Ava?"

"You were always part of the family, son. Just wrong daughter to begin with." Lex turns to Will with an amused expression. "Sorry to rub salt in your wound, but nevertheless, rather true."

Romano lets out an annoyed huff, glaring at Lex because he can. The two of them are more like best friends than father-in-law to son-in-law. Yet rightfully so, their persona is just that of a controlling billionaire who always gets their way. It's a completely different world, nothing at all like practicing medicine.

"I wouldn't even know where to begin with getting her to talk to me, let alone proposing."

Barely thinking straight, a thousand thoughts are running through my mind. We're talking about Ava here. I can't just propose marriage, especially since she was there the first time I attempted to propose marriage to someone. This has to be special and meaningful. Then there's the matter of the ring. Again, it's Ava. I've spent enough time with her to know her taste in jewelry is refined.

"I'll help you," Romano intervenes, his eyes finally meeting my gaze. "Just as long as you promise me to never ever hurt my sister. You understand me?"

I look him in the eye, the man I once considered my arch-nemesis.

"What do you have in mind?"

TWENTY-FIVE

AVA

In just a heartbeat, everything is ruined between us.

I leave Austin standing in the corridor, his face crestfallen at my callous words. The moment between us is a blur, like my body is standing there, yet my mind is elsewhere, so far in this mess I created inside my head. I've hurt the one person who means the world to me.

But even as the words leave my mouth, I know I've made a mistake. I've allowed it all to consume me, the lies, the media frenzy, and the worst offender of all—my insecurities.

Now it is all too late. The damage is done, and I've crushed the man I love.

When I get back to my apartment, Eric takes one look at me with sympathy in his eyes. He stuck around to babysit Emmy when I lied and said I had to take care of something. He brought his laptop, so balanced watching her and dealing with this media mess. When it comes to unwarranted scandals, Eric knows exactly how to handle it.

Shaking my head in silence, I sniffle as my eyes cloud and my words choke on the sobs stuck in my throat.

"Ava, sweetie, sit."

Eric brings me a bottle of water as I sink into the sofa, throwing my head back and reliving it all. I don't understand what came over me. This need to protect what is mine. But that's the thing, Austin isn't mine. He's Emmy's father and the man I've been intimate with.

But that's where it ends.

"I don't want to talk about it, Eric," I mumble.

Eric checks his watch. "Okay, listen. I have our legal team on this, and you bet we'll sue whoever's ass started this mess."

"What's the point, Eric? It's always going to happen no matter who I'm with."

With his arms crossed, Eric stands up. "Ava Edwards, I know you're upset. But you need to stop this damn pity party of yours. This isn't the woman I admire, and god damn it, I refuse to keep watching you destroy yourself because you can't wake up and admit the truth. Where is the great Ava Edwards, huh?"

"Eric," I stammer, "I don't know what's happening with me either."

Eric releases a collective sigh of frustration, and I don't blame him—I'm frustrated with me too.

"Listen, I'm already running late to a meeting. As soon as it's done, I'll call you. But please, for the love of God, pull yourself together."

Eric leaves my apartment as I sit here, lost with what to do. It isn't out of character for Eric to dish out tough love. In so many ways, we're alike. I have zero patience for self-pity, but when you're the one walking in those shoes, it's a whole other ball game.

While Emmy continues to sleep, I do nothing but stare at the wall. For how long, I'm not sure. When she stirs, I change and feed her, then place her back down for another nap.

Just so I can go back to staring at the wall again.

My phone sits on the sofa beside me. There is no missed call from Austin, not even a text message. There are several from other people, but I ignore them and hit dial to call Millie. When the call connects, I can't even talk.

"Ava," Millie calls softly. "What did you do?"

I shake my head, though she can't see.

"I ruined it, Millie. I hurt Austin, accused him of all these things which I know in my heart aren't true, but I don't know what came over me."

If anyone knows me, it's my flesh and blood.

My sister.

"Do you think the self-sabotage is because you're scared?"

"I'm scared, Millie." I swallow the hard lump inside my throat, twisting the corner of the cushion anxiously with my fingers. "I'm in love with him."

As tears fall down my cheek, Emmy stirs in her bassinet again.

Leaving the phone on the sofa, I keep Millie on speaker while cradling Emmy in my arms. Her eyes open faintly as a small yawn escapes her.

"Falling in love with someone is the most exhilarating feeling, but also the scariest at the same time. Your heart is at its most vulnerable, and sometimes we do crazy things..." Millie adds, then remains quiet.

"Are you angry with me?"

"Angry you're in love with Austin?" she questions, then sighs. "Gosh no, Ava. If there is anyone worthy of your heart, it's Austin Carter. I just wish you would be honest with yourself and stop listening to this inner voice which thinks you're not good enough."

"I saw him, with Lane. They were coming out of the storage room together. I accused him of being with her and still in love with you," I admit, with a crack in my voice.

"Oh, Ava. Why would you say that?"

"Because I'm stupid, that's why."

The buzzer rings on the door. I have no choice but to walk and not run, with Emmy still in my arms. "Hold on, Millie."

I press on the intercom. "Yes, Harry?"

"Your brother-in-law is here to see you."

"Send him up."

I walk back over to grab my phone, then unlock the door and hold it open for Will.

"It's Will," I tell her.

"Call me later tonight before bed, okay?"

Will exits the elevator, still dressed in his suit. I half expect him to be pissed from the articles, but he looks calm.

"Millie," I say, handing Emmy to Will, who cradles her. "How do you ignore the noise? The lies?"

I can almost hear her smile on the other end. "In the end, no one knows what goes on behind closed doors. It's just you and the man you love. That's all you'll ever need."

Will leans in to speak closer to the phone. "I love you too, Mrs. Romano."

"Such a gentleman," Millie teases, then clears her throat. "Ava?"

"Yeah?"

"I know the timing isn't perfect, but..." she begins with then stalls, only for Will to beam beside me. "You're going to be an aunty again soon."

My eyes widen as my lips curve upward in disbelief.

"Oh, my God! How? When?"

She laughs over the speaker. "Well, I think out of all people, you know how a baby is made."

I half-hug Will since he still has Emmy in his arms. It explains why he looked so calm and didn't barge into my apartment with a chip on his shoulder.

"How far along?"

"Ten weeks, so still keeping it under wraps. No one knows, not even Mom and Dad. We just want to pass the twelve weeks, especially since I've miscarried before."

"But I thought you guys weren't having sex back then?"

Will shakes his head with a smug expression. "How about you ladies have this conversation when I'm not around?"

"Okay, okay," I mouth, still elated over this amazing news. Despite my own mess, this is such a blessing, and I know how much they both want this. "Call me tonight, Millie. I need details of when exactly he shot his load, and you got knocked up."

Will presses his lips together with a less-than-amused expression but keeps his opinion to himself.

"Promise, sis. And chin up, okay? It will work out."

I glance at Will with my shoulders slumping. "How do you know?"

"It always does, Ava bear."

Will follows me to the living room, where we both take a seat on the sofa. He's talking to Emmy, and who would have thought a billionaire could be so smitten with a baby.

"Will, are you angry with what those media outlets posted?" I ask, though fully aware I am stepping into treacherous waters. "You know, what they said about Austin and Millie, plus those pics. You trust your wife, right?"

"Yes, I trust my wife," he answers without hesitating.

"I'm not pleased with the lies and have my legal team investigating who was behind this. But also, I have a pregnant wife who doesn't need any stress in her life. So, if that means I need to suppress my anger, then that's what I will do."

I admire Will for remaining so calm since he is usually the opposite of calm. He's come a long way from the controlling billionaire who came back into our lives seven years ago, but I guess this is the power of love. It'll change you no matter how much you think it won't.

"I'm really happy for both of you," I say with ease. "Ashton finally gets a brother or sister. It's so much fun having a sibling."

Will chuckles, his entire face lighting up. "It's hard for me to relate. Beau was born when I was already a teenager. The closest thing I had to siblings was you and Amelia."

"Oh, that sounds so wrong." I laugh too. "You know, because you married her."

As we both take a deep breath to come down from the laughter, Will glances my way with a relaxed grin.

"Why don't we go for a walk? It's a nice afternoon."

"I don't think it's a good idea we get seen together, not after today and everyone assuming we're involved in some partner swap. Besides, the paparazzi are outside."

"So?" he questions with slight annoyance. "Are you going to stop living your life because of other people? Since when have you ever done that? If anything, you've always lived your life for yourself."

"Okay, fine. Can I at least get changed, so I don't look like an overtired mother?"

"Whatever makes you happy."

I quickly get changed into something a bit nicer—a pair of jeans, sneakers, and a white knitted sweater. Before we leave, I change Emmy into a onesie, and bring the blanket which belonged to Austin, to cover her. I decide to use the carrier instead of the stroller, wanting to keep her close to me. She's still small, and the weather has cooled of late. The last thing I need is Emmy getting sick, especially because she was born prematurely.

We walk down the street, talking about the city, and of late, how it's changed. Will has always been a Manhattan boy, born and bred on the Upper East Side. But his move to LA for Millie has definitely been a positive change though you can't deny he still misses being here.

"This place will never leave you," I tell him wistfully.

"No, it never will. I'm glad we kept our brownstone here for when we stay. Probably the best decision we made."

"You've both made it work just like Mom and Dad. You've both sacrificed and compromised at the same time."

Will lowers his head, his movements slowing. "You know, Ava, if this is about Austin..."

I shake my head. "This is about me, Will. For the first time in my life, I have two people who have become my entire world. So it's not just about what I want. It's about what's best for everyone, not Ava Edwards and her selfish needs."

"So, what's the answer?"

"I miss my family. I don't want Emmy growing up without her grandparents or cousins."

"Move to LA then."

I lower my eyes, knowing what I'm about to say can go two ways. After all, we are talking about Will Romano here. "I won't go without him, Will."

Will rubs his chin, then looks toward the sky. "I don't think you have to."

My glance focuses on Will's serious expression as something passes between us. He stops here on the sidewalk, and as I look around, the surroundings look familiar. I've been here before, an odd memory of laughing while walking down this very street. And then, I turn to see the building.

Alistair's.

"This pub is where—"

"Where you and Austin spent New Year's Eve?"

"How did you know?"

"I'm gifted, sixth sense or something like that. Shall we go in? For a pint or something less alcoholic for you."

The place looks dark, only a faint glow coming from inside. "I think they're closed anyway."

Will grabs my hand, then twists the handle of the door with his other.

"Will, I don't think we should be trespassing. Alistair is married to an Aussie. His wife has probably taught him how to fight with crocodiles, and it's likely he carries a knife. I mean, didn't you watch *Crocodile Dundee*? That's not a knife. This is a knife..."

"Ava?" Will turns to me, narrowing his eyes. "Can you shut up for just one moment?"

"Just because you're a billionaire doesn't mean you can boss me around."

Inside the pub, music plays. It's some lame song, but then it continues to a remix of the music Alistair played on New Year's Eve. The same night...

Then, the lights come on, and standing in the middle of the dance floor is Austin, dressed in a navy-blue suit, looking so handsome it hurts to be standing apart from him.

"Austin?" I gulp, my heart racing from seeing him. "What are you doing here?"

He moves close to me and strokes my cheek gently. I take a large savoring breath, closing my eyes at his touch.

"I don't like what happened this morning between us, Ava."

I shake my head. "I know, I was an idiot. I feel stupid for acting so—"

"Crazy?"

"Amongst many words which can be used to describe me."

Austin reaches out for my hands, holding onto both of them. His stare is unwavering, deep, and reaching every part of my soul.

"You were standing right beside me the first time I proposed marriage to someone. I had no idea what I was doing or thinking, but I thought it was the right thing to do, even though something inside was bothering me. I was trying to prove a point to everyone, and marriage should never be about anyone else." He takes a deep breath, but his hands remain steady, then slowly, a grin spreads across his face. "With you, Ava, everything is wrong yet so right at the same time. I feel like I've known you my entire life. We're more than just two people who stumbled into this bar looking for something to take away the pain."

I watch his soft gaze, the way his lips move when he talks, to how vulnerable and raw his words are.

"You are more than the mother of my beautiful daughter. You're the reason I breathe, Ava. My life has never felt so complete until now. I'm not going to hold back anymore, nor be afraid of you running from me. I love you. I can't stop thinking about you, and when we're apart, it's you I want. You I crave. I don't care what people think. I care about what is right for us."

Austin releases his hands from mine to reach into his

pocket. With his stare still fixated on me, he removes the ring from the box and places it on my finger without even a pause, nor the traditional stop and wait for the woman's reaction.

"In so many ways, Ava, I've always loved you. And I never want to ever stop. I want to build a life with you. I want to grow our family. I want to see us both follow our passions, and most importantly, I want you in my arms every day for as long as I breathe.

"Ava Edwards, I give you this ring to symbolize my commitment to making you my wife. There is nothing else I want, so please... " Austin's breath finally hitches as his eyes soften, only for tears to stream down my cheeks. "Listen to what your heart is telling you, and tell me your forever is me by your side as your husband."

I nod, unable to choke back my tears, my mouth hurting from the grin bearing so wide.

"You are my forever," I whisper, touching his lips with my fingers. "I would be honored to be your wife."

Austin's hazel eyes shimmer as his entire face beams with pride. He cups my face to place a kiss on my lips, the warmth of his touch spreading throughout me. How did I get so lucky to fall in love with such a beautiful man who knows exactly my fears yet protects me from falling prey to them?

We pull away for Austin to place a kiss on Emmy's head.

"I love you, Ava," he whispers.

"You don't know how much I needed to hear that."

"I do," he tells me, then continues, "I was scared of pushing you but knew my hesitation only made you doubt my love for you."

"I admit it, Austin. I thought I wasn't good enough, but instead of listening to my heart, I hurt you."

"You did, but it made me fight harder for you."

I kiss him once again, basking in the happiness of finally allowing myself to fall in love.

"How did you do all this? And the ring, my God, Austin, it's so beautiful."

"See, when you have family around who know how to pull strings, it makes life a little bit easier."

"Family?"

I turn around, forgetting Will was standing at the bar all along and only noticing now that he is with Alistair and a pint.

"Lex and Will organized this place, and Eric helped me with this stunning piece of jewelry on your hand." Austin glances at Will, giving him a slight nod in which Will raises a glass.

"See, my strength is saving lives. So I'll stick to what I know best and let the billionaires and fashionistas do the rest."

I throw my arms around him, though careful not to squash Emmy. "You're perfect as you are, Dr. Carter."

"Right back at you." Austin grins, then plants another kiss on my lips. "My crazy, stubborn, yet beautiful fiancée."

TWENTY-SIX

AVA

"Do you remember when we rode our bikes up that hill?" I point to the steep hill on my left. "And we accidentally saw a couple having sex against the man's Porsche?"

Austin's face breaks out into a wide grin with one hand on the steering wheel, his other is resting on my knee. Wearing a white polo, his arms look so defined. I squeeze my legs shut because I am this close to ditching this house viewing and mauling him in the car instead.

"I remember because the man was pushing sixty, and the chick had the tits of a nineteen-year-old."

"Trust you to notice," I tease, to roll my eyes. "Such a guy."

"Aw, you jealous, baby?"

"Nope, I've got the ring." I wave my hand in the air proudly. "Oh! And the baby."

Austin laughs, shaking his head. "Forget again?"

I punch his shoulder gently at the same time he pulls into the circular driveway. The realtor's car is already here—

a fancy Mercedes, of course, because it's all about the status in Beverly Hills.

"So this is house number five?" Austin scratches his chin. "Lucky number five."

"Look, none of the houses we've looked at have been right."

"No." He's quick to intervene. "None of the houses we've looked at have been right for you."

"Is it wrong of me to want the perfect house for our family? And close to the hospital, so you don't have to commute, especially when you're on call?"

"Don't give me that face," Austin warns me playfully. "With that smile and a lick of your lips, like I haven't noticed you squeeze your legs how many times on the drive over here?"

I remove my seat belt, releasing a frustrated groan.

"It's been two whole weeks of the quietest sex we've ever had while under my parents' roof," I remind him. "I'm going insane."

"First of all, it's been one week. And before we left for LA, I fucked you into oblivion because we both knew it would be strained for a few weeks until we get settled into our own home."

"Strained would be an understatement," I mutter beneath my breath.

Austin raises my hand to his lips, kissing my knuckles gently.

"You're cute when you're sexually frustrated."

I let out a groan. "Let's go before I really show you what cute is."

Austin reaches out for my hand as we walk together, admiring the front yard. It's hard to compare when you've grown up in LA and your parents have the most beautiful home. Austin's parents also have a nice home in Thousand Oaks, decorated beautifully since his mother owns a furniture store.

"Dr. Carter, Ava," our realtor, Margaret, greets. "It's nice to see you again."

"Fifth time is a charm, Margaret."

Margaret takes us inside, presenting the stunning main foyer. There are stained oak floors and pristine white walls. The staircase is gorgeous but not overly grand like my parents' place. I didn't want something too big where I'd lose Emmy once she started moving around, but enough for our family to grown in.

"It's a nice size," I comment with a nod. "And the kitchen?"

"Is right through here."

The kitchen is grand, with every appliance I'll need. Mom gave me a list of things to ask, which I do, all of which Margaret answers to my satisfaction.

"And then we have the patio, pool, and guest house."

The view is impressive, with lots of trees for privacy and a luscious green lawn that sprawls around the pool. There is enough room for a trampoline, playhouse, and even a basketball court if Austin wants one since he loves to play.

"I'll show you the bedrooms."

Upstairs has six bedrooms and four baths plus a large lounge area connecting the rooms, making it a perfect play area for Emmy. Downstairs, there is also a large room for my home office. Thankfully, Austin's work remains at the hospital. As for me, technically, I run my own show but being in LA is somewhat less stressful for photoshoots given there are so many great locations. Before coming here, I sent

Eric pictures of the property. He responded with a thumbs up and ideas for shoots around the pool.

"Do you mind if we have a look around?" Austin asks.

"Certainly. There's a basement downstairs, and if you take a sharp left, you'll also find the cellar."

"Sounds perfect," Austin responds with a mischievous grin.

"I need to make some calls. Just find me when you're ready."

Austin doesn't delay, taking my hand and almost dragging me downstairs. The basement is completely finished, perfect for storage and products samples which I usually have lying around my apartment.

We take the sharp left into the cellar.

"Oh, wow," I mouth, walking into a fully finished room with glass doors and lights to showcase rows of wine. Some appear refrigerated behind the glass doors, plus a few barrels. Some bottles are lying flat on the wine racks. I move closer to the glass door to get a better look at what wine they're storing. The couple who owns this place has a vineyard in Napa Valley, something Dad and I discussed investing in together.

Behind me, there's a warm sensation as Austin leans into my back, his lips close to my ear.

"Did you do as I said, Miss Edwards?"

I nod with a knowing grin, pressing my thighs together to suppress the throbbing between them.

"When I check... " he says with a ragged breath, "... there better not be anything beneath this dress of yours. I demanded your pussy be bare and exposed."

"I always listen to doctor's orders," I murmur.

Austin slides his hands beneath my dress until he reaches between my legs, causing me to gasp.

"Hands on the glass," he demands.

Placing my hands on the glass door, I hear his belt buckle unclip. Then, he slowly enters me as I try to quiet my moan. With each thrust, I'm on the verge of exploding as Austin pulls the strap of my dress down and exposes my bra.

With his lips kissing my neck, he keeps his thrusts hard, then demands, "Take your tits out for me, just the way I like them."

I pull my bra down as they fall out for his groan to echo in my ear. He doesn't waste time, grabbing them and tugging on my nipples which causes them to leak. Fuck, this is going to get really messy quickly.

My hands still press against the glass as I stick my ass out. Austin commands I come with him, my body shivering in delight, the same time he grips my hips tightly.

We both catch our breaths, trying to come down from the high. Austin slowly pulls out of me while kissing my shoulder.

"You came inside of me," I remind him, basking in his juices between my legs. "How am I supposed to walk outside now?"

Austin turns me around, then presses me against the glass. My back shivers from the glass, cooling my heated skin.

With a penetrating stare, he runs his thumb against my bottom lip. "It sounds to me like you're not finished."

I shake my head teasingly. Austin drops down between my legs, running his tongue along my clit as my hands wrap around his hair. It doesn't take me long before the sensation rips through me again, and I fall into a deep orgasm, the ripples of pleasure spreading throughout every inch of my body.

My eyes close while I try to catch my breath. We kiss deeply before Austin helps me straighten my clothes. He runs his hand through his hair to neaten it, then we hold hands and make our way back upstairs.

When we see Margaret, she glances at us furtively to wait for our response.

The house is just right.

And we just made it *perfect*.

I turn to gaze at Austin, then nod with a smile.

"We'd like to put in an offer," he informs Margaret. "Now, let's talk numbers."

It's Christmas Eve, and Mom has cooked up a storm with my help, of course. While staying here, she's been teaching me to cook. Back in Manhattan, I either dined out or ordered in, barely using the kitchen.

Austin, however, is a great cook. His mother taught him well.

We can't all be a perfectionist like him, but my stuffing sure looks good.

I wash my hands in the sink when Austin walks into the kitchen on a call. He says goodbye, then breaks out into a wide smile.

"We got the house."

"We did?" I wipe my hands, then jump up into his arms. "Lucky number five."

"I'm proud of you both," Mom congratulates, embracing me, then Austin. "We need to celebrate with our best wine."

Dad walks into the kitchen with Emmy in his arms. He's a big old softy, even asking Mom to buy one of those bouncer things for his office when it came to babysitting. One of the perks of staying with them.

"What are we celebrating?"

"We bought a house, Dad!"

Dad's eyes reflect with relief. "Excellent news. Now, is this the place near the hospital?"

"Yes," Austin confirms while leaning back against the countertop. "A ten-minute commute. It helps when I'm on call though Chief Robinson wants to discuss me moving into a specialty. I've been considering cardiothoracic surgery, but I need to weigh my options on the studying aspect once again.

"Cardiothoracic surgery is something I once too considered," Dad mentions softly.

"Really?" I ask with curiosity. "You wanted to mend broken hearts?"

As I wait for a response, Mom watches Dad with a nostalgic gaze. She always wished he continued with medicine. However, Lex Edwards has done so much good in the world with the wealth he has created. He's responsible for giving so many people jobs, and the charities both my parents are involved in are endless. Not only that, Dad has helped Uncle Julian and Aunt Adriana fund local villages in Central America, building schools, shelters, and basic things we take for granted.

He may not be a heart surgeon, but he's done just as good in this world.

"Something like that." Dad smiles, then follows with, "Eventually, you could move into your own practice. It is Beverly Hills, after all."

I laugh as everyone watches me with curiosity. "As long as he's not a plastic surgeon. Boobs and vaginas all day long? No thanks."

"They do make an awful lot of money, Ava," Dad teases.

Mom furrows her brows. "Why on earth would they be looking at vaginas?"

"Haven't you heard?" I question with a sneer. "It's the latest trend. Vaginal reconstruction."

Both Addy and Alexa walk into the kitchen, no doubt smelling the food.

"What's going on?" Addy asks, grabbing a bowl and dumping some Lucky Charms in there even though we're yet to eat. "Sorry, I'm starving and need something small to tie me over."

"Mom didn't know vaginal reconstruction is the latest trend."

Addy presses her lips flat, unimpressed with this conversation.

"Oh, yeah," Alexa says while grabbing a bottle of water from the refrigerator. "A few of my friends have got it done."

"What exactly did they get done?" Mom questions.

"Labia tightening. Just makes it look less creepy."

Austin hides his smirk at the same time. Dad pinches the bridge of his nose, then groans.

"This is what I get for living in a house full of women. Labia reconstruction before dinner." His tone is less than pleased, and his smile from before disappears as our conversation takes a nosedive. "Now, if I can pass off my princess, I'll fetch that bottle of wine from the cellar."

"Do you need help?" Mom asks, eyeing Dad as he hands Emmy to Austin. "A few bottles were moved, so you may not find it."

"Always, Mrs. Edwards."

My parents disappear as Will, Millie, and Ashton come through the back door. Millie is starting to show, the bump looking so cute on her. It makes me miss being pregnant and the newborn phase. Emmy is close to four months now and getting chubby. But then, I remember how Mom said this would happen. I shake my head, willing these crazy thoughts to stop.

Ashton runs to Austin, desperate to see Emmy. He's so excited to be a big brother, telling everyone his mommy has a baby girl inside, too, although they have decided not to find out the sex of the baby.

"What's happening, people?" Will asks, digging his hand into the bowl and scooping up Addy's Lucky Charms, much to her annoyance.

"We were discussing how labia reconstructions are really hot right now," I tell them.

"It is?" Millie asks.

"Yeah, we're trying to convince Austin to get into plastic surgery," Alexa casually mentions. "It's a moneymaker."

"First of all, we weren't convincing him. If anything, I said yes to any other specialty but not anything that's got to do with boobs or vaginas."

"So, wait a minute." Millie raises her hand. "What are they doing to the labia?"

Alexa continues her story of her friend, Ella, who had it done only recently. She goes into detail about the excess tissue being removed from the enlarged labia minora or majora.

"It makes sense," Will deadpans, with a mouth full of cereal.

Millie places her hands on her hips. "How does it make sense?"

"Well, frankly, no man likes an ugly pussy."

"William Rockford Romano, I can't believe you just said that in front of our son," Millie berates him.

Thankfully, Ashton is too busy trying to tickle Emmy, who's giggling every time he digs his tiny fingers into her chin.

"Is this true?" I turn to Austin.

"I mean, look, yes. Unfortunately, some women aren't gifted in that area," is all Austin says.

Addy smacks Wills hand again, grabbing the last Lucky Charm. When she finally wins, she joins in the conversation. "I guess in comparison, it's like a man having an ugly penis."

"What does an ugly penis look like?" Alexa asks while scowling.

Everyone turns to look at me. Then, with an inward gaze, my lips press flat.

"I have no idea why you all just looked at me. You should respect my fiancé, who is standing right beside me."

Austin almost snorts, his smug face not running to my defense at all. "C'mon, Ava. You were the wildest one here. Even I know that. Surely, in your younger days, you've encountered one."

My eyes glare at him as I cross my arms in defiance. "Listen, this isn't exactly how I expected to spend Christmas Eve with my family."

Everyone laughs, and it's impossible for me not to join in. So what if I slept with a fair few men in my younger years? It's not like Austin and Will were saints. Millie is a commitment girl. As for Addy, I'm still not sure what is happening with her since she never talks about any man like ever.

And well, Alexa, she isn't a virgin but clearly hasn't encountered an ugly penis yet.

"Where are the parentals?" Millie asks.

"They went to the cellar together to get a bottle of wine," I muse.

"Oh, God." Millie shakes her head with a grimace. "I don't want to know."

"I dare any of you girls to go down and find them," Will challenges.

"Hell no, from me," I blurt out. "I'm still scarred from that time I snuck in late after a party and heard mom say 'Daddy', followed by a disturbing giggle."

Millie shudders. "More so than 'spread your legs, Charlotte. I need to taste you.' Huh?"

"Um, how about, 'turn around and give me that ass now,' then you hear the sound of a slap," Addy complains, flinching.

We all groan. My parents are the worst, but then, we all turn to look at Alexa.

"Why are you all looking at me?" She releases a huff, and before she says anything, my parents walk back in with a bottle of wine.

Mom's cheeks look red, and I could've sworn she had her hair parted to the left, not centered, earlier on. As for Dad, he seems rather pleased with himself.

"Everyone is here, so what are we discussing? Hopefully, we dropped our earlier discussion?"

"Actually, Mom," I say, Austin lowering his head with a smirk, the same as Will. "Alexa will tell you."

"Argh, I hate being the youngest..."

As we all laugh, even though my parents have no clue why we're laughing, I can't help but thank the Universe for blessing me with every single person in this room.

For my parents, my sisters, my brother-in-law, and my nephew.

And of course, my soon-to-be husband in just over a week and our little girl.

Emerald Charlotte Edwards-Carter.

Also, for teaching me how fairy tales may endure heartache but how they should end.

Happily ever after.

Inside this very room, I have exactly that and more.

New Year's Eve

"Get your fucking dick out of my face!"

Rocky yells to Eric as the both of them are once again embroiled in the game of Twister. The same thing happened last year. After all these years, I should be immune to this, but it is still entertaining to watch from the sideline.

"How about you get your hairy gorilla balls out of my face," Eric counters with his face turning bright red.

"I told you, dude, I get my balls waxed."

"You wax your balls?" Adriana blurts out, then covers her mouth with disapproval. "Why on earth?"

Rocky grins from his awkward pose. "My wife likes it that way."

Will swipes the bottle of tequila, drinking straight from it. Still in his suit, like the rest of us, he has removed his jacket and appears desperate to erase what he just heard. I don't blame the boy. I'm still in shock.

"You're fucking kidding me, Dad," Will shouts, wiping

his mouth. "You said you were doing that for a prostate exam?"

"Yeah, kid. I say a lot of things to you."

Nikki is sitting with Charlotte and Kate, keeping very quiet on the matter. But then, she leans in and whispers something for the women to laugh.

It's New Year's Eve but also Austin and Ava's wedding day. When they asked if they could have the ceremony here, with only close family and friends, of course, I wasn't going to say no.

You see, I'm not one for lavish affairs, and I prefer to keep my family close to me.

In the end, that's all that matters.

I drop my gaze to meet the smile of my precious princess. In my arms, her emerald eyes shine brightly, just like her mama's.

"What do you think, princess? Was it a good day for you too?"

She responds with a coo, a simple sound that makes my heart sing.

Before Emmy was born, it was a long while since I'd held a baby girl in my arms. For the longest of time, I never knew any different. Charlotte and I had been blessed with four beautiful daughters, each one unique in their own way.

Beside me, Ashton tries to tickle Emmy's feet.

"Grandpapa, when is my sister coming?"

"Ashton, remember how we told you inside your momma's tummy is maybe a boy or girl?"

His big brown eyes stare at me. "There are two babies inside?"

"No, buddy. Just one. But maybe it's a baby brother."

"But I don't want a brother because then Daddy and Momma won't love me lots and lots," he sulks.

I motion for him to sit on my lap while I juggle the two of them.

"That's not true. Look at your mimi and me," I tell him, referencing the affectionate name he calls Charlotte. "We had four girls, and we love them all equally."

"Even Alexa?" He scrunches his nose. "She got angry at me because I went into her room. I played with her phone. But then I dropped it."

"That sounds like Alexandra," I mutter beneath my breath.

Charlotte joins us, offering me a plate of food. I motion for her to place it on the table beside me as she sits on the chair and scoops Ashton into her arms. He puts his thumb in his mouth, the same thing Andy would do as a child.

"Andy used to put his thumb in his mouth," I say wistfully.

"I remember. It drove Adriana crazy." Charlotte laughs, then sighs. "It was a beautiful day. You held up well, Daddy."

I lean in and kiss Charlotte's hair. "It's not easy giving your baby girl away."

"No, it's not," she agrees, stroking Ashton's hair as he closes his eyes. "You and Ava have always had a special bond, but trust me, she'll never leave you. Why do you think she's pushing you to partner in the winery together?"

We have been discussing it of late. Ava and I have always been passionate about wine. She managed to find a vineyard which listed on the market only yesterday and even contemplated delaying her honeymoon to get this project started.

"I didn't think of it that way."

"She's always going to be a daddy's girl. That doesn't

stop just because she's married. So now, you've got another little princess to worry about."

I look down at Emmy, who has fallen asleep in my arms. "No one is going to touch this little girl. I will protect her for the rest of my life if I have to."

Charlotte grins beside me. "How you ended up with four daughters is beyond me. I think the Universe really wanted to test your patience."

"I have sons too." The both of us shift our gaze toward where Andy stands. He's near the back door in what appears to be a heated argument with Jessa.

The two of them have always been close, but according to Addy, that was until Jessa moved to London last year.

"What's going on there?" I ask Charlotte.

"I would say they seem to be embroiled in some argument, and judging by the way Andy is running his hands through his hair, I'd say he's jealous over Jessa's new fiancé."

"Fiancé? Since when?"

"Since that's why she flew over, to tell Noah and Kate."

I purse my lips, still in shock. It only felt like yesterday Jessa was born, and she's always been a massive part of my girls' lives. After all, she is their cousin.

"Wait a minute, rewind back to Andy being jealous? They're cousins."

Charlotte releases a breath. "They're not technically cousins. They are cousins to our girls, but not each other. It just feels that way because they spent so much time together, like Will and Amelia."

Charlotte has a point, though as I watch Andy in what I'll agree appears to be a jealous stance, I can't help but feel sorry for him. We've all been there, done that. Thank God I never have to go through that again. The woman I love is all mine, and that's all she'll ever be.

"I'm going to take Ashton to bed. Then I'll come back for Emmy." Charlotte stands up slowly, careful not to wake Ashton. Before she leaves, I quickly stop her.

"I love you, Charlotte. Thank you for building this life with me."

"It's been quite some life, huh?"

"Worth every moment."

She leans in to kiss me, careful not to drop Ashton, then takes him inside to place him in the room we've set up and decorated as his.

As I watch on, Twister has progressed to Noah and Julian joining in. With three men now surrounding Eric, even though Tristan is watching on the sideline with Adriana, he shouts with too much enthusiasm. "This is even better than Pornhub!"

I can't hide my laughter as all the men shout profanities at Eric before hopping off the giant Twister mat.

Austin walks toward me and offers to take Emmy to bed.

"Perfect day for a wedding," I tell him with a smile. "You both look very happy."

"I am." Austin grins while appearing relaxed. "We are."

I extend my arms as Austin takes his daughter. She stirs slightly, but he gently rocks her.

"Goodnight, princess," I whisper, stroking her hair.

Austin checks on her, and she's fallen asleep again.

"Lex? I just wanted to tell you I made a decision."

"Oh?" I cross my arms, raising my brows with curiosity. "What's that?"

"I've decided to go ahead with cardiothoracic surgery. Ava and I had a lengthy discussion, weighing up the pros and cons but it's something I want to do. I know it'll be a long road ahead, but Ava is supportive, and that's all that matters."

I nod, proud of this kid for following his dreams.

A dream I once had.

"I'm proud of you, son." I beam with pride. "We're both here if you need us, and if you need help with Emmy or anything. We're all in this together."

"I know," he says with a knowing grin. "I think you said that to me when I tried to marry your other daughter?"

We both laugh as Ava and Addison join us. Ava has stayed in her wedding dress, a beautiful laced gown Adriana designed especially for her.

"Did he tell you, Dad? My husband is going to be a heart surgeon. A mender of broken hearts. If that's not a tagline, I don't know what is."

"Put it on my business card." Austin smirks, then tilts his head to kiss Ava's cheek. "I'm going to take Emmy to bed. Addy, control your sister. She and Will have hit up the tequila, and I don't want to deal with hungover Ava on a flight to Aspen tomorrow."

As Ava and Austin both walk toward the house, Addison nods, only for Ava to laugh at something really loud, then join Will at the poker table Rocky has set up.

"Here's the rule, no dicks out," Rocky warns with a serious tone. "Tits are welcomed."

"That's so crass," Amelia tells him. "And sexist."

Addison sits beside me, leaning her head on my shoulder instead of stopping her sister from drinking. We watch on as Austin returns, and Noah makes him drink a shot. There's more laughter and more rounds of shots.

"Two down, two more daughters to go."

I chuckle softly, kissing the top of Addison's head.

"Between you and me, I always knew Amelia and Ava

would end up here. Maybe not with the people they're with, but still here."

"Really?" Addison questions. "So, what are your predictions for me?"

I purse my lips, thinking quietly. Addison is different from her sisters. Growing up, she loved playing sports but was a quiet achiever at the same time. She excelled in her studies, so it didn't surprise us when she wanted to study for a degree in psychology. Of all the girls, she is the only sane one, never bringing a boy or boys home. From what Charlotte says, Addison isn't one to focus on her love life. I've even heard her older sisters tease she's still a virgin.

The perfect daughter.

"I think you are going to graduate and make me proud."

"I promise you, Dad. I've watched my sisters enough to know that being on my own is exactly what I want. And there's absolutely nothing wrong with focusing on myself."

"You're right, Addison," I say, then gently warn. "But no matter how intelligent you are, when love strikes, it's a force to be reckoned with."

Addison laughs, releasing a shallow sigh. "Since when did the great Lex Edwards become an advocate for love?"

I watch her from across the garden, my beautiful wife, Charlotte.

"Since the moment I crashed into the one and only Charlotte Mason inside my parent's hallway," I murmur, remembering the moment as if it happened just yesterday. "That's when I knew my life would change forever."

SNEAK PEEK

THE TROUBLE WITH HER

Andy

Two years ago

"Will you just stop and talk to me for a minute?"

My hand is clutched around Jessa's bare arm, desperate for her to ease into my touch but instead, her muscles tense.

Inside my heated grip, she lowers her head to avoid my persistent stare while her chest rises and falls beneath the ivory-laced dress she's wearing. Jessa's signatory bronze curls fall to the side as she continues to remain silent. So much of me aches to reach out and tug on a strand, just as I've done a million times before. She hated it with a passion, even though I loved it.

But that was in the past when we were the best of friends and when we couldn't go a day without talking to each other.

Then—it all changed between us.

I silently plead with her to look me in the eye, but the

longer we stand here, the more she retreats, almost as if she can't stand to be next to me.

"What would you like me to say?" Jessa questions in a dull tone.

Letting go of her arm, I run my hands through my hair in frustration. No matter how it plays in my mind, I don't understand how we got here. How can two people who have been in each other's lives since they were kids can stand here unable to communicate in a mature manner?

"How about you begin with the truth? Why you left home, to begin with?"

Around us, the music is blaring as Eric insists on going back to an era I don't care for. However, the oldies seem to enjoy it, laughing while drinking copious amounts of alcohol. My mother is the worst offender, singing out loud to then accidentally spill her glass of red wine all over Eric's patent white leather shoes.

I wait for Eric's dramatic outburst, but he's so far gone even to notice.

If anyone was going to throw a party like this, of course, it had to be Ava. Given it's her wedding day, our families are having the time of their lives. The majority of them are drunk or in a food coma from the banquet served at dinner.

The only one who appears to be in control is Uncle Lex, as usual. Somehow, he got babysitting duty, though it looks like he's enjoying his time with Ashton and Emmy.

Everyone is in the best of spirits, adding to the occasion of it being New Year's Eve.

All but the person with a massive chip on her shoulder.

"God, Andy." Jessa throws her hands up in the air. "Why do we have to go over this? I left because I wanted more. Believe it or not, there's more than just LA."

I cross my arms in defiance. "Yeah, I know, that's why I moved to Manhattan."

"Exactly, you moved away, so why is it a problem that I did too?"

How can I tell her the problem is how she left? We had a big fight, and the next minute, she packed her bags to rediscover herself supposedly. Jessa didn't care how I felt about her, despite me trying to communicate my feelings. Instead, when I found the courage to say anything, she pushed me away before I could even get my words out, like she sensed what I was going to say before I said it.

"God, Jessa!" I yell, then bite down to control my anger, cautious of our family overhearing. "You walked away from us like we were nothing. Then you don't talk to me for a year, and suddenly, you're back? Oh, but let's not forget that I found out you were engaged to be married through Alexa, of all people."

Slowly, her gaze lifts until her eyes meet mine. For the longest time, the light green orbs brought me comfort, laughter, and a sense of security in a world full of uncertainty.

But now, they belong to a stranger.

"I wanted to tell you in person," she admits, her voice low. "But it didn't seem right to call you out of the blue and announce such a thing."

All of this hurt more than I care to admit. The pain ran deep, but I suppressed it like everything else I couldn't control—my biological father's death, the dreams which still plague me when I see his face even though I never knew him. According to Mom, we only had ten days together, and in those days, he managed to hold me only once—his fragile body too far deteriorated to even cradle a newborn baby.

The only person I ever confided in about these dreams

was the very person standing in front of me—the only person I trusted with these thoughts of mine.

There's no changing Jessa's mind. She ran away and fell in love with some British man who, according to Alexa, is the perfect prince charming—rich and handsome.

The same kind of guy Jessa and I would make fun of all the time.

"You're right," I tell her, still keeping my gaze fixed. "It would've been weird to call me out of nowhere, but what doesn't make sense is you getting married. We made fun of guys like this, and you, of all people, thought marriage was a ridiculous notion."

"I'm not the same person you once knew, Andy..." she trails off.

"No, you're not, Jessa," I responded hastily. "Because the girl I knew wouldn't have run off on her own. She'd have begged me to pack my bag and abandon my responsibilities, so we could chase cheese rolling down a hill in Gloucester."

She drops her gaze, unable to look at me any longer. My eyes gravitate toward the diamond ring sitting on her finger. It's big and no doubt an expensive piece of jewelry, all the things Jessa never cared for until prince charming rode his horse and carriage in.

Yet, it represents everything another man offers—a life together, marriage, a possible family—all of the things I'll never be able to give her because the timing was never on our side.

Not when we're family.

And being romantically linked is something her father won't approve of.

"Tell me, Jessa, what does Noah think of this?"

"My father is fine."

Cocking my head, I release a disturbing laugh with my

gaze shifting to Noah on the dance floor with Rocky. "Really? He doesn't look fine since he's trashed tonight, and Kate is trying to get him to sober up."

Jessa crosses her arms beneath her chest. "What are you getting at? My father has no choice. I love Benedict and will fight for him if I have to."

My stomach hardens, the hurt rippling to every part of me at her willingness to fight for another man—the words, sharp like a knife, cut deep into an already open wound.

Jessa will fight for a man she's known for five minutes.

But what we've built over a lifetime is over in a heartbeat.

"Well, I guess you've gotten everything you want," I say, ignoring the tightness inside my chest. "Happy New Year, Jessa."

I don't linger, just standing beside her is too unbearable. I need anything to numb the pain, anything at all.

With wide steps, I hit up the makeshift bar in Uncle Lex's patio. The bartender responsible for serving the liquor kindly asks what I'd like to drink.

"Fireballs... make it a tray."

Beside me, a body knocks into me. I turn briefly to see Millie as she rubs her pregnant stomach.

"Fireballs, uh oh," she mentions, then releases a sigh. "What happened, Andy?"

As I shake my head, my lips curl. "Nothing, nothing at all. She's getting married to some British playboy, and that's it."

"I'm sorry, Andy. I don't know what she's thinking. Both me and Ava are surprised this happened. We had no idea she was even seeing someone."

"Well, now everyone knows."

Taking the glass in my hand, I then throw it back. The

cinnamon-flavored liquor burns for just a moment, but I don't stop there.

"Andy, maybe you should slow down. If you want to go somewhere..."

I drown out Millie's words with another shot, this drink less potent.

"You know what I want?" I tell her with a rasp in my throat. "I want to get out of here."

"Sure, of course, but is it safe for you to drive? How much have you drunk?"

"I'm fine."

"Look, Andy. I know you're angry but don't bullshit me. How much have you drunk? Because I'm not allowing you to drive anywhere like this."

Again, I refuse to listen and throw back another drink. Then, just when I think Millie's silence means she'll leave me alone, I see her motion to Dad to come over.

Great.

I let out an annoyed huff, throwing back another as he places his hand on my shoulder. "I'll take you home, son."

"You want to take me somewhere?" Fine. But not home. Take me to Melrose."

"Why Melrose?" Millie questions.

"Any club where I can find a woman to make me forget tonight ever happened."

Millie looks at Dad, but he doesn't say anything, and I don't expect him to. He doesn't involve himself unless he feels his opinion is of value, unlike Millie, who in many ways is just like my overbearing mother.

"If that's what you want, I'll take you," Dad informs me.

Across the patio, Jessa is dancing with Ava and Luna. Her body moves freely with a smile permanently fixed and an occasional break into laughter.

But then, as if she senses me staring, her gaze shifts, and the smile on her face disappears. I can work it in my head in so many ways, assume the furrowed brows and drooping shoulders express the hurt she feels. Maybe, the down-turned mouth and pained expression is the regret over how she handled us.

No matter how I break it down, it all comes down to this.

Jessa Bentley-Mason is marrying someone else.

And there's not a goddamn thing I can do about it.

Printed in Great Britain
by Amazon

83163872R00192